LICHFIELD

THE U.S. ARMY ON TRIAL

LICHFIELD

THE U.S. ARMY ON TRIAL

JACK GIECK

THE UNIVERSITY OF AKRON PRESS   AKRON, OHIO

All inquiries and permissions requests should be addressed to the publisher, The University of Akron Press, Akron, OH 44325-1703.

Manufactured in the United States of America
First Edition 1997
01 00 99 98 97   5 4 3 2 1

Library of Congress Cataloging-in-Publication Data
Gieck, Jack.
     Lichfield : the U.S. Army on trial / Jack Gieck.—1st ed.
        p.   cm.
     Includes bibliographical references (p.).
     ISBN 1-884836-26-7 (cloth).—ISBN 1-884836-27-5 (pbk.)
     1. Trials (Military offenses)—England—London.   2. Courts—martial and courts of inquiry—United States.   3. Prisoners—Crimes against—England—Lichfield.   4. United States. Army—Prisons—England—Lichfield.   5. United States. Army—History—World War, 1939–1945.   I. Title.
KF7641.G54   1997
343.73'0143—dc21   97-6216
                                                                                        CIP

To Vicki, my wife and my best friend

CONTENTS

Photographs

HEADQUARTERS
UNITED KINGDOM BASE
APO 413, US ARMY

SPECIAL ORDERS   1 Dec 1945
NUMBER 316

E X T R A C T

*

   4. A General Court-Martial is aptd to meet at such places and times within the UK Base as may be directed by the President thereof for the trial of such persons as may be properly brought before it.

DETAIL FOR THE COURT

COL LOUIS P LEONE, 015350, Inf, Hq, UK Base
President
LT COL FAYETTE G HALL, 0270317, DC, 232nd Sta Hosp
MAJOR WALTER E HOPPER, JR., 0351669, Inf, 6856th American Tech Sch Ovhd Det Law
Member
MAJOR WILLIAM J SHEA, 0301242, CAC, HQ, UK Base
MAJOR WILLIAM L TAYLOR, 0455932, TC, 4th Group Regulating Station
MAJOR BENJAMIN E PERS, 0512283, MC, 1st Hospitalization Unit, 6th Field Hosp
CAPT JAMES L CHAVASSE, 011011781, CE, Hq, UK Base
CAPTAIN MILTON BLUM, 0416576, MC, 312th Station Hospital
MAJOR LELAND SMITH, 05183289, QMC, Hq, Seine Section, TDY w/Hq UK Base
Trial Judge Advocate
1ST LT HARRY A SCHWAGER, 01557978, JAGD, Hq, UK Base
Asst Trial Judge Advocate
1ST LT JOHN J O'KEEFE, JR., 01004654, JAGD, Hq, UK Base
Asst Trial Judge Advocate
1ST LT FRANK M JOHNSON, JR., 0639967, Inf, 2D Reinf Depot, TDY w/Hq UK Base
Defense Counsel
1ST LT JOSEPH E CASSIDY, 01895036, AUS, 20th Reinf Depot, TDY w/Hq UK Base
Asst Defense Counsel

   All arraigned cases in the hands of the Trial Judge Advocate of the General Court-Martial aptd by par 2, SO 289, this Hq, cs, will be brought to trial by this court. Tvl directed by the President of this CM in connection with the functioning thereof is auth and is rec in the mil sv.

BY COMMAND OF BRIGADIER GENERAL THIELE:

JOHN S MALLORY,
Colonel, GSC,
Chief of Staff

Prologue

It was a brisk but not cold February morning in London. A hazy sun filtered through the light overcast, glinting off the slate rooftops, highlighting fresh repairs on the smoke-stained Victorian buildings. Although it had been more than a year since German buzz bombs had hit the city, it had been only eleven months since the last of the silent, supersonic V-2 rockets had devastated entire neighborhoods, and I had seen some of the remains of their massive destruction as I walked through the cobblestone streets of the Soho and Mayfair districts.[2]

A young replacement officer in the Army's 78th Division in Bremerhaven, Germany, I had been granted a ten-day leave to London, where, on this, my second day in the city, I planned to spend the morning attending a public session of an American court-martial being held in the British capital. But I needed help getting there amid the labyrinth of streets in that part of London.

"Excuse me, sir, can you direct me to Grosvenor Square?" I asked the man walking toward me.

"Well, it might be a bit hard to find," the Englishman said. "I'd better walk you there." And he did, reversing his course, leading me through Berkeley Square, turning left on Mount Street while asking friendly questions about where I'd served during the war.

The gentleman's response was typical of the British attitude toward Americans at the time. It wasn't the first time I had been personally escorted to my destination by a stranger. Here in England, my U.S. Army uniform conferred a privileged status—an honor that was being publicly called into question at the tribunal I was headed for. It was a military trial that all of us in the Army of Occupation had read about in *The Stars and Stripes,* the army's outspoken GI newspaper.

Written by army enlisted men, some of whose names subsequently became familiar by-lines in *Time, Newsweek,* and AP dispatches, *The Stars and Stripes* kept the rumor mill grinding—albeit discreetly, on the paper's last page. The front page of the daily was devoted to the Nürnberg (or Nuremberg) trials, which had recently begun amid the rubble in that German city.[3]

War-weary soldiers waiting to be shipped home derived real satisfaction from reading the detailed accounts of surviving "Nazi war criminals," charged with murder, enslavement, looting, and other felonies, being faced with their crimes and getting what they deserved.[4] The articles had almost as wide a readership as Milt Caniff's daily cartoon strip, "Male Call," featuring the fantastic Miss Lace.

But when GI readers turned to the back page of the same paper to read the conclusion of the front page Nürnberg articles, many were disturbed by the irony of small, juxtaposed items which mentioned other hearings by the Army's Judge Advocate General into allegations of physical brutality and even murder—atrocities said to have been committed by Americans against Americans who were prisoners in the guardhouses of the army's 10th Reinforcement Depot near Lichfield, in the county of Staffordshire, in England's Midlands north of Birmingham. Some who had spent time on the post vented their anger in letters to the "B-Bag" column (a reference to the cleaned-up version of standard barracks advice to a complaining GI: "Blow it out your B-Bag!"). Several letters included references to an unidentified "Beast of Lichfield" at whose hands at least one death was said to have occurred.

The story finally broke into the open on the front page of the December 5th, 1945, issue of the paper, when readers learned that "Each of nine prisoner guards, formerly stationed at the Lichfield (England) depot, are facing separate trials on charges of 'cruel and inhuman disciplinary treatment of stockade prisoners during the winter of 1944–45.'" The article went on to detail allegations which suggested practices that went well beyond the usual tough disciplinary regimes for which army guardhouses were well known.[5]

The world had just been through a trial of another kind. It had been a war unique in American history. Unlike those which succeeded it (with the questionable exception of the 1991 Persian Gulf War), World War II was characterized by a unanimity of national spirit—an absence of polarization, once the war had begun. It has been called "the last good war," one in which it was easy to tell the good guys from a classically execrable enemy. The Germans had overrun and subjugated most of Europe and systematically exterminated millions of Jews. The Japanese, without warning or declaration of war, had inflicted thousands of casualties and epic devastation in their surprise bombing of Honolulu's Pearl Harbor—newsreel scenes we have all witnessed many times since on television.

Responding with a moral outrage unknown decades later, hundreds of thousands of teenagers volunteered before they were drafted. Many of us in college signed up for Advanced ROTC courses in our junior year in the hope that, instead of being deferred as engineering students, we would be called up before we graduated. And almost all of us were. While we impatiently waited for our orders, grades in our other courses sagged. I remember our Field Artillery gunnery instructor at Iowa State, a Regular Army first lieutenant, lecturing us one day in 1942. "The trouble with you guys," he scolded, "is that you're afraid the war will be over before you get in. Well, I can assure you there'll be plenty of war left when you get there." He was right on both counts. Many of us were idealistic innocents. And a number of my classmates would have their names carved in the marble walls of Memorial Union's Gold Star Hall.

I had arrived in London the first week in February, 1946, staying in a room arranged by the Red Cross at a hotel on Duke Street, not far from Piccadilly Circus. On my second morning in the city, thanks to my British guide, I eventually found Grosvenor Square—a quadrangle of buildings enclosing an area of motley foliage that might once have resembled a village green. But after years of German bombing, it looked nothing like the handsome site of today's U.S.

Embassy. In a dingy two-story structure of smoke-stained brick facing the square, I found the temporary courtroom.

In a room with dirty windows and a bare wooden floor, the members of the court sat behind a long table on a dais, facing the spectators' gallery. A full colonel, the president of the court, sat in the middle of the group, at the peak of the rank pyramid, with the grades of the remaining members tapering off in descending order to two captains, one at each end. The officers wore customized "Eisenhower jackets," regulation green "blouses" that had been cut off below the waist by local tailors. These helped a little against the chill in the barely heated building, a carryover from London's wartime fuel shortage.

At a smaller table, next to a first lieutenant who was his defense counsel, sat the defendant, Sergeant Judson H. Smith. He had been a provost sergeant in charge of the guardhouses at the army's Lichfield replacement depot. He was personally charged with mistreatment of American soldiers who were serving time in the Lichfield stockade, many of them combat-wounded returnees recently discharged from Army hospitals.

At another small table sat a major who was the "trial judge advocate" (TJA), or chief prosecutor. His assistant, a captain, was questioning a witness when I slipped in and took my seat. The assistant prosecutor wore Army Air Corps insignia and pilot wings.[6] He looked a little old for an Air Corps pilot, I thought. He was at least forty years old.

The captain seemed to be investigating whether some two thousand troops received at the 10th Reinforcement Depot had been treated differently from other transients being shipped from Lichfield as replacements into combat units on the European Continent. Some of these soldiers, it developed, had been transferred from guardhouses in the United States, their sentences having been automatically commuted when they sailed for England. But when they arrived at the Lichfield depot, they had been billeted in its guardhouses.

The witness, a full colonel in his fifties, squinted (*scowled* is more like it) at his questioner through the round, steel-rimmed lenses of his government-issue glasses.

"Were they to be treated the same as other prisoners or differently from other prisoners?" the assistant TJA asked him.

"There was no distinction made," the witness answered petulantly. "When they were assigned, they were assigned as replacements. They were no longer prisoners."

"Weren't they kept in the stockade?" The captain sounded surprised.

"There was no stockade at Lichfield," the colonel snapped. It was a highly technical quibble. That the facility had three guardhouses behind barbed wire was a matter of record.

"They were in the status of prisoners when they were with you?"

"No! They were only in custody."

"You distinguish custody from other forms of imprisonment? In what manner? How do you distinguish between being in custody and being a prisoner?"

"They were turned over to the detachment commanders for safe delivery to their destinations."

This was a considerable euphemism, I thought. *The Stars and Stripes* had reported that they had been "put on board ship under gun."

"They were kept under guard, weren't they?" the assistant prosecutor persisted.

"I wouldn't be at all surprised if some of them were." The colonel's scowl turned to a sly grin as he sneaked a quick glance toward the spectators to gauge his audience's reaction.

"I move that the answer be stricken," the assistant TJA said in even tones.

The president of the court, a full colonel himself, was not quite so calm.

"I am going to ask you to answer the questions of the prosecution and not wander off on any side remarks," he told the witness. "You have come into this court and displayed a very hostile and belligerent attitude, which is certainly not in keeping with the attitude expected of a colonel in the United States Army. You have embarrassed the court. We have a sergeant on trial here and we are trying to get this case over. Please assist the court in expediting the case."[7]

"I am asking you what you did with them as commanding officer of the depot," the assistant prosecutor resumed. "You placed them under guard. Is that correct?"

"I turned them over under guard, yes."

"Will you tell the court just what difference there is in your mind between a man being under guard and a man being in prison? What is the difference?"

"That would only be an opinion on my part," he said breezily, with just the hint of a grin again. He had not been humbled. The captain ignored it.

"*Is* there any difference between a man who is restrained in a depot under guard and a man who is imprisoned in a depot? He's a *prisoner*, isn't he?"

"Yes, he's a prisoner." It was a grumpy answer.

"So, when you told the court a few moments ago that he was not a prisoner that wasn't so, was it?"

The colonel just sat there.

"Will you answer the question?

The witness flushed.

"I refuse to answer the question. The trial judge advocate is trying to embarrass me—" The law member cut him off.

"The remarks of the witness will be stricken from the record and the witness is directed to answer the question."

Before the morning was out, the witness would rise from his chair, shouting, "I'm not the defendant here!"

As it happened, I had arrived in the midst of an historic confrontation between Captain Earl J. Carroll of the prosecution and Colonel James A. Kilian, former commandant of the 10th Reinforcement Depot at Lichfield. He had originally been called by the defense as a character witness for Sergeant Smith, but he was now recalled to spend seven days on the witness stand under the prosecution's relentless cross-examination.[8]

It was a confrontation that would be sensationalized in *The Stars and Stripes*. Unheard of in a military court-martial, the assistant prosecutor seemed to be shifting the blame from the defendant to the *witness*, implying that the sergeant's brutality had been a product of the command policies of the Lichfield depot's administration—an administration headed by Commandant Kilian, whose orders Smith had merely been carrying out. It was the kind of twist that Andy Griffith, as the fictional lawyer Matlock, would resort to almost every week in a television series forty years later, except that this scene was devoid of the lightheartedness that characterized that TV series. These two powerful personalities had, by this point in the trial, become the only gladiators in the arena. The roles of everyone else in the room were reduced to bit parts.

The ensuing courtroom drama proved so addicting that I not only came back after lunch that day, but I also returned the next morning—and the next—until I had used up half my leave glued to a spectator's chair in the court. My rail trip to Scotland, together with the rest of my vacation plans, were abandoned to the spell of the trial and the epic struggle that was taking place in that room.

Each morning, as Captain Carroll, a San Francisco lawyer in civilian life, began spinning his web of carefully crafted questions, I watched the face of the aging cavalry officer gradually turn from a weathered tan to a ruddy pink to beet red as his anger and frustration mounted. By the time the president of the court adjourned the session for lunch, Colonel Kilian would be almost purple.

Lunch, perhaps accompanied by at least one drink, seemed to restore the witness's color and demeanor, but by five o'clock he would, once more, look like a man in danger of a heart attack or stroke. Under Carroll's incessant, seemingly insubordinate interrogation (Carroll was, after all, only a captain while Kilian was a full colonel), the former commandant came off as a stereotype; he seemed an arrogant, hard-nosed field grade officer of limited ability—an overbearing peacetime commander who had been promoted beyond his competence in wartime, and who had, perhaps, been given a noncombatant role to keep him out of trouble. That Colonel Kilian could withstand seven days of such aggressive questioning was, if nothing else, a testament to his stamina.

But it was only the beginning. This trial was to be the first of a series, the frontispiece of an emerging scandal that the press on both sides of the Atlantic would call the "Lichfield trials." Repercussions from Lichfield would be felt all the way to the White House. General Dwight D. Eisenhower, Army Chief of Staff, would personally order an investigation.

Partly, I think, the chronology that follows is about what war does to people—and what people are obligated to do to win a war in which the survival of the country is at stake (indeed, the survival of western civilization may well have been at stake). The book also explores the classic Nürnberg defense: a soldier's right—or, indeed, his obligation—to refuse to obey an unlawful order.

There are no unblemished heroes in the story of Lichfield. But there do emerge some highly motivated, sometimes colorful characters who fought each other fiercely at the time for what each believed to be right and in the best interest of the country. The last two chapters and the book's Epilogue describe what eventually happened to some of them.

This project has taken longer than I intended—half a century, if you start by counting the day I entered the courtroom. The contents of the book have been distilled from fourteen volumes of court records, two years of daily issues of the European editions of *The Stars and Stripes*, contemporary articles in *Time, Newsweek, U.S. News and World Report,* and the *New York Times,* supplemented by interviews with contemporary journalists as well as some of the principals and their associates at the time. The collected writings of Don Doane of the Associated Press, later with the Washington Office of *U.S. News and World Report,* were particularly helpful. Doane sat through much of the lengthy trial of Colonel Kilian, the last of the Lichfield trials.

The author is also indebted to attorneys Joseph Robinson, Thomas Foley, and, especially, to the late Earl Carroll. Major M. K. Beedle,

Regimental Secretary, Prince of Wales Regiment, Whittington Barracks, Lichfield, Staffordshire, England, provided invaluable historical
data. Other sources include the Center of Military History, the Library
of Congress, and the National Archives, Washington, D.C.; the U.S.
Army Judiciary, Falls Church, Virginia; state and county vital statistics records in Blair and Omaha, Nebraska, as well as Harlan and
Frankfort, Kentucky; the *Historical Register & Dictionary of the United
States Army,* and its successor, the *Official Army Register;* the California
State Bar Association, Los Angeles, California; and William Manchester's *The Arms of Krupp* (Boston: Little, Brown and Company, 1964).

In 1978, my wife and I visited and photographed the site of the
story, the century-old Whittington Barracks facility in Staffordshire,
long after it had returned to British control. Several of these pictures
are reproduced herein. Other Lichfield photos include the actual pictures presented as evidence by the prosecution in the Smith trial.
Shooting of these photographs was personally directed by Earl Carrol
who, upon being named assistant prosecutor, visited Whittington
Barracks, taking an army photographer to the former Lichfield depot.
At the deactivated site, he apparently posed a few army service personnel in his pictures, in order to give the court more than words.

The candid portrait of the aging Earl Carroll I shot "live," by available light, during our last interview in his study. With his permission,
I also took down from his wall the framed vintage photo of him in his
Air Corps uniform and copied it, hand held at a fifteenth of a second,
by the lamp on his bedside table. Although these pictures are not,
consequently, this photographer's best work, I was lucky to get them
at all.

As documented in the Epilogue, I had two memorable interviews
with assistant prosecutor Earl Carroll, forty years after he exposed
Lichfield to the world press, unleashing a torrent of public outrage
that many believe changed the United States Army, and especially its
judicial system, forever. But Earl Carroll had his doubts.

LICHFIELD

THE U.S. ARMY ON TRIAL

HEADQUARTERS
UNITED KINGDOM BASE
APO 413, US ARMY

SPECIAL ORDERS   6 Dec 1945
NUMBER 320

E X T R A C T

*

2. CAPT EARL J CARROLL, O512149, AC, Hq, US Forces, European Theater, TDY w/this Hq, is detailed as Asst Trial Judge Advocate of the General Court-Martial apt by Par 4, SO 316, this Hq, cs.

3. CAPT EARL J CARROLL, O512149, AC, Hq, US Forces, European Theater, TDY w/this Hq, is detailed as Asst Trial Judge Advocate of the General Court-Martial apt by Par 17, SO 264, this Hq, cs, as amended.

BY COMMAND OF BRIGADIER GENERAL THIELE:

JOHN S MALLORY,
Colonel, GSC,
Chief of Staff

1

THE TRIAL

Army Air Corps Captain Earl Carroll smiled when he read the mimeographed order lying on his desk at the army's United Kingdom Headquarters. This time, "by command of General Thiele," he would be on the *prosecution* side. Since VE Day in May, 1945, Carroll had been engaged in what amounted to a military hobby while he accumulated enough points to be sent home. A lawyer in civilian life, he had been volunteering as defense counsel for GIs who found themselves facing a court-martial for overstaying a pass, getting drunk, or, if they were in the Army of Occupation, for "fraternizing" with German civilians. His Perry Mason courtroom manner had grossly displeased more than one field grade officer who had sought to make an example of one of his troops.

It didn't help that Earl Carroll wore his limp service cap cocked at a jaunty angle and shoved back on his head. All Air Corps personnel customarily removed the circular springs from their leather-billed, eagle-crested caps, ostensibly so that cockpit headphones could be clamped over them—but the "20-mission crush" was really a badge that distinguished flyers from old-army Infantry "grunts" and Field Artillery "red legs." For a maverick like Carroll, it made an appropriate statement. Earl Carroll was described many years later by William Manchester in *The Arms of Krupp:* "Brash, likable, and genially Irish, Carroll had an instinctive gift for publicity, plunging eagerly from one controversy to another. . . . *Newsweek* had described him as 'flamboyant.' Others called him insubordinate."[2]

Born in San Francisco on March 23, 1904, Carroll's interest in the law was forged in his youth when his father, a salesman who lost a leg in a railroad accident, never received any compensation for his injury. A proud man, the senior Carroll refused to accept charity, and his resulting hardship may have been partly responsible for his son's lifelong advocacy of underdog causes.[3]

During the 1930s, Earl Carroll worked his way through law school as a musician in several San Francisco orchestras, where he played banjo, saxophone, and the bugle. Admitted to the bar in 1941, the same month the Japanese bombed Pearl Harbor, he began practicing law in the Mockadnock Building on Market Street in San Francisco with a partner, Thomas L. Foley of Hayward, California.

Carroll's hobby—his consuming passion—was flying airplanes. He eventually became an instructor in advanced aerobatics for the San Francisco Flying Club. In 1942, this led to a job in Sacramento as a civilian instructor for the Army Air Corps, and he persuaded the Air Corps to admit him to the service as a result. At thirty-eight years of age, Carroll was too old to be a fighter pilot, but he managed to wangle a job ferrying planes to Europe.

Some have suspected that Carroll's assignment to the London court was the result of manipulation by personnel in the army's UK Headquarters who had heard about events at Lichfield, and who wanted to see justice extended to more than a few scapegoats of enlisted rank. More likely, since Carroll's job ferrying aircraft had evaporated and his service record indicated he had been trained in the law, it was simply a logical assignment when 1st Lieutenant Harry A. Schwager was excused as assistant TJA. But Brigadier General Claude M. Thiele would regret having approved Special Order No. 320 appointing Captain Carroll as assistant trial judge advocate in the Smith trial.

The trial had begun two days earlier. Shortly before 1:30 P.M., on the afternoon of December 3, 1945, Sergeant Judson H. Smith, smartly dressed in his "Class A" uniform, entered the courtroom at 44 Grosvenor Square. The room had a musty smell, the result of its having been unoccupied for some time. The bare windows and peeling plaster walls were unrelieved by decoration of any kind.

Because of the seriousness of the charges, this was to be a *general* court-martial, the army's highest kind of tribunal, the others being "summary" and "special" courts-martial.

Smith walked up to the dais, faced the members of the court seated behind the long wooden table, and saluted. His salute was solemnly returned by the president of the court, a full colonel.

Executing an about-face, Sergeant Smith repaired to his place as the "accused," at a smaller table where two junior officers were seated: his defense counsel, 1st Lieutenant Frank M. Johnson, Infantry, and the assistant defense counsel, 1st Lieutenant Joseph E. Cassidy, AUS.[4] Although the army's *Manual for Courts-Martial* then in force did not require it, both Johnson and Cassidy had received legal training in their civilian lives. They were, however, relatively inexperienced recent law school graduates.

Judson Smith had been a coal miner in Harlan County, Kentucky, when he enlisted for his second hitch in the army in 1942. Born in Pittsburg, Georgia, population 310, on May 24, 1913, he had received an eighth-grade education before enlisting in the army for the first time in November, 1928, at the age of fifteen—perhaps as a ticket out of Cumberland, the little Kentucky mining town in which he grew up. He had been discharged from his first period of service in 1935, after which he ended up working in Kentucky coal mines after all.[5]

After his second enlistment on May 14, 1942, at Fort Thomas, Kentucky, Smith took the army's new General Classification Test (often called an intelligence test, although it actually measured a variety of skills and aptitudes), scoring in the second lowest of its five classifications. Until his indictment, however, he had an unblemished service record, with a consistent performance rating of "excellent."[6]

The court which Sergeant Smith faced was presided over by Regular Army Colonel Louis P. Leone, Infantry. As president of the court (always the senior officer present), he would function as chairman and chief judge. Seated next to Colonel Leone was Major Walter E. Hopper, Jr., law member. Regardless of his rank, the law member always sits next to the president. He serves as a kind of legal parliamentarian and referee, ruling on all questions of law and procedure. By regulation, he is preferably assigned by the office of the Judge Advocate General.

On either side of the president and his adjacent law member, in order of descending rank (if an officer happens to receive a promotion while he is serving on the court, the seating order is changed) were Major William L. Taylor, Transportation Corps; Major Benjamin E. Pers, Medical Corps; Captain James L. Chavasse, Corps of Engineers; and Captain Milton Blum, Medical Corps. These members of the court constituted the panel of judges in the case.

Major Leland Smith, Quartermaster Corps (and a lawyer in civilian life), was trial judge advocate (TJA), a role that is primarily that of chief prosecutor. First Lieutenant John J. O'Keefe, Jr., of the Judge Advocate General Department (JAGD) had initially been assigned as assistant trial judge advocate. He, together with another assistant TJA, 1st Lieutenant Harry A. Schwager (also JAGD), had been excused from serving by the office of the Judge Advocate General at UK Headquarters the day before. Both would be replaced with the assignment of Captain Earl Carroll. This seemingly innocuous personnel change would later alter the course of the trial.

To achieve a conviction before a court-martial, it is necessary to prove, first, that the accused did, indeed, commit the offense described in the charges and specifications, and, second, that the offense described is in violation of and punishable under the Article of War cited in the charge.[7]

In contrast to the tiers of law books in civilian courthouses and law offices, the Articles of War at the time were contained in just twenty-seven pages of the *Manual for Courts-Martial,* and consisted of a total of 121 laws, of which only forty-five "Punitive Articles" governed the conduct of U.S. military personnel. For American soldiers everywhere in the world, these eight pages of the manual constituted The Law. Indeed, when troops began acting restively at some military installations it was not uncommon for first sergeants to preempt their free time by literally reading them the Articles of War—not exactly a long version of the Ten Commandments, but sometimes close.

With such a compression of the world of law into so few pages, many of the Punitive Articles broadly collected a wide spectrum of offenses. The 93rd Article of War, for example (one of the articles under which Smith was to be tried), lumps together an assortment of crimes, including "manslaughter, mayhem, arson, burglary, housebreaking, robbery, larceny, embezzlement, perjury, forgery, sodomy, assault with intent to commit any felony, assault with intent to do bodily harm with a dangerous weapon, instrument, or other thing. . . ." And, in case of doubt, there was the catchall 96th Article of War, under which Sergeant Smith was also charged, stating "Although not mentioned in these Articles, all disorders and neglects to the prejudice of good order and military discipline, all conduct of a nature to bring discredit upon the military service . . . shall be . . . punished at the discretion of [the] court."[8]

Although courts-martial have a reputation for summary justice (the expression, in fact, derives from the army's one-man "summary" court-martial for minor offenses—an extra duty often performed by a company commander), it is a perception not altogether deserved. While it is true that military courts have a very high conviction rate, this is not usually the result of deliberate trampling on the rights of the accused. Rather, very few cases are brought to trial that are not likely to result in conviction. Having a case solid enough to achieve a guilty verdict is the responsibility of the investigating officer, who performs the role of a grand jury after charges are initially prepared. Indeed, any investigating officer who permits a weak case to come to trial is automatically in trouble. Military courts find losing cases an embarrassment.

The charges against Judson Smith were phrased in the standard jargon prescribed by the *Manual for Courts-Martial* extant at the time:[9]

CHARGE I: Violation of the 96th Article of War.

Specification 1: In that Sergeant Judson H. Smith . . . of Guard Pool, 302nd Reinforcement Company, 37th Reinforcement Battalion, 10th Reinforcement Depot did, while serving in the capacity of a Provost Sergeant, in conjunction with [eight others] between 1 August 1944 and 31 March 1945, wrongfully and unlawfully impose, cause to be imposed, and permit to be imposed cruel and inhuman disciplinary treatment upon the prisoners under his supervision and control, namely . . . [six are named] . . . and other prisoners whose names are not known by:

a. Causing said prisoners to stand facing a wall with their nose and feet touching the wall and requiring them to double time [run in place] for a period of more than two hours;

b. Forcibly causing said prisoners to eat an excess amount of food and thereafter causing castor oil to be administered;

c. Causing said prisoners to be placed in a room without proper lighting;

d. Causing said prisoners to scrub concrete floors with a brush and cold water for long periods of time and under such weather conditions as to cause great physical discomfort;

e. Causing said prisoners to extend their arms and retain them in a constrained position for long periods of time;

f. Forcibly causing said prisoners to eat and consume cigarettes;

g. Causing other unnecessary and extreme physical discomfort to the prisoners.

Specification 2: In that Sergeant Judson H. Smith . . . did . . . about the latter part of November 1944, wrongfully and unlawfully strike Private William D. Sims, then a prisoner under his control, upon the head with his hands, causing the prisoner's face to strike the wall, and strike him on the buttocks.

Specification 3: In that Sergeant Judson H. Smith . . . did . . . unlawfully strike an unknown garrison prisoner under his control.

CHARGE II: Violation of the 93rd Article of War.

Specification 1: In that Sergeant Judson H. Smith . . . did . . . about the latter part of November, 1944, with intent to do bodily harm, commit an assault upon Private Saul L. Russ, then a prisoner under his control, by willfully and feloniously striking the said Private Saul L. Russ on the body with a dangerous weapon, to wit, a club.

Four more specifications follow, identical except for the substitution of names. Victims of the beatings are cited, over a period extending from August, 1944, to March, 1945. They include Staff Sergeant James B. Gallardy, Private Aubrey L. Richey, General Prisoner Daniel MacMillan, and General Prisoner Gaspar Furnari.

These were the formal charges against Smith. The trial would bring out more odious details of guardhouse punishment at Lichfield. By the end of the month, the allegations began reverberating in the press back in the States. A *Time* writer seemed shocked when, in the December, 1945, issue, he described "men found with cigarets [sic], forced to eat them; men asking to go to the latrine, dosed with castor oil. Another allegation: Negroes in the mess hall were forced to crawl and bark like dogs before they were fed."

The writer's concluding paragraph was prophetic: "There were others besides Judson Smith facing trial—other enlisted men, some junior officers. The trail of trials might not stop there. The U.S. Army was on trial."[10]

2

THE DEPOT

The scene where these events were said to have taken place might have come directly from the pages of a Dickens novel. Built for the British Army in 1880, Whittington Barracks is characteristic of that forbidding Victorian style of architecture that was later copied by some American reformatories and asylums. Some modern architects explain it as a repudiation of the Georgian style and its preoccupation with prettiness. Others call it "classic orphanage."

Arranged in a lopsided quadrangle, the multistoried, interconnected buildings of this army post near Lichfield, England, were originally constructed of red brick. But a century of weathering has randomly stained the clay, giving the place a worn, haggard look. In the clocktowered headquarters facade, the brick is set in severe, frowning-eyebrow patterns over arched windows which peer out just below the sharply gabled roof line. The steep, steel-gray slate roofs are studded with hundreds of baroque brick chimneys, harking back to a time when the entire complex was heated by fireplaces. Built some time later, satellite clusters of auxiliary barracks buildings—long, one- and two-story corridor structures—surround the main quadrangle.

The entrance to the complex is dominated by a ponderous, foursquare fortresslike structure, Guardhouse No. 1. It is the only remaining guardhouse of the three in service during World War II. Replete with battlements and slotted windows in its corner towers, it is reminiscent of some of the surviving castle fortresses in Wales, a hundred miles to the west, that were built in the thirteenth century.

Although it is depressing even today, Whittington Barracks is obviously much better cared for now than it was during the war. *Time's* description of Lichfield in its December 31, 1945 issue painted a grim picture:

> The ugly red brick buildings, begrimed by industrial smoke, sat on a treeless limestone hogback. Most of the barracks windows were broken. There were no lawns or plantings around the camp. Worse than the looks of the place were the ugly reports that came from there:
>
> The newcomer saw a line of men double-timing along the walks. Even men who could barely walk, because of leg wounds received in combat, were forced to double-time to their cold, bleak barracks. Those who faltered were clubbed across the shins by guards.[1]

During Sergeant Smith's trial, Assistant TJA Earl Carroll would dispatch a photographer to the facility, ostensibly to document evidentiary material, but, perhaps more important to his own agenda, to capture the stark ambience of the place.

Whittington Barracks had been turned over to the American forces by the British late in 1942 as a staging area for the Allied invasion of Normandy on June 6, 1944—the greatest military amphibious landing operation in all history, launched from the shores of England. After D-Day, the facility became a "reinforcement depot," a U.S. Army post where individual, or "casual," replacement soldiers were sent to be processed for reassignment to combat units which had become depleted because of casualties. Between September, 1942, and September, 1945, when the base was returned to the British, some 340,000 American troops had passed through the Lichfield depot. Although most of the transients lived in the ancient brick barracks of the main complex, the overflow survived in pyramidal tents on what had been a golf course.

A significant portion of these replacements, especially in later years as the war ground on, were men who had been wounded in combat, and who had recently been released from army hospitals. Understandably, many of these veterans were less than enthusiastic about returning to their own or any other combat unit. Many went AWOL (absent without leave). Similarly, as the war heated up and Allied forces were driven back by the Germans during the Axis's last-ditch Battle of the Bulge (December, 1944), many casual draftees, exported to Lichfield from replacement training centers in the United States, also went "over the hill," as the GIs in the barracks called it.

Soldiers who were apprehended while absent without leave, or even those who returned a few hours late from pass or furlough, found themselves confined to the Lichfield guardhouse awaiting court-martial. Sometimes missing a single roll call was interpreted as prima facie evidence of absence without leave and proved to be a ticket to the stockade. There the offender found himself surrounded by convicted felons whose crimes ranged from theft of army property to rape and murder.

The attitude of the permanent cadre of the depot had been thoroughly soured by their experience with the first waves of replacement soldiers from the U.S. Under the unofficial "shape up or ship out" policy of many stateside army installations, the misfits, malcontents, and incompetents naturally formulated the first lists that entered the minds of commanding officers and staff NCOs when it came time to fill their replacement quotas. In fact, some of the early shipments to Lichfield were actually made up of *prisoners* who had been convicted by military courts in the U.S. of armed robbery, assault, rape, car theft, burglary, and other criminal offenses. Often literally put on board ship under guard, these felons deserted at their first opportunity. Lichfield cadre learned to be tough as nails in handling their temporary charges, and they did not distinguish between individuals.

Thus, the operation of prisons turned out to be a significant part of the daily business of the United States Army's 10th Reinforcement Depot. In addition to its function as a temporary jail, Guardhouse No. 1 was also the post provost marshal's office during the years the facility was occupied by U.S. troops. There were two other long, two-story brick buildings designated as Guardhouse No. 2 and Guardhouse No. 3. These ancillary structures have since been torn down, but photographs of their bleak exteriors and squalid interiors became some of Earl Carroll's prosecution exhibits and are reproduced in this book. Recently sentenced convicts, together with personnel awaiting trial, flowed into these prison buildings at the rate of fifty soldiers per day.

Army guardhouses and stockades have deliberately cultivated the image of a place to be avoided. Some, like Honolulu's Schofield Barracks Guardhouse, immortalized in James Jones's *From Here to Eternity*, were infamous. Early in World War II, a stockade at Fort Custer, near Battle Creek, Michigan, consisted of pup tents behind barbed wire—in midwinter.[2] Obviously, the Lichfield command did not want its guardhouses to be perceived as a comfortable retreat in which to avoid combat. Such a refuge would have been counterproductive to the mission of the facility.

In keeping with that objective, the physical facilities in the Lichfield guardhouses were spartan indeed—especially the plumbing. Two had no urinals at all. Each building had one toilet per wing, and, in contrast to the popular spit-and-polish image of army latrines, prosecution exhibit photos showed them to be filthy, with broken toilet seats and with leaking pipes and fixtures.

The temperature in the buildings frequently fell below freezing, with scrub water on the bare concrete floors turning to ice. Guardhouse No. 2 had a dark, bricked-up hole at the end of a row of cells which was used for solitary confinement. For these and other reasons, the testimony of Captain Roy E. King, post sanitation officer, Captain Rudolph E. Warnecke, medical officer, and Major Herbert W. Bluhm, post inspector, would be sought by the defense.[3]

Commanding officer of the Prison Company at Lichfield was Captain Joseph A. Robertson—though prisoners rarely saw him. On the organization chart, he reported to Major Richard E. Lo Buono, Post Provost Marshal. Prison officers directly in charge of the guardhouses were 1st Lieutenant Leonard W. Ennis and 1st Lieutenant Granville Cubage. But, for the most part, direct operation of the prisons was in the hands of noncommissioned officers and other enlisted personnel, nominally in charge of whom was Acting Provost Sergeant Judson

Smith. Often, noncommissioned officers who were casual transients being processed through the depot were temporarily assigned to guard duty in the Lichfield prison complex, even though they might hold a higher rank than the permanent personnel to whom they reported.

In command of the 10th Reinforcement Depot at Lichfield was Colonel James Alphonse Kilian, a tough, dedicated, Regular Army Cavalry officer whose permanent rank, in 1945, was lieutenant colonel. He had been promoted to the temporary rank of colonel early in the war in May, 1942, and he wore silver eagles on his shoulders.

Kilian had been born in a small town near Omaha, Nebraska, on July 27, 1891, the son of an Army Militia officer, Julius Nicholas Kilian. The elder Kilian was a captain in the Nebraska Infantry when his son was born, and he was later promoted to major.

Like his father, James Kilian made the military his life. He first enlisted in the army on June 8, 1907, a month before his sixteenth birthday. After being discharged sixteen months later, he briefly attended Virginia Polytech before enrolling at the University of Missouri in 1910. There he opted for military instruction instead of gym.

Upon attaining the age of twenty-one in 1912, Kilian quit college and enlisted as a private in the Missouri National Guard, which assigned him to active duty at Fort McKinley in the Philippine Islands. When his father died at sea the following year, he returned briefly to his mother's home in Blair, Nebraska, after which he reentered the University of Missouri. There he rose to the rank of cadet major in the university's Cadet Officer Corps in 1913, and to cadet colonel the next year, thus achieving the highest rank attainable in the Missouri State Military School—the equivalent of today's ROTC. He graduated in 1914, receiving a B.S. in agriculture with a minor in animal husbandry.

After his college graduation, Kilian became a second lieutenant, Infantry, in the Missouri National Guard. Discharged as a captain in

1919 after service in World War I, he then entered the Regular Army. By 1920, he had become a first lieutenant in the Cavalry, attending the Cavalry School's basic course in 1921, and completing the branch's advanced course in 1928. Two years later, he graduated from the prestigious Command and General Staff School, a coveted entry in a career officer's resumé, and he attained his Regular Army rank of lieutenant colonel in 1939. By 1944, Colonel James Alphonse Kilian, a soldier's soldier who had earned the Legion of Merit during World War II, was stuck in a dull, behind-the-lines administrative job at Lichfield—or so it seemed.[4]

3

THE CASE FOR THE PROSECUTION

Before Captain Earl Carroll reported to the court on December 6th, Major Leland Smith, trial judge advocate, had already rested the case for the prosecution, even though the trial was only three days old. After checking into the Cumberland Hotel at the northeast corner of London's Hyde Park the previous afternoon, Carroll began by reading the transcribed trial record to date, together with related documents. The latter went back to Judson Smith's arraignment in early October. In the file he found dozens of letters and telegrams, initiated by a temporary special defense counsel, 1st Lieutenant George W. Lamprolos, demanding the appearance of key Lichfield personnel to testify for the defense. But soon after that list of witnesses was submitted, a number of these officers received travel orders to be "redeployed" to the U.S. at once, thus occasioning such telegraphed responses from the army bureaucracy as:

OFFICERS REFERRED TO BEING NO LONGER SUBJECT TO ORDERS OF THE THEATER COMMANDER ARE PRESENTLY UNAVAILABLE AS WITNESSES.

When the defense pressed for depositions to be taken in lieu of testimony, the replies became even more vague. The witnesses were "believed to be in the United States," but were "unlocatable."[1]

Witnesses which the defense had sought to call included 1st Lieutenant Leonard W. Ennis, Infantry, who had been in direct charge of the guardhouse; Captain Rudolph E. Warnecke, Medical Corps, who had been the depot surgeon (the chief medical officer); Major Herbert W. Bluhm, Quartermaster Corps, the post inspector; and finally, Colonel James A. Kilian, commanding officer of the 10th Reinforcement Depot at Lichfield at the time the alleged events had taken place.

It appeared that the defense planned to claim that any wrongful acts committed by the defendant were the result of policies set at a higher level—possibly in compliance with direct orders. It was a defense not unlike the ones being offered in the Nürnberg trials being held across the English Channel at precisely the same time, facsimiles of which were offered once again almost half a century later in the trial of Oliver North and others involved in the Iran-Contra scandal of the 1980s.

Ultimately, the file revealed that the army, perhaps to avoid unfavorable press, had relented and agreed to call the witnesses asked for by the defense. After assimilating this background, Carroll read as much of the three days of trial transcript as had been transcribed. Carroll began warming to his new assignment. But he would enter the trial with a hidden agenda of his own—an agenda that would not always support the simpler objectives of the court.

Major Smith's first prosecution witnesses had been prisoners. The stories they told in the first person came off much uglier than the words in the charges and specifications. Questioning by Colonel Leone, president of the court, revealed that the daily schedule for the prisoners consisted of three and one-half hours of continuous calisthenics, from 8:00 A.M. until 11:30, after which they were marched in formation to a mess hall, where they stood outside at attention until their row was marched into the building. Inside, the prisoners were given twenty minutes in which to go through the chow line, eat their meal, and return their trays.

As subsequent testimony revealed, this left the prisoners no more than ten minutes in which to eat. Those at the end of the line got less time than that. After lunch, they were returned to the prison yard between the guardhouses, and by 1:00 P.M. they had commenced an additional four to five hours of calisthenics. This routine, it developed, was a seven-day-a-week schedule, Sundays included.

It was also revealed that the prison guards carried eighteen-inch billy clubs and other weapons, and used them freely. If a man was perceived to be not exercising vigorously enough, he got into trouble. Sergeant Saul L. Russ, the first witness, was still recovering from wounds he had received in combat when he ran afoul of Provost Sergeant Smith. Under questioning by the prosecutor, Russ described what turned out to be a typical occurrence:

The accused [Sergeant Smith] would walk between the lines of men as they "double-timed" [ran in place] and usually he would tell a tall man to pick up his legs higher if they weren't high enough for calisthenics. He came to me and my legs weren't high enough, and he ordered me to stand nose and toes against the wall. We faced the guardhouse as we double-timed. It was a brick wall.[2]

What happened next was repeated almost word for word by witness after witness. The prisoner was required to keep his nose and toes against the brick wall while he double-timed. If he, indeed, kept his nose to the wall while he ran in place, the soldier crashed his knees into the wall. So the prisoner would try to hop gingerly from one foot to the other, whereupon Sergeant Smith would order him to lift his legs higher. Unable to comply to the noncom's satisfaction, the prisoner would be struck from behind with a billy club.

Other witnesses testified that this kind of harassment—and beating—continued for twenty to twenty-five minutes before they were returned to the calisthenics ranks. Many limped back to the guardhouse in the evening with severe contusions that, as was developed in later testimony, received no medical attention.

Many minor infractions resulted in the "nose-and-toes" treatment. One of the "exercises" in the calisthenics classes consisted of standing at attention while holding one's arms straight out continuously for twenty minutes or more. If a prisoner's muscles gave way too early, he would be struck with a billy club and sent to "the wall" for the special treatment described.

The defense counsel's initial strategy during its cross-examination had simply been to attack the credibility of the witnesses because they were prisoners. This worked with at least one witness, Daniel MacMillan, a confessed car thief who was still a general prisoner and who admitted to having been convicted by courts-martial no less than seven times in two years. But other witnesses had been model soldiers until they had returned a few hours late from pass and were summarily charged with being AWOL. Even if one was physically present on the post, failing to attend any formation (especially if his absence caused him to miss a packet ship across the channel) could be an automatic ticket to the stockade.

More than one witness testified that the treatment he then received in the guardhouse actually provoked his going AWOL again upon being released. One man explained that he had gone AWOL to hitchhike into Birmingham to buy bandages and medication to treat injuries he had sustained in the stockade. Whether picked up by military police, or returning voluntarily, each man had received a substantially more severe sentence. And when he was returned to the guardhouse he was accorded the special treatment reserved for "repeaters." Sergeant Smith, the prisoners testified, frequently turned the man over to other jailers with instructions to "work him over."

Although the prosecution witnesses had been sequestered, they told essentially identical stories—about their own experiences and about the treatment of other prisoners, whom they named. Their third-person testimony about punishment inflicted on *others* helped deflate the defense's ludicrous argument that a prisoner could not positively identify who it was who struck him while his nose was against the wall, since the person wielding the club would have been behind him at the time.

When so challenged, witnesses testified to recognizing Sergeant Smith's unmistakable voice yelling obscenities, even though they were not permitted to turn their heads to look at him. Under cross-questioning, defense counsel Cassidy managed to get an admission from Sergeant Russ that at times he had withdrawn his nose an inch or two from the wall, making the point that the witness was not really "nose-and-toes" while he was double-timing as he had stated.

Reading the trial transcript as an experienced litigator, Earl Carroll found the defense's nit-picking tactics small-minded and silly.

Witnesses were asked whether they had ever tried to report the treatment they received at the hands of their jailers. The army, after all, maintained an office of the Inspector General which regularly visited army posts, including the guardhouse facilities at Lichfield. But even relatively moderate complaints reported anonymously to visiting IG officers resulted in retribution. Private Anthony R. Calogero testified about one such incident:

"It seemed that the major came up and wanted to know if any of the prisoners had any complaints, and he asked if we were getting enough food to eat. One of the prisoners told him we were getting enough food, but we didn't have enough time to eat the food. Then one of the jailers came in and asked what fellows didn't get enough time to eat their food, and about seven or eight of us went down. Later they turned the question into we were not getting *enough* food to eat."

"So what happened as a result?" the TJA asked.

"He [Sergeant Smith] brought us over to the mess hall and filled our trays up with food, and the ones who were giving out the food were told to make sure our trays were filled up.

"After we had consumed the first tray of food we were told to go up and get seconds, and the trays were filled up with a like amount of food. We came back to the table and sat down. Some of us couldn't finish it and we were told if we didn't finish it it would be shoved down our throats with a club."

"Then what happened?" Major Smith asked.

"Then we were taken back to the stockade and stood against the wall for about two hours and Sergeant Smith told the jailer to feed us castor oil."

Further questioning by Major Smith elicited Private Calogero's description of how he was made to scrub concrete floors with a GI brush in January, when the weather was so cold that the water sometimes froze on the floor and on the scrub brush as well. This punishment had been meted out "for not standing still in formation," he said. And he was by no means alone in scrubbing the floor. It was often scrubbed several times a day by prisoners who had "done something wrong."

Major Smith asked him why he had not reported this kind of treatment to prison officers.

"It wouldn't do any good," Calogero asserted. "Things that were going on were evident and they didn't need to be reported, and I didn't want the consequences if I was found out for reporting it.

"I knew if it was found out that I said anything I'd get beat up," Calogero declared, "and I decided it was healthier to keep my mouth shut—and a lot more comfortable."

In cross-examination, the defense counsel did his client little good by again attempting to intimidate the witness. As Private Calogero stuck to his guns, his apparent personal conviction invited further questioning by members of the court:

DEFENSE (Lieutenant Johnson): I want you to remember that you are under oath when I ask you this question. You have testified that you were afraid of what the consequences would be if you reported this. Did you know what the consequences would be?

WITNESS (Private Calogero): Yes, sir.

DEFENSE: You actually knew that you would be mistreated if you reported it?

WITNESS: Yes, sir.

DEFENSE: Now that you have sworn you actually knew that, I want you to tell the court why you knew this. Why do you swear today that if you never did report it and you never were mistreated for reporting it?

WITNESS: Because I don't consider myself any different from others who did report it. I was no exception. I expected that what happened to me would be the same as happened to the others who reported it and I'm positive of that. There were no exceptions in that place.

CAPTAIN BLUM (Medical Corps officer, interrupting): What happened to the others when they reported it?

WITNESS: I seen two of them who did report it and they were all marked up and cut. There was a bruise around the face, and the fellows complained that they couldn't walk. They were hit in the ribs. I couldn't see any of the body marks, but I could see the marks on their faces.

A procession of witnesses repeated similar stories of brutality. After each witness completed his testimony, the defense co-counsels would attempt to impeach his testimony because the man had been a prisoner at the time and consequently had an ax to grind.

But then Major Smith introduced a witness with no possible motivation for shading the truth: Staff Sergeant Ashur H. Baizer, who happened to have been assigned to temporary duty working in the prison while he was awaiting reassignment at the replacement depot. Sergeant Baizer's former unit, moreover, had been the Staff Judge Advocate's Section at U.S. Army Headquarters, United Kingdom Base.

Straightforward and articulate, Ashur Baizer's testimony contained the first indication that Lichfield brutality might actually represent the execution of policies set at a higher level. He had worked in the guardhouse for five or six weeks during October and November, 1944. He identified Sergeant Smith as the provost sergeant, and testified that he had seen Smith administer "nose and toes" discipline during calisthenics on numerous occasions. The calisthenics, he said, were continuous "from approximately 8:00 in the morning until about 11:30; and then for a like period in the afternoon."

When asked about the treatment of a Private Sims, Sergeant Baizer became the first witness to implicate Lichfield's prison officer, 1st Lieutenant Leonard W. Ennis:

"Sims was ordered to stand with his nose and toes against the wall and double-time against the wall, and in the process of double-timing he was struck on the sides of the head repeatedly by the provost sergeant on the order of the prison officer or assistant prison officer."

"Who was that?" Major Smith asked.

"Lieutenant Ennis," Baizer responded without hesitation.

While Sims was "nose and toes" against the wall, Sergeant Baizer related, Lieutenant Ennis ordered Sergeant Smith to "work the prisoner over." This, he said "was a routine phrase that meant administer physical punishment."

Major Smith asked what kind of physical punishment.

"Well, after Sims stood against the wall, Sergeant Smith ordered him to double-time. Sims made no move for a while to comply with that order. Sergeant Smith repeated it, and Sims turned his head. Evidently he was going to explain why he wasn't following the order, and Sergeant Smith struck him from the other side with his bare hand against his head; and after he had struck him several times the prisoner began to double-time.

"This continued for about ten minutes. At the end of the time the prisoner was sobbing, and evidently the provost sergeant had exhausted his anger and demanded an explanation of why he had not followed the order—which was that the prisoner had an excuse from the post hospital that he had a sore foot.

"When the punishment was over, Lieutenant Ennis ordered the prisoner to go back out in the yard where the others were having calisthenics."

Although Major Smith never followed up on Sergeant Baizer's statement that Sergeant Smith was following orders from Lieutenant Ennis, this allegation was not lost on the defense counsel, as became apparent when Lieutenant Johnson picked up the questioning.

"Start at the beginning from the time when Sims was taking exercise and tell us what happened," he ordered.

Sergeant Baizer complied:

"In the course of the calisthenics period Sims raised his hand. Lieutenant Ennis and Sergeant Smith were both in the yard then, supervising the exercises. After Sims was recognized, Lieutenant Ennis ordered him to come to him—to Lieutenant Ennis—on the double. Sims limped over to him or started to, and Lieutenant Ennis repeated the order. Even with that repetition, Sims continued to limp to him, at which time Lieutenant Ennis ran up to him.

"Sergeant Smith was in the center of the group of men in the front rank. Lieutenant Ennis brought Sims back to Sergeant Smith and said: 'Take this man inside the guardhouse and work him over.'"

Lieutenant Johnson questioned whether Sergeant Baizer had been close enough to accurately witness what was going on, and he asked where he had been standing.

"I should say five or six feet away," Baizer replied, adding that he had clearly heard Lieutenant Ennis order Sergeant Smith to "work the man over."

The defense counsel then asked a series of questions that sounded a great deal like a lead-in to the Nürnberg defense.

"Would Sergeant Smith have hit Sims if Lieutenant Ennis had not given him that order?"

Sergeant Baizer didn't know.

"Was Lieutenant Ennis the type of officer from whom a noncommissioned officer who worked under his command would refuse an order—*even though the order was wrong?*"

"It wouldn't be likely," the witness acknowledged.

"If you had been under the command of Lieutenant Ennis and he had given you an order to work Sims over, would you have worked him over?

"I couldn't say, sir," Baizer responded. "That was a question in my mind at the time."

Sergeant Baizer was excused, having made a significant impression on the court.

Major Smith's next witness also had been on temporary duty as a guard while stationed at Lichfield. Staff Sergeant John M. Newlands of the 135th Signal Engineers Company was sworn in and took the witness stand. He readily identified the accused Sergeant Smith. During his testimony, Newlands would be the first witness to suggest that the policy of prison brutality probably extended all the way up the chain of command at Lichfield.

The prosecutor asked the witness to describe an incident that (it would later be alleged in *The Stars and Stripes*) had resulted in a fatality.

"It was about 8:00 o'clock one morning," Newlands testified, "during that period at the time when the prisoners were outside of Guardhouse No. 2 in formation, waiting for their assignment to various details around the post. Sergeant Smith selected one of the men of this formation for no apparent reason and told him to stand against the wall of the guardhouse with his nose and toes against it and start double-timing.

"The prisoner was doing that for a short length of time, and the procedure of assigning other prisoners to detail went on. Shortly thereafter, Sergeant Smith returned to this prisoner and said he wasn't double-timing fast enough, and he told him to go faster. The prisoner apparently couldn't, and Sergeant Smith raised his hand and shoved the prisoner's head against the wall as hard as he could, striking the prisoner at the back of his head with his hand.

"The prisoner turned sideways after the impact just long enough for me to see that his nose was apparently smashed in. He was bleeding from what seemed to be his eyes, his nose, and his mouth."

The anonymous prisoner was probably Eril Bolton, who later died of a massive intercerebral hemorrhage.

Lieutenant Cassidy's cross-questioning for the defense was inept. His nit-picking questions tended to reinforce rather than impeach Sergeant Newlands's testimony. The assistant defense counsel's interrogation was interrupted by Lieutenant Johnson, who picked up the questioning:

"Was that act that Sergeant Smith did to this unknown prisoner up there revolting as far as your sense of human treatment of one person to another was concerned?"

"Yes, sir," Newlands testified, "it certainly was."

"Then why didn't you stop it? You were a staff sergeant, and Smith was only a sergeant."

"Because it was well known on that post that any action of that sort which was taken would be better not discussed; because it was by common knowledge authorized by the officers in charge of the guardhouse, and perhaps by those in charge of the post."

The defense counsel had elicited an answer that would play into Captain Carroll's hand as the trial proceeded.

The witness was asked when he had first reported what he had seen.

"After the war," Newlands replied. "I believe it was after 'V-E Day,' when one of our men in my particular unit had written a letter to some higher headquarters, and an officer from the Inspector General's Section in Paris came down to interview us and find out what we knew about this case. We had heard that investigations with regard to the 10th Replacement Depot had been made, and no satisfactory results had been obtained. [But] when this captain came to interview us, I was hopeful that finally something would be done to clarify the whole mess."

Even then, the sergeant said, he had some misgivings.

"I had the idea that certain officers of the 10th Replacement Depot were very influential, and that action might possibly be taken—not against me, but perhaps against friends of mine who were more closely connected with it."

"So you were interested in protecting the guards and prisoners who were your friends down there, and you were only interested in having Sergeant Smith tried for mistreatment?" Cassidy's tone was sarcastic.

"I was only interested in having those responsible for brutal treatment tried," the staff sergeant shot back.

Major Smith had saved his strongest witness until the end of his case for the prosecution. On Wednesday morning, December 5th, Private Aubrey L. Richey took the witness stand. His story would become a major issue in the case.

Twenty-two years old, five feet seven inches tall, and weighing about 135 pounds, Private Richey had been sentenced to the stockade for having been AWOL from the Lichfield post. But after a week in the guardhouse, he was hospitalized with tonsillitis (suggesting that he must have been very ill indeed, since the prosecution had already produced a number of other witnesses who testified that prisoners on sick call were almost always brushed off by the dispensary doctors and immediately returned to duty).

Richey had been hospitalized for fourteen days, during which he seems to have had a tonsillectomy. That an escaped prisoner should have a restful two-week vacation in a hospital bed upon his return apparently did not sit well with Lichfield cadre. Encouraged by Major Smith, Private Richey told his story:

"I came out of the hospital around the fifth or sixth of December. I was brought over by guard from the hospital, and when I walked into the door Sergeant Smith said, 'Well, I see you're back.' And he pushed me with a club. He put me up against the wall and wanted me to double-time. He asked me 'what'ya say?' And I told him I couldn't double-time. Of course I wasn't in too good a shape. I knew I was too weak to double-time."

"Had you ever had occasion to double-time before, under Sergeant Smith?" the prosecutor asked.

"Yes, sir," the witness replied. "More than once—for anywhere from two hours to three hours."

"Go ahead and tell the court what happened after this."

"We were standing right outside the office and he came on inside with me and he jabbed me with a stick in the ribs as I started in the door. When I got into the office I didn't notice who was in there, but I know there were two or three officers—or it might have been one officer and two or three sergeants.

"Sergeant Smith said, 'So you're not gonna double-time?' And when he said that he hit at me and poked me with this club he had in his hand. I threw up my hand and he hit me on the hand. Then, before I could do anything else, these other guys were coming over. I didn't know who they were. I turned around to look at them and Sergeant Smith hit me about two times on the head; and then I took about four licks. At about the fourth lick I was knocked out. I was going down and that's all. I was knocked out."

"What was the next thing you remember?"

"When I woke up I thought I was in solitary, but I was upstairs in No. 2 Guardhouse. I had a blanket under my head and I was lying on the floor. I was bleeding. My head was busted open in three places. I was too weak to get up at the time.

"I looked around and there were two or three guys standing around me. They didn't offer to help me up or anything. I looked over and Sergeant Smith was standing a little ways from me. Then they picked me up and sat me on the bed on the end of a bunk. I was sitting there with my head busted up and it was bleeding awfully bad and I was pretty weak. This lieutenant—I don't know his name, but he wears a 1st Division patch [the uniform worn by Lieutenant Ennis]—came up there and grabbed me up by the collar.

"I was put into this solitary confinement in No. 2 Guardhouse with my head still bleeding in two places. I've still got the scars on my head. There were two colored boys in there at the time. I don't know exactly how big the room was, but it was very small. They didn't have any heat and there was no light in there. I think they had one blanket for three men and we all slept together. You got one loaf of bread a day—and water—and you had to urinate in a bucket."

Richey added under questioning that he had received no medical attention for his injuries either before or after his confinement.

When it was the defense's turn, Lieutenant Johnson attempted to reduce the impact of Richey's testimony. He began by challenging the witness's statement about punishment he had received at the hands of Sergeant Smith.

"You testified a few minutes ago that Sergeant Smith made you double-time for two or three hours with your nose and toes against the wall?"

"He did."

"Before you went to the hospital?"

"Yes, sir."

"For how long?"

"For two or three hours at a time, and so were a lot of other guys."

"Nose and toes to the wall?"

"Yes, sir."

"Was your nose actually touching the wall?"

"I don't know whether it was actually touching the wall. It never did."

"Were your toes actually touching the wall?"

"Yes, sir. If they weren't, they came around and made you touch it."

"Will you demonstrate to the court how they did it?"

Private Richey left the witness chair and walked over to the wall of the courtroom, facing the wall with his toes touching the molding.

"Put your toes against the wall like *that*, and you kept them there. If you didn't, they would poke you in the stomach or the ribs. There were two or three guards on one side, and two here, and you couldn't do anything about it. You stood there double-timing or they hit you."

The defense counsel was not helping his case.

"You *cannot* double-time with your nose and toes against the wall, can you?" the lawyer demanded.

"My nose and toes were not touching the wall all the time. Common sense tells you that."

Lieutenant Johnson turned and addressed the court. "Let the record show that it is physically impossible for a man to double-time with his nose and toes against the wall."

Major Smith rose in response as Private Richey returned to the witness chair.

"The phrase," the prosecutor explained, "according to the testimony of the witness, does not mean that during the time when the person was double-timing his nose and toes would be against the wall because that would be an impossibility. The phrase 'double-timing with nose and toes against the wall' means that the prisoner had his nose and toes against the wall, and he was told to double-time as nearly in that position as he could be if he were double-timing."

Major Hopper, the law member, spoke up. "I think that the court is aware of the actual meaning of that."

Defeated in pursuing that line of questioning, the defense counsel switched to casting doubt on the witness's ability to estimate time accurately while he was double-timing against the wall. He began by challenging the accuracy of the witness's recollection of the dates involved:

"Are you sure that the time Sergeant Smith hit you was in December?"

"That's right, sir," Richey answered.

"If Gallardy comes on the witness stand here and testifies that he saw you whipped by Sergeant Smith in January, will that be a lie?"

"Well, it would have to be, I guess."

"It would have to be, wouldn't it?"

"Yes, sir."

"If Claim comes on the stand here and swears that you were whipped by Sergeant Smith in January, will that be a lie?"

"Well, I couldn't say, sir."

"You don't know whether or not you were whipped?"

"It wasn't in January."

"Then if he says that he saw you whipped in January, that's a lie, isn't it?"

"I don't know what anybody else says."

"You said that you were not whipped in January. If anybody says that you were, it's a lie, isn't it?"

"That's right, sir."

Members of the court were getting restless. Finally, Richey himself spoke up.

"I would like to ask you something, sir. I would like to ask the court just what that has got to do with this trial, sir?"

However appropriate it might have been, there was no applause from the spectators' gallery.

Again, Major Hopper responded, explaining to Private Richey that when anyone takes the witness stand it is the right of the defense to attack his credibility.

Lieutenant Johnson again changed the subject, switching to an examination of previous offenses committed by the witness. The defense counsel read from a sworn statement Richey had made to the court's investigating officer. In the statement, Richey admitted he had been absent without leave more than once.

"Do you remember saying that you were AWOL sixty-five days?" the defense counsel asked.

Richey said he did not remember. He did recall telling the investigating officer that he had never gone AWOL until he arrived at Lichfield, "when I was treated like I was."

Because Richey had signed the sworn statement, Johnson suggested that he had committed perjury, since sixty-five days was not a correct count of the number of days he had been AWOL.

This was too much for the law member. Major Hopper addressed the defense counsel, sounding like an impatient law school professor.

"When you are endeavoring to impeach the testimony of the witness by referring to a sworn statement, it should relate to matters to which he is testifying on the stand."

Major Smith asked to make a statement "for the record and for the benefit of the defense counsel":

"It will be my submission that you cannot impeach the witness on this collateral matter unless he denies that he made that statement. . . . A man may get drunk and a man may get into a fight. Those things are not convictions which affect his capability as a witness. Of course, if he is himself on trial, they can be introduced against him if he is convicted. But this man is not on trial. He is a witness, and only those convictions which he has had which affect his capability—that is to say, those which involve moral turpitude, are admissible against him."

"With the permission of the court, I will withdraw what I said," the chagrined defense counsel offered.

Before dismissing the witness, Colonel Leone asked Private Richey to approach the table where the members of the court were seated so they could examine his scars, some of which were concealed by his hair. The law member asked Major Pers and Captain Blum, the two

Medical Corps doctors, to examine Private Richey and to describe his injuries for the record.

Separating the witness's hair with his fingers, Major Pers dictated his findings to the court reporter:

"There is a lateral scar on the forehead about two and one-half inches long over the front parietal area. It is a scar two to three inches long—a healed scar. There is another scar about three inches long over the right parietal region; and there is a healed scar on the scalp about three inches long over the left parietal area of the scalp."

Perceiving the empathy of the court, Major Smith had Richey put his height and weight into the court record (five feet seven inches tall, 135 pounds—probably less at the time he was released from the hospital).

Major Smith's next witness, Private Louis L. Kardon, corroborated Richey's testimony. Having made a statement to a major in the Inspector General's office about conditions at Lichfield after his own reassignment, Kardon had actually received a cablegram from General of the Army Dwight D. Eisenhower, commander of U.S. Occupation Forces in Germany, ordering him back to England from Germany to be a witness in the trial.

Major Smith first established that Kardon had known Richey for about two and one-half months when they were both prisoners. The witness testified to having seen Richey being forced by Sergeant Smith to double-time against the wall for as long as "an hour or two," and to seeing him otherwise brutally treated. He had seen him being dragged upstairs in Guardhouse No. 2 by Smith and others and shoved into "the hole," as they called the solitary confinement cell. As it happened, Kardon's bed was right next to "the hole," so he was in a position to know that Richey had been in solitary for just over two weeks, and he had seen him in his weakened and battered condition when he was finally released from the bricked-up cubicle.

When the assistant defense counsel had his turn, Lieutenant Cassidy (who, typically, had questioned whether the windows had been sufficiently clean to permit witnesses to clearly see what they testified to) went immediately to the impossibility of Kardon's knowing what had gone on in that dark, windowless room.

But the defense was in for a surprise. Kardon explained that there had been a secret loose brick in the wall of the solitary cell right next to his bed, and at night he and Richey opened this breach in the wall to talk with each other. In fact, he said, other prisoners had supplemented Richey's diet of bread and water with food they smuggled back from the mess hall, passing it through the hole.

When the next witness, Pfc Robert W. Schwerftberger, was sworn in, he told a particularly chilling story. While he and two other prisoner had been taking showers in an adjacent building, one of them was using forbidden hot water. Sergeant Smith and Sergeant Jones, another jailer, burst into the shower room and beat the wet, naked man into unconsciousness with their billy clubs.

The prosecution's last witness, General Prisoner Gaspar Furnari, testified to having been beaten with clubs for at least fifteen minutes by five jailers at the same time—Sergeant Smith and four others. He claimed their action was without provocation. They had begun by pushing him from one man to another, he said, "trying to get me mad, so they could really work on me. But when I didn't, they got angry instead."

Under further questioning by the prosecution, Furnari stated that all of his attackers, including Sergeant Smith, participated in the beating, and that they had continued to beat him after he fell to the floor. The soldier offered to show the court where the beating had taken place in the Lichfield guardhouse.

Lieutenant Johnson rose to cross-question the witness. Seeking to minimize the effects of the punishment Kardon had described, the defense counsel asked him how long he had spent in the hospital after the beating.

"I didn't go to the hospital," Furnari responded.

"How long was it before you went to the dispensary?" Johnson asked.

"They didn't take me to the dispensary."

"Do you mean to tell this court that five guards and jailers whipped you and you didn't go to the dispensary or the hospital?"

"That's right."

"How long after you were whipped did you report it to officers?" Johnson now demanded.

"I understood that everybody who gets whipped keeps it to themselves," the witness explained; "don't report nothing to no one, unless they want to get beat up again."

The defense counsel had succeeded in making things worse for his client. Since the members of the court had no questions, the witness was excused.

At 11:25 A.M. on December 5, 1945, less than two full days into the trial, after presenting fourteen witnesses, Major Smith rested the case for the prosecution. That same day, *The Stars and Stripes* featured its first headline about the trial:

YANKS TELL OF BEATINGS AT LICHFIELD TRIAL

Stars and Stripes staff writer Ed Rosenthal, who had been present in the courtroom, described how prisoners at the 10th Reinforcement Depot guardhouse were "locked up, cut, and hit in the ribs." His piece went on to describe Calogero's "castor oil treatment," the fact that "he was forced to scrub a concrete floor with cold water and a GI brush during bitterly cold weather in January, 1945," and that "the water froze on the floor and brush." Rosenthal, obviously shocked by the testimony, wrote of "three solid hours of calisthenics without a break until lunch time, and another three hours in the afternoon," and concluded his December 4, 1945, dispatch from London with these details about the case:

Pvt. Anthony R. Calogero, a 1st Division Infantry combat man, testified at the reopening of the Lichfield general court-martial here today. . . . The first trial opened yesterday after a six-week delay to summon witnesses, including Col. James. A. Kilian, former Lichfield CO, from the U.S. and the Continent.

Dressed neatly in a sun-tan shirt and Eisenhower jacket with three hash marks and six overseas stripes on his sleeve, Sgt. Judson H. Smith of Cumberland, Kentucky, was the first of nine MPs to be tried in the Grosvenor Square Courthouse. His trial is expected to last about a week.[3]

But, as subsequent events proved, Rosenthal was more accurate as a reporter than as a seer.

SOUTHERN GERMANY EDITION

One Year Ago Today
The Germans retired on the Siegfried Line and the Allies advanced swiftly on a front of nearly 200 miles.

THE STARS AND STRIPES
Unofficial Newspaper of U.S. Armed Forces in the European Theater

The Weather
Today: Fair. Maximum temperature 41.
Tomorrow: Little change.

Volume 1, Number 193   20 Pfennig   Tuesday, November 20, 1945

20 Top Nazis Go on Trial Today

80th Inf. Div. To Sail Late In December

PARIS, Nov. 19—The 80th Inf. Div. has been alerted to go home as a Category IV unit and should sail during the latter half of December, the G-3 Section of USFET Rear announced today.

The 80th Div., now on Category I-T (temporary occupation) assignment with the 3rd U.S. Army in Czechoslovakia, was given a readiness date of Dec. 15. Redeployment officials said, however, that a man assigned to the outfit should not expect to be home by Christmas.

Theater Service Forces headquarters, meanwhile, announced that Camp Lucky Strike, largest in the Le Havre POE staging area, had been closed for major redeployment use. It had expedited the return of more than 330,000 soldiers to the U.S.

To Be Used in Emergency

In the future Camp Lucky Strike will be used only in emergencies. It consists of non-winterized tents.

Not Us, Russians Say Of Black Market Deals

MOSCOW, Nov. 19 (UP)—U. S. and British troops, and not Russians, are operating the black market in Germany, the Soviet magazine New Times charged yesterday.

Rejecting "malicious slander against the Red Army," the magazine asked, "what travelers haven't seen British and American soldiers boldly selling cigarettes and other goods, sometimes even military weapons?"

New Times listed specific instances and dates of Anglo-American black marketing, and asserted, "It's no secret that not only privates engage in such trade." The magazine said that on Oct. 26, Soviet patrols "were compelled to detain" an American brigadier general and a British colonel for selling watches.

Reds Rebuffed, De Gaulle Wins Confidence Vote

By RICHARD PRYNE
Staff Writer

GI Dragnet Again Out In Germany

By ROBERT MARSHALL
Staff Writer

FRANKFURT, Nov. 19—Germany was being combed today for evidence of resistance to occupation forces, black market dealings, and other illegal activities as the Army went into the final phases of its second "Operation Tallyho."

The operation went into action at dawn Sunday with all available troops in the American zone taking part in the dragnet. In groups of varying sizes, armed soldiers raked through civilian populations for evidence of unlawful actions.

Search for Weapons

With strongly-manned road blocks and roving patrols, the operation was intended to uncover anything which might indicate individual or organized resistance to the occupation, such as illegally possessed weapons or ammunition. Searches were also being made for fuel,

First Frau in Jail

Ex-Himmler Aide Ailing, Can't Appear

By ARTHUR NOYES
Staff Writer

NURNBERG, Nov. 19—The International Military Tribunal announced tonight that 20 members of the Nazi hierarchy accused of multitudinous war crimes would go on trial as scheduled at 10 a. m. tomorrow.

There would have been 21 defendants in the prisoners' dock, but Ernst Kaltenbrunner, former right-hand man of the late Nazi hangman, Heinrich Himmler, suffered a cranial hemorrhage last night. U.S. Army physicians said he had recovered sufficiently yesterday to mumble his "regret" that he would not be able to face trial tomorrow.

The tribunal's announcement that the trials would open on schedule came at 7:30 tonight, after a day of indecision in which four motions before the tribunal made it appear possible that the trials might be postponed at the last minute. The French had asked for a rehearing

---

SOUTHERN GERMANY EDITION

One Year Ago Today
In the Aachen area Allied patrols were within sight of the Roer River which was backed by a strong enemy defense belt.

THE STARS AND STRIPES
Unofficial Newspaper of U.S. Armed Forces in the European Theater

The Weather
Today: Fair. Maximum temperature 41.
Tomorrow: Snow.

Volume 1, Number 194   25 Pfennig   Wednesday, November 21, 1945

Charges Read in Trial of 20 Nazis; Defendants to File Protest Today

Once More the Leaders Sit Together, but as the Conquered and Accused

Indictments Bore Many Of Accused

By LESTER BERNSTEIN
and STODDARD WHITE
Staff Writers

NURNBERG, Nov. 20—The hour of reckoning came today for 20 kingpins of the Hitler gang, and, sitting before the International Tribunal that is trying their cases and will pass upon them the judgment of the Allied world, they resembled nothing so much as an oversized jury of business men.

Twenty political fanatics, militarists and financiers whose mad plans to take Europe and remake it after their own designs nearly succeeded, displayed boredom, concern and sarcastic amusement as they shifted back and forth on the hard wooden benches facing four judges and alternate judges.

Headlines in *The Stars and Stripes* on the first and second days of the Nürnberg trials, whose proceedings paralleled those of the Lichfield trial in several ways. (Courtesy of the Library of Congress)

Headquarters and main quadrangle of Whittington Barracks near Lichfield, Staffordshire, England, home of the 10th Reinforcement Depot during World War II. Colonel Kilian's office was in the clock-tower building. (Photograph by the author, 1978)

Barracks structure similar to Guardhouses Nos. 2 and 3 at Lichfield. (Photograph by the author, 1978)

Barracks buildings in the Lichfield complex. (Photograph by the author, 1978)

Captain Earl J. Carroll, Army Air Corps, c. 1943. (Photographed from the original by the author, 1979)

Colonel James A. Kilian, commandant of the 10th Reinforcement Depot at Lichfield. (Associated Press)

4

THE DEFENSE BEGINS

On Thursday morning, December 6th, Captain Earl J. Carroll was sworn in as assistant trial judge advocate. In less than an hour he began entering objections to the form of questions put by the defense. His first utterance, as he interrupted Lieutenant Johnson's interrogation of Major Richard Lo Buono, Lichfield provost marshal, was a harbinger of things to come:

"If it please the court, it is all right to summarize questions on cross-examination, but this is *direct* examination. Counsel is putting answers in the witness's mouth."[1]

By afternoon Carroll began conducting some of the cross-examination for the prosecution. The emotional temperature in the courtroom went up perceptibly as he clashed with both the defense and the court. Perhaps fueled by his reading of the trial transcript the night before, he was more than a little testy in protesting a ruling by the court's law member, Major Hopper, about his aggressive questioning of Major Lo Buono:

"This witness climbs on the witness stand and and he tells this court 'We had definite programs. They were all laid out. I knew exactly what they were. We had these men do this, that and the other thing. None of these men were mistreated. I knew exactly what they were assigned to.' And you get into cross-examination and he knows nothing. Or, if he knows it, he refuses to reveal it. You pin him down on one thing and he squeezes out."

Although Major Hopper once again instructed him to drop his belligerent, antagonistic manner in cross-examining the defense witness, Carroll refused to let the evasive provost marshal "squeeze out." He continued hammering away at the officer until the defense counsel finally complained:

"I would like the record to reflect that the prosecution have been three times directed by the court to restrict his testimony, but he insists on following the same line of testimony and questioning."

Before the day was out, the new assistant prosecutor had earned a stinging rebuke from the law member:

"Captain Carroll, you have been instructed by the court in regard to this testimony. You have also been vitally instructed twice that the court is not interested in sarcastic remarks to the witness or the defense, and the display of loss of temper on your part has nothing to do with it."

Lieutenant Frank Johnson, Sergeant Smith's defense counsel, had begun his case the day before with a series of motions. He immediately won a dismissal of the the charge of "forcibly causing said prisoners to eat and consume cigarettes" because the prosecution had presented no evidence to support the charge. After registering the complaint that a requested witness, Major Herbert Bluhm, depot inspector at Lichfield, had yet to show up, Johnson called his first witness, 1st Lieutenant Donald Ridge.

The defense had called Ridge in an apparent effort to impeach the testimony of Daniel MacMillan—the felon who had been convicted of car theft, among other things, and who had testified for the prosecution. But when Johnson began to put questions to his witness seeking to establish MacMillan's poor reputation for veracity in his former unit, the 113th Infantry Regiment, Major Smith objected at once, arguing that "anything the witness might have observed about the man while he was in that company at a different time and a different place than the events testified to is immaterial." The prosecution's objection was sustained and the defense's first witness was summarily excused.

Lieutenant Johnson's next witness merely presented some pictorial layouts of the Lichfield compound in order to enter them into the record. But then the defense introduced 1st Lieutenant Granville Cubage, Field Artillery, one of the two 10th Reinforcement Depot police and prison officers. (1st Lieutenant Leonard Ennis was the other.)

Tall, blond, twenty-seven years old, Lieutenant Cubage was the son of a university president and was a student in civilian life. One journalist who met him expressed the opinion that "Granville Cubage was a decent officer who, given a choice, would have put the job of serving as police and prison officer at any location at the bottom of his preference list."[2] But Lieutenant Cubage had been assigned the job at Lichfield from December, 1943, until March, 1945, and since Lieutenant Ennis left the post in December, 1944, Cubage was the only police and prison officer at Lichfield thereafter.

Lieutenant Cubage testified that he interviewed every prisoner sent to the guardhouse, later admitting that would have meant at least fifty interviews a day, and that he regularly talked to many of them while they were incarcerated. The only complaints he ever heard, he said, had to do with inadequate mail service, lack of toilet articles, and other minor beefs. He swore that he had never seen Sergeant Smith mistreat a prisoner and that the only prisoner he ever saw Smith strike was Private Richey. Cubage told a very different story about that incident from the one the prosecution had presented:

"It was about the middle of December. Richey had recently escaped from the guardhouse. I believe he had just been apprehended. [Richey, it will be remembered, had testified to having just returned from sixteen days in the hospital.] I asked to see him, to see how he managed to escape, or what were the conditions of how he escaped, and I called for him. Sergeant Smith was in the office, and he went down to get Richey.

"I was sitting in the office behind the desk. As the door opened I heard Sergeant Smith say 'Get inside.'

"When I looked up I saw Richey turn around and hit Sergeant Smith in the face. Sergeant Smith stumbled back over the coal box, and immediately Richey was on top of him. Sergeant Smith hit Richey with a club, and someone on the left of me grabbed hold of Richey."

The confrontation seemed unlikely, considering the difference in build of the two adversaries. When Richey was on the witness stand, not far from the defense table, it had been apparent that Sergeant Smith was three inches taller and at least forty pounds heavier than the witness. Richey, moreover, had just returned from the hospital at the time of the incident, having testified that he was still very weak.

Lieutenant Cubage continued his narrative:

"Someone ran across the room and grabbed Richey. At the same time someone was coming in the door. Two people—I don't know if they were guards or duty sergeants—grabbed Richey and took him out."

Lieutenant Johnson asked whether the prisoner had been taken directly to solitary confinement. Cubage said he didn't know.

"Immediately after it was over with, Sergeant Smith's mouth was bleeding a little," the witness said. "He came over and sat down by the fire. I sent someone over after Captain Robertson, and Captain Robertson came over with Lieutenant Ennis, and they examined Richey and Sergeant Smith."

This last statement seemed to contradict Cubage's own testimony moments before when he said Richey had been immediately taken away by two men and, thus, would no longer have been present. Major Smith missed this point in his cross-examination, probably because it was delayed until the next day.

The witness seemed to become rattled when the prosecutor asked whether Richey had received any medical treatment. Changing his testimony, Cubage now claimed that he had ordered Richey taken to the dispensary. When reminded that he had earlier "assumed the two guards took the prisoner to solitary," he lamely suggested that perhaps the guards didn't hear his order.

To clear up the matter, Major Smith asked whether Richey's name had been entered in the organization's "sick book," or on the set of three-by-five index cards kept on each prisoner. Cubage was certain it had been entered in both. These records, the TJA observed, would also settle the confusion about whether Richey had just returned from the hospital as he claimed, or from being AWOL as Cubage claimed. The prosecutor suggested that the records should be submitted to the court.

"The organization has been abolished and I don't know where these records are," Cubage said.

In his redirect examination, Lieutenant Johnson had the former prison officer fix exactly where the altercation had taken place, using the blueprints of the building plans that his earlier defense witness had brought in—perhaps to lend credibility to his witness's testimony with precise physical detail.

When the defense turned to the matter of serving food to the prisoners, Lieutenant Cubage testified that, although there were many problems associated with feeding eight hundred prisoners in a mess hall which seated only two hundred, he always made sure everyone got enough to eat. To assure that, he was usually present for least one meal a day.

The defense counsel repeated his question about men eating excessive food.

"I observed that the prisoners could take as much as they wanted, and they could eat as much as they wanted to. I believe that they consumed a ration and a half to two rations. It varied from time to time."

"There has been some testimony to the effect that castor oil was administered to the prisoners," the defense counsel asserted. "What, if anything, do you know about that?"

"We had several cases of dysentery in the guardhouse. I had been sending them down to the dispensary. Captain Warnecke, the medical officer at the dispensary, called me up and told me to come down and get a bottle of castor oil and to administer this to the prisoners myself personally. He wanted an officer to do it. The reason was because the dispensary was overloaded with men, and it would cut down the confusion in the dispensary. So I sent a man down after the bottle, and for two or three days I gave them castor oil according to the amount he wanted given, which was two tablespoons from the mess gear."

"Was any prisoner ever administered castor oil without them volunteering for it?"

"Never."

"Was any prisoner ever forced to eat an excess amount of food in that mess hall while you were prison officer?"

"Never!"

In his later cross-examination, Major Smith would fail to explore the medical wisdom of prescribing a cathartic like castor oil for dysentery (which is characterized by hemorrhagic diarrhea, due to an ulcerated lower bowel).

Lieutenant Cubage was asked about the rules for incarceration and the conditions associated with solitary confinement. The only persons authorized to place a prisoner in solitary, he said, were Major Lo Buono or himself. Sergeant Smith was authorized to take such an action only in an emergency, "in case of violence or for the safety of other prisoners and the guards." The sergeant had exercised such authority only once, Cubage said, during an attempted prison break in Guardhouse No. 3.

As prison officer, Lieutenant Cubage personally inspected the solitary cell three or four times a week, he said, together with any prisoners confined there. As he described it, the room was identical with other cells.

"There was no difference whatsoever." It was, he said, fifteen feet square—the same size as his own office downstairs. Its walls were not bare brick; they were covered with plaster and had even been painted. Although there was no electricity in the room there were "two very large windows, probably a total of six feet across and six or eight feet high."

Because there was no way to heat the room, the officer explained, and because some of the glass was broken, the windows were partially covered by blackout blinds; but it was never totally blacked out. At one time, it was true, these blinds had been nailed down to help keep out the cold, but at the recommendation of the sanitary officer, Captain King, the nails had been been removed.

"No person was ever placed in solitary confinement where that solitary confinement was darkened." The way Cubage described it, "the hole" didn't deserve its pejorative nickname. The defense counsel then had the witness deny for the record that there had been any "loose brick," which would have been impossible if the wall had, indeed, been plastered and painted.

When questioned about prisoners in solitary being required to sleep on the floor with only a single blanket (and with neither a bed nor a mattress), Cubage explained that the room originally "had beds that the British used, but the prisoners didn't like them. We used those for probably six months. The prisoners said they would rather sleep on the floor."

In any case, he was positive the men had been warm enough at night. The prisoners were issued as many blankets as they wished, he said, and it was common for them to take as many as seven blankets each. (In subsequent rebuttal testimony, Aubrey Richey repeated that he was issued a single blanket at 10:00 or 11:00 P.M. each night, and this cover was taken away at 6:00 A.M. the following morning.)

Recalling that Private Richey had testified that while in solitary he had been required to urinate in a bucket, Colonel Leone interrupted with a question.

"What sanitary facilities did you have available for the prisoners?"

"The prisoner was allowed to go to the latrine, which was ten feet from the solitary door."

"How could he get permission?" The colonel's tone was skeptical.

"Just tap on the door and the jailer would open it for him. There was always a guard within a few feet of the door to the solitary cell—twenty-four hours a day."

The defense finally got to the matter of calisthenics. According to

Lieutenant Cubage, "During the long summer days they could get in an hour of exercises in the morning. Then, the prisoners, after they came in off their [work] details, would take a little close order drill or calisthenics for about an hour in the afternoon." The calisthenics were given right out of the Infantry Drill Regulations, he said, and the prisoners were given a fifteen-minute break after each fifteen minutes of calisthenics. But in winter there could be no calisthenics at all because the days were too short.

It was true, the prison officer acknowledged, that there were occasions when a man was ordered out of formation to stand facing the wall of the guardhouse. But he made it sound like the grade-school punishment of standing in a corner. If, for example, a prisoner heckled the guards, he might be ordered to stand facing the wall until all the others had been marched into the mess hall; then he would have to eat last. But there certainly was no "nose and toes" business or double-timing or anything of that description.

Cubage further declared that he had given the guards an order "against race discrimination, using profanity, or abusing prisoners—taking advantage of a prisoner's rights. I tried to impress on them to respect the prisoner to obtain respect." And prisoners could come to him any time they wanted to with their grievances, he insisted. On one occasion, he testified, he had actually cashiered and transferred out of the organization a guard who admitted to using profanity toward a prisoner who had later complained about his language.

The way Lieutenant Cubage described it, Lichfield sounded not much worse than the U.S. "country club prisons" for white collar crime that were criticized decades later.

Reading the trial transcript of the foregoing, Earl Carroll's suspicions were aroused. He found Cubage's testimony much too pat—virtually unbelievable in the face of the army's own investigation. Had the witness been coached? Was he being intimidated? Who, he wondered, would have the temerity to suborn perjury by an army officer in a public trial of this magnitude? Certainly not the meek defense lawyers.

The next day, December 7th, *The Stars and Stripes* revealed that 1st Lieutenant Granville Cubage would himself face court-martial, "to be tried on charges of prison brutality after the nine enlisted guards stand trial on the same offenses"—as would 1st Lieutenant Leonard W. Ennis, who had been charged on December 4th.

Cubage's credibility was not improved by reappearances of Aubrey Richey and Charles McGinnis, both of whom were recalled by the court. Using the charts of the facility introduced by the defense, McGinnis pointed out exactly where he had seen Sergeant Smith club Richey.

"They gave him up for dead," McGinnis testified. "Everybody thought he was dead."

5

THE CHAIN OF COMMAND

About an hour after Captain Carroll was sworn in on December 6th, the defense called Major Richard E. Lo Buono, provost marshal at the Lichfield depot from November, 1943, to June, 1945. Inexplicably, Lo Buono hedged when Lieutenant Johnson asked whether that service had been continuous. The former provost marshal gave high marks to Sergeant Smith's performance as a noncommissioned officer under his command. The rating on Smith's service record had always been "excellent," he said. When asked about the guardhouse prisoners' calisthenics, Lo Buono characterized these as "a few setting up exercises in the morning."[1]

But those were just about his only straight answers. He could not say which cells were used for solitary confinement. Different cells, he said, were used at different times. After some equivocation, the former provost marshal seemed to agree with Lieutenant Cubage's description of the cell in which Private Richey had been confined. It was not only spacious and pleasant with a large window, but it even had a fireplace, and was sometimes used for a summary courtroom. He inadvertently differed with Lieutenant Cubage, however, on the capacity of the mess hall, where, he claimed, all of the prisoners could usually be accommodated at one time. Because the mess hall seated only two hundred, Cubage had said the eight hundred guardhouse prisoners had to be served in shifts.

Major Lo Buono acknowledged that there was no heating in the guardhouses, but was quick to point out an exception: a water heater that gave off some heat—although it was not in the part of the building where the cells were. The rest of the post had coal-fired fireplaces or potbellied stoves. But their operational schedule was also unclear:

"We were not supposed to have fires up to a certain period in the day, depending on the time of year. It varied according to the time of year."

When Captain Carroll began the cross-examination of the former provost marshal after lunch, the major obviously didn't want to put *anything* solid on the record. Much like a situation comedy in which a character tries to avoid saying a forbidden word, what follows is an abbreviated sample of the rambling, sidestepping equivocation Major Lo Buono put into the court record:

PROSECUTION (Captain Carroll): You testified that there was some sort of a schedule made up for calisthenics. Is that correct?

WITNESS (Major Lo Buono): That's right.

PROSECUTION: Who would actually prepare the schedules?

WITNESS: Either Lieutenant Cubage or myself.

PROSECUTION: When Lieutenant Cubage prepared a schedule, would you see it?

WITNESS: It would depend.

PROSECUTION: Do you have a recollection of any of the schedules that were in force during the period I just mentioned?

WITNESS: Yes, I think the last one I made myself.

PROSECUTION: Can you tell the court, to the best of your knowledge, what that schedule consisted of?

WITNESS: Yes. It consisted of just the program for the day. I can't recite it off; it's been some time since I've seen it.

PROSECUTION: To the best of your memory, how did you start the day off?

[The assistant prosecutor was trying to establish that the daily program began with calisthenics.]

WITNESS: There was a formation in the morning. Usually reveille formation and chow.

PROSECUTION: At what time?

WITNESS: That varied according to the time of the year. We couldn't take the prisoners out in the dark.

PROSECUTION: What *time of day* did the program start?

WITNESS: As I say, it depended on the time of year. As I recall, I think it was 5:30 or 6:00.

PROSECUTION: At 5:30 or 6:00. *How* did the program start?

WITNESS: The men got up and they fixed their bunks, usually, and fell out for chow. But they had a period in there of about an hour that they stayed in their barracks cleaning up—getting ready to go to chow.

PROSECUTION: So from 5:30 in the morning until 6:00 or 6:30 they spent in the barracks?

WITNESS: No. They went to chow; and some of them did their barracks after they came back from chow.

PROSECUTION: What happened at eight o'clock?

[Controlling his frustration, Carroll asked the question in a slow, deliberate cadence, dropping one word at a time.]

WITNESS: They had a formation to send them out on a work detail, or whatever they were going to do for that day. Maybe it was calisthenics for that certain group, or maybe they were going to classification, or they might be going for a further clothing issue. Each prisoner had a day. Some men had to report to the investigating officer.

PROSECUTION: What was the program that you had set up for those prisoners who were not assigned to some detail?

WITNESS: Some of them didn't do anything.

PROSECUTION: Didn't you have *anything* prescribed for them in your program?

WITNESS: Yes. There were different things they could do.

PROSECUTION: Tell us what your program was for those.

WITNESS: They had their calisthenics in the morning.

[Carroll brightened. The assistant prosecutor had finally elicited the answer he had been struggling to produce.]

PROSECUTION: Starting at what *time?*

WITNESS: Any time in the morning. It just depended what the man's setup was. He might be going out that same day. Or he was held over there, maybe, for some formation.

PROSECUTION [Trying to get to it]: Didn't you provide a *calisthenics* program for those that remained in their cells?

WITNESS: Yes.

PROSECUTION: The calisthenics program started *when?*

WITNESS: Usually after the formation in the morning. After that eight o'clock formation.

PROSECUTION [Speaking slowly in a raised voice, as if talking to a foreigner unfamiliar with the English language]: Approximately *when* would that calisthenics program start?

WITNESS: They can vary, depending on how many details went out in the morning or what was on the schedule for that day.

PROSECUTION: You made up a *schedule* for calisthenics, did you not?

WITNESS: Yes.

PROSECUTION: You provided in that schedule that those men not assigned to other details would attend calisthenics, did you not?

WITNESS: Yes.

PROSECUTION: And you provided that the calisthenics would start at a certain *time?*

WITNESS: That's right.

PROSECUTION : What *time* did you provide that they would start?

WITNESS: Some time after eight o'clock in the morning. It was listed as 8:00, but lots of times we were handling a lot of men and we were not always right on the dot—at eight o'clock, at nine o'clock, or ten o'clock, for any formation. We tried.

PROSECUTION: I am asking you what your *schedule* provided for. As I understand it your schedule provided that those not assigned to other details would attend calisthenics at eight o'clock in the morning. Is that right?

WITNESS. Not right at 8:00. It called for that.

PROSECUTION: That *is* what your schedule provided, did it not?

WITNESS: Eight o'clock or nine o'clock or ten o'clock in the morning.

The president of the court lost his patience.

"Let's get this straight," Colonel Leone ordered. "Take your time on answering these questions. Think of exactly what the question is, and try to answer the question as close as you possibly can to the specific thing [asked], and not all these exceptional things, so that we can carry on."

"There were a lot of exceptions, Colonel," the major protested.

The president's frustration showed.

"We're not interested in the exceptions. Just answer the question! We've had five minutes trying to find out that at eight o'clock in the morning the prisoners got out."

Colonel Leone's lecture had little effect.

PROSECUTION (Captain Carroll): Do you have a copy of one of these schedules you prepared?

WITNESS (Major Lo Buono): There are plenty of copies. I don't have one right with me.

PROSECUTION: Could you *get* one for this court?

WITNESS: I don't know whether I could or not. They were left at the depot in the files.

PROSECUTION: As the president has suggested: Everybody in the prison has been assigned; you have got the men left that are going to do calisthenics. What did you prescribe on a piece of paper as your *schedule?*

WITNESS: Calisthenics.

PROSECUTION: "Calisthenics, eight o'clock?"

WITNESS: And drill.

PROSECUTION: How long were the calisthenics to go on? From eight o'clock to when?

WITNESS: It was broken up into periods. Usually if there was an interruption—

PROSECUTION [Breaking in]: What did you put down on a piece of paper was to happen to them at *nine o'clock?* Calisthenics, you say, were from 8:00 to 9:00.

WITNESS: I didn't directly supervise the program for the day myself.

The record went on like this for many more pages, during which Earl Carroll's anger and frustration mounted, eventually earning him his rebuke by the law member. After being asked about his calisthenics schedule for at least the twentieth time, Major Lo Buono's response indicated yet another blind alley:

"There was nothing on the schedule," the former provost marshal now stated, "because you couldn't designate a certain period for them. You never knew definitely when that period would come, that the man was going to be available."

The assistant prosecutor asked a different question.

"*Who* was it that determined whether they had calisthenics or whether they cleaned up the barracks or *what* they did if they were not assigned by the duty sergeant to a detail?"

"It wasn't the duty sergeant."

"Well, who made the assignment?"

"It could be one of the officers who were present or one of the jailers would come and tell probably one of the officers that they had some men, and if there was any request for a detail, he usually took the request for details out to the men and picked them up wherever they were."

Carroll eventually gave up.

When the president of the court asked the witness about responsibility for prison operation, Lo Buono attempted to remove himself from the chain of command. Although he was sure he had been provost marshal at Lichfield, and although he regularly inspected the guardhouses, he explained that the prison was really operated by the 316th Replacement Company, under the command of Captain Joseph Robertson, who, he said, reported to Colonel Kilian, commandant of the post—thus skipping over himself. When asked about his background, Lo Buono revealed that he had been a graduate student pursuing an advanced degree before entering the army. He had to be a smarter man than this vague, bumbling, catatonic person on the witness stand, Carroll thought. Why was he acting like this?

The next defense witness was Captain Joseph A. Robertson, commanding officer of the 316th Replacement Company, the prison company that really ran the guardhouses, according to Lo Buono. In civilian life, Robertson had been the proprietor of a dry cleaning shop in Toledo, Ohio. When asked about reporting relationships in his company, he attempted the same leapfrog trick that Major Lo Buono had introduced, claiming that Lieutenant Granville Cubage, prison officer, was responsible not to Robertson himself, but to Colonel Kilian.

When the defense counsel asked him about the Richey incident, Captain Robertson's version differed significantly from Lieutenant Cubage's:

"I got a report one day that there had been some kind of a fight over at the guardhouse. I went over immediately. I went upstairs to the second floor of the guardhouse, and Richey was up there, upstairs. [Lieutenant Cubage had said Robertson examined Richey downstairs in his office.]

"When I got up there I questioned Richey. I examined him to see how bad he was hurt, and when I satisfied myself that he was not injured in any way [some of the court members exchanged glances] and did not need any further treatment, I talked to him. I asked him what was the trouble and he told me.

"He said that Sergeant Smith had said something to him that he didn't like. I said: 'Did you hit him first?' He said 'Yes, sir, I did.' Then I sent everyone out and I talked to him. I told him about his temper, and he said: 'Yes, sir, that's what it was. I just lost my temper. I couldn't take what he said to me, or the way he said it, because I just couldn't control my temper.' So I cautioned him that he is a prisoner now, and he had better change his attitude, and that was the last of it so far as I was concerned."

"Could he [Smith] have put a man in solitary without your having knowledge of it?" Johnson asked.

"Unless you lay a foundation that he is psychic, I don't see how he can answer it," Carroll broke in, interrupting the defense counsel.

Some spectators smiled. Members of the court did not.

When asked about his personnel, Captain Robertson said he had put his own executive officer, Lieutenant Ennis, into the guardhouse as prison officer when he took over as CO of the prison company. (Earlier he had stated that Lieutenant Cubage was the prison officer and he reported to Colonel Kilian.)

Although he was not as evasive as Major Lo Buono, Captain Robertson was careful not to incriminate anyone—including, and especially, himself. When Major Pers asked him whether Major Lo Buono "had the privileges and rights to go into the guardhouse at any time to see what was going on," the CO of the 316th Prison Company quickly passed along responsibility for the prison.

"Yes, sir," the captain responded. "And if anybody came in to investigate, they would go to Major Lo Buono as the one in charge."

The first witness called the next morning, on December 7th, was Lieutenant Colonel Stephen F. Barron, a Catholic chaplain of considerable rank for the Chaplain Corps. The defense's foundation for calling him had been laid when Captain Carroll had asked Major Lo Buono whether the Lichfield chaplain had given him an itemized list of the interviews he had in the stockade each day, and whether the priest gave him a "little synopsis of what the man had come to see him about." In a moment of rare forthrightness, Lo Buono had said that although the chaplain was not required to do that, he always did. In fact, the provost marshal also received a copy of the monthly report that Father Barron sent to his commanding officer. Earlier, Major Smith had condemned the practice as a violation of the privileged confidentiality of conversations between a clergyman and his parishioner. But the defense sought to show that, although he might have had other personal problems, no prisoner had ever complained to the chaplain about mistreatment—so there must not have been any.

Lieutenant Cassidy took over the questioning for the defense, which Johnson may have asked him to do since he was Catholic. When Cassidy asked the chaplain whether he had received reports from any of the prisoners as to discipline in the guardhouse, Major Smith was on his feet at once.

"The Father visited these guardhouses in his capacity as a *chaplain*," the TJA protested. "That is, to give help, religious guidance to those who chose to talk to him. Now, if a soldier confided in Father Barron, that is a privileged matter. If he did *not* confide in him, that is equally a privileged matter. Under no circumstances should those matters be made the source of testimony in court!"

The assistant defense counsel attempted to persuade the court that "only purely spiritual matters connected more with the confessional" were privileged. He lost. And that ended any useful testimony by Father Colonel Barron, or by the next witness the defense had called, another chaplain, a captain bearing the unlikely appellation of Father Comfort.

The next several witnesses, all stockade cadre, seemed intent on confirming the story told by their former boss, Lieutenant Cubage (calisthenics, they said, lasted half an hour at most, with frequent breaks; no one was ever physically punished). The remarkably close match of their testimony with that of the prison officer got one of them into trouble. Staff Sergeant Jim L. Duncan, a detail clerk in the guardhouse, made statements on the witness stand that were substantially different from the record of what he had earlier told the investigating officer in his own sworn statement before the trial.

First Lieutenant Warnham E. Hays provided more insight into the assembly-line justice system at Lichfield than the defense may have intended in calling him to the witness stand. Although he had no legal training, Hays's assignment at the depot had been that of defense counsel for *all* the accused who were tried in the special courts-martial that pumped prisoners into the guardhouse, eventually swelling its ranks to 1,002 soldiers. Hays "defended" thirty to sixty clients per week. His interviews with the accused men in preparation for the trials were compressed into his two visits per week to the guardhouse, each roughly four hours, which gave him fifteen to twenty minutes of consultation with each client before trial.

Johnson and Cassidy were not scoring many points for their client. But they had reason to believe that their next witness would be more effective.

6

THE COMMANDANT APPEARS

The next witness for the defense, much anticipated by the press, was Colonel James A. Kilian, Cavalry, commanding officer of the 10th Reinforcement Depot at Lichfield from November 11, 1942, until January 18, 1945. Interviewing him outside the courtroom, a *Time* correspondent found him "disarmingly forthright."[1]

In Kilian's first appearance before the court, the former commandant bore an air of confidence and military bearing befitting his rank and his three decades of distinguished service. The magenta and white colors of the Legion of Merit stood out in the single row of ribbons above the left pocket of his Eisenhower jacket. In his answers to the defense counsel, who was four grades his junior, Colonel Kilian was courteous, articulate, precise in his testimony, and unflappable. Observing protocol, he addressed the equal-rank president of the court as "sir," although he had significantly more service in the Regular Army than did Colonel Leone.

For a commanding officer of a large, complex facility, the witness seemed to have an amazing grasp of detail. In contrast to the evasion that characterized the testimony of his provost marshal, the colonel answered logistical and organizational questions in exhaustive detail. For example, in describing the scope of his authority, Colonel Kilian explained:

"I had military jurisdiction over the country surrounding Lichfield for approximately twenty miles in all directions, with the exception of Burton-on-Trent and Birmingham. I touched the outskirts of Birmingham and Sutton Coldfield and Walsall. All the booking was done in No. 1 Guardhouse. The policy was that every man would be cleared from No. 1 Guardhouse by noon each day; that is, any man apprehended this afternoon would be cleared from No. 1 Guardhouse by noon tomorrow. Is the court really interested in all these details?"[2]

The young defense counsel, Lieutenant Johnson, seemed somewhat intimidated by the colonel's strong presence and easy cognizance on the stand. His questions had a tentative, deferential tone:

"During this period in the fall of 1944, what policies did you have set up in regard to the punishment that soldiers would receive for certain offenses? If you remember, sir, please say."

Colonel Kilian described a "three-by-five card file" made up on each prisoner. "If it was his first offense, or a minor offense—such as being out of the post without a uniform, or for a short period—that man was released to his company. Sometimes these minor offenses were even punished under the 104th Article of War [which, typically, might put him on KP for a week, or restrict him to quarters], and a report—a blank mimeographed form—was made up stating why the man had been arrested, and the number of offenses that he had had."

The commandant went on to explain why the numbers in the guardhouse increased after the invasion of Normandy, and how he gradually tightened his policies as the mission of his replacement depot was threatened:

"At that time we were packaging hospital returnees. We were very busy. They were coming in very fast. To start with, shortly after D-Day, in those packages going out there would be a number of AWOLs in each package. To safeguard that, I adopted, first, the policy of having ten percent overload in each package. We were taking three hundred at a time to start with, and there would be approximately a full platoon of twenty-five to thirty men. As the men were absent without leave from the packages, first I tried the policy of merely repackaging them and sending them in the next package. That did not have the desired result, so that we we began to be a little more severe. If a man were absent without leave from the package, he was tried by a summary court. Then we had to adopt the policy of a special court as these men were going absent two or three times. Eventually, I adopted the policy in severe cases—where a man was a known package jumper, as we termed him at that time (in other words, he had done it persistently)—of attempting to try them under the 58th Article of War [desertion, or conspiracy to desert]. That congested the guard-house."

In answering questions about whether the barracks—and especially the guardhouses—had been adequately heated, Colonel Kilian again appeared to be thoroughly knowledgeable about the subject, differing substantially with his provost marshal on the adequacy of the heating. His testimony seemed to indicate that he actually gave priority to the guardhouses over the rest of the compound:

"The building was constructed to be heated by fireplaces. In 1943 we had a slight epidemic of nasal pharyngitis. At that time I secured two-hundred-odd Sibley stoves. (I had had canvas [tents] allotted to me, and I got the stoves for the canvas.) I first installed those stoves in the mess halls, one for each fireplace. The next building in which those stoves were installed was Guardhouse No. 2, known as the Dyott Building. We installed one for each fireplace—one new-model bell-type Sibley stove.

"Until I got more stoves, which took me several months, the other barracks were heated by the fireplaces. Some of the barracks never did get stoves. Some of those stoves were used in tents.

"I had set some tents out. We had a good level place. I put those tents up and I installed a stove in each of those tents so that the men could go in those tents—everybody in the depot—and thoroughly warm up in the morning. That was the recommendation of my surgeon, and we stopped that epidemic in less than 48 hours."

On the central subject of punishment of prisoners by the guards, Colonel Kilian indicated that officers and noncoms were expected to maintain discipline in their organization and, for the most part, simply used moderate extra-duty type of punishment often prescribed under the 104th Article of War. But they *never* used calisthenics as punishment. "In fact," he added, "I don't believe we were very rigid, and I think that that was one of the troubles." There certainly had been none of the "nose and toes" business that had been described by former prisoners. And guards never struck anyone with their billy clubs. They carried them, he said, "as a symbol of authority—instead of wearing a weapon."

The commandant frequently inspected the guardhouses, he said, and he personally interviewed twenty to thirty prisoners a day. Although he heard complaints about family troubles and other personal problems, he never heard one about mistreatment. His analysis purporting to account for the high percentage of AWOLs at the Lichfield depot was not convincing:

"The thing in which I was interested in as regards the prisoners when I talked to them in the guardhouse was their background. 'Why are you here, absent without leave many times?' Often I would see a familiar face; a man would be there two or three times. I would stop and talk to him about that. The usual complaint was that they were detaining him and he wanted to get back to the fighting line."

Conscious of the image he was projecting, Kilian had made two deliberate points in his testimony. First, he—and absolutely no one but he—could authorize putting a prisoner into solitary confinement. His other intended message was quoted verbatim in newspapers and magazines on both sides of the Atlantic, including *The Stars and Stripes:*

"I personally observed Sergeant Smith, and I knew who he was and I knew the job he was doing. I knew the type of personnel that he was handling. Every time the rearrangement of personnel came up, there was always a request that Sergeant Smith stay on the job he was on. I personally think, and I state, that Sergeant Smith is one of the best noncommissioned officers that I have seen in my entire service of over thirty-three years. He had a tremendous job and he did it. I personally would rather have had Sergeant Smith on that job than seventy-five percent of the lieutenants who came through the Depot."

Major Smith conducted a bland cross-examination of the commandant. The otherwise irrepressible Earl Carroll never got out of his chair. But Colonel Kilian would be recalled.

Following Colonel Kilian's testimony, the defense called two Medical Corps officers to the witness stand, Captain Rudolph E. Warnecke, who had been post surgeon at Lichfield, and a physician on his staff, Captain Norman B. Tannahill. Both doctors testified that, although they saw a great deal of evidence of combat wounds in the prisoners they examined, they had never seen evidence of beatings. Asked about injuries, they said that they had seen bruises and abrasions about the head on some men, but there had always been an explanation that such contusions were the result of an accident. In one case, for example, a laceration above the eye had been caused when "two colored prisoners were tossing a board from one to the other, and accidentally the board slipped out of the hands of one of the colored prisoners and struck this prisoner in the face" while he was lying on his bunk.

The medical officers also indicated that there were many malingercrs among the men they saw on sick call, and that they were quick to screen these out and mark them for duty so they could be shipped out.[3]

Court was adjourned at 5:00 P.M. The defense counsels had finally had a good day. But their star witness would be recalled. And Colonel Kilian would display a very different demeanor when he next entered the courtroom.

7

THE BEAST OF LICHFIELD?

Despite their lack of experience, defense counsel Frank Johnson and his assistant, Joe Cassidy, had reason to believe they had done a creditable job up to this point in the trial. While their witnesses had not always been convincing, all had presented testimony tending to refute the charges of brutality leveled against their client. Then, however, the defense swore in 1st Lieutenant Leonard W. Ennis, former Lichfield depot prison officer. His testimony would prove to be a turning point in the trial.

An Associated Press journalist, in an interview years later, described Lieutenant Ennis as "beefy, florid-faced, tough; not very bright."[1] Earlier in his army career, the prison officer had been a provost sergeant in Hawaii, home of the infamous Schofield Barracks. His service record included a history of psychological problems, and the rumor mill had identified him as the probable "Beast of Lichfield."

After the witness was sworn, Lieutenant Johnson went at once to the Sims incident, about which Staff Sergeant Ashur Baizer had testified. Johnson invited Lieutenant Ennis to tell his version of what happened.[2]

"Up in the 10th Replacement Depot I was in the prison block observing calisthenics," Ennis began. "I observed after a couple of exercises that one man was not exercising, this man being Sims, a tall colored boy [an almost universal appellation used by witnesses and members of the court when referring to Negro soldiers]. I told Sims to double-time to me. When I got Sims before me, I asked Sims: 'Sims, what seems to be your trouble?' He said: 'My legs are bothering me and I can't do the exercises.'

"I asked him if he had a medical excuse. He said no, he had no medical excuse. I knew that he had no medical excuse because I had sent him on sick call twice before this, and Captain Warnecke had sent down that there was nothing physically wrong with this man Sims, and so I told him to get back in the ranks and exercise. He refused to do so. I ordered him inside to the guardhouse. As he turned about, Sergeant Smith followed in the back of me.

"When I got in I told Sims that he was giving me a lot of trouble. He was agitating [sic]. I said it couldn't be done in the block amongst prisoners and that I wasn't going to stand for it. I said: 'Get double-timing, Sims,' and he refused to double-time. I turned around and said to Sergeant Smith: 'Smith, get that man up against the wall and see that he stays there.' On that order, Sergeant Smith turned the man around and he pushed him against the wall. I went to the main office at the gate. I was a little angry. On the way through I saw one prisoner, Sims, facing the wall."

Lieutenant Johnson asked the witness to demonstrate how Sergeant Smith had pushed Sims. Ennis's pantomime made the action look firm but restrained. He explained the action.

"Sims was talking to me and the sergeant was on the other side. He took him by the shoulder like *that* and he said: 'Get up against the wall.' The man's head didn't hit the wall. I saw him brake it with his hands."

That ended the defense's direct examination of Prison Officer Ennis, and it was the prosecution's turn. Major Smith had obviously referred to the court record of the testimony of Staff Sergeant Baizer, the casual guard. Sergeant Baizer had testified that he heard Lieutenant Ennis order Sergeant Smith to "take this man inside and work him over," and that Sims "was struck on the side of the head repeatedly by the provost sergeant on the order of the prison officer."

Major Smith asked Ennis whether he had a short temper. The officer denied that he did, but he admitted that Private Sims had made him angry. The TJA then inquired whether Ennis had ever challenged men to come out and fight him. This time the witness denied it, "to the best of his knowledge." Asked whether Sergeant Smith carried a billy club, Ennis couldn't remember.

"If he [Sims] had been ordered to double-time against the wall, he would have carried it out—or something else would have been done?" The TJA was getting to the meat.

"Yes, sir," Ennis responded.

"You wouldn't stand for either you or Sergeant Smith giving an order and its not being carried out?"

"Yes, sir."

"On occasions men were double-timed against the wall as an aid to discipline, were they not?"

The question brought the defense counsel to his feet.

"I object to the question," Lieutenant Johnson interjected. "The witness has not testified to anybody double-timing against the wall [in direct examination]."

But the law member permitted the question.

"They were double-timed facing the wall as an aid to discipline," Ennis admitted straightforwardly. But he defined the "usual distance" from the wall as "about a foot and a half."

Staff Writer Art White reported the breakthrough in the trial in the next morning's *Stars and Stripes:*

First Lieutenant Leonard W. Ennis, formerly a prison officer at the 10th Reinforcement Depot, admitted today that he had ordered prisoners to stand 'nose and toes' against a wall, and to "double-time up to one hour as punishment."[3]

After the defense's careful orchestration of sworn testimony denying that such punishment had ever taken place, it seemed ironic to Earl Carroll (who had so far stayed out of the cross-examination of this key player in the Lichfield drama) that a defense witness against whom charges had already been filed would be the one to publicly reveal that it had, after all, been common practice.

Ennis got in deeper as his cross-questioning under Major Smith continued. Having written evidence showing that the prison officer had once disciplined Sergeant Smith for fighting with a prisoner, the TJA began weaving another trap for the officer.

After having the witness deny ever having seen Sergeant Smith hit anybody inside the guardhouse "at any time under any circumstances," the prosecutor reminded Ennis of the sworn statement he had made to Colonel Swope of the Inspector General Department during the IG's investigation of Lichfield. He read the statement Lieutenant Ennis had signed at the time:

"'There was a colored boy. Sergeant Smith, provost sergeant, was in the cell block and he carried a club. He was having the man exercise, and he took the club and hit him in the body. The colored boy turned around and hit Sergeant Smith and he took action.'"

Ennis remembered having made the statement to Colonel Swope, but his explanation came as a surprise:

"At that time there were several Smiths working in the guardhouse, and I confused Sergeant Smith, the accused, without seeing the accused in person, with the other sergeant when I was asked the question. I couldn't determine which sergeant he meant, but I do remember the incident."

"You say now that this was not the Sergeant Smith who is being tried here?" Major Smith sounded skeptical.

"It is not," Ennis asserted. "The Sergeant Smith who I meant was a *technical* sergeant, three up and two under [describing the stripes on his shoulder]."

"Was this other Sergeant Smith also provost sergeant?"

"He was a jailer."

"When you said, 'Sergeant Smith, *Provost Sergeant,*' you meant *another* Sergeant Smith who was *not* the provost sergeant?"

Lieutenant Ennis was becoming edgy. He attempted to deflect the question.

"I referred several times to provost sergeants in there."

"So when you said, 'Sergeant Smith, Provost Sergeant,' you were not referring to the Sergeant Smith who is being tried here?"

"No, sir."

"About which Sergeant Smith were you talking when you were answering these questions which were put to you by Colonel Swope? Were you always talking about this other Sergeant Smith?"

"No, sir."

"We had better go through it again, question by question. Evidently we have got two Sergeant Smiths."

"I believe that we had more than one. With the guards there were quite a few."

"Whether there were one or two or a dozen, I want to find out, when you say 'Sergeant Smith' here, to which one you are referring, and whether you are *ever* referring to the Sergeant Smith who is being tried here."

With that, the TJA sat down and Captain Carroll picked up the questioning for the prosecution.

It was classic Carroll. His relentless interrogation of the now sweating Ennis seemed to draw sympathy from the court's law member, who eventually limited Carroll's questions and actually threw out some of the testimony.

Carroll began reading the detail from Ennis's interview with Colonel Swope. Each time he came to a reference to a "Sergeant Smith," he asked the witness which Sergeant Smith was intended. Then he came to a line in Ennis's sworn statement, "We have had several men who turned on Sergeant Smith. We would have them stand against the wall, nose and toes, sometimes as long as an hour. We had others double-time in place. In that they face the wall and double-time."

The Sergeant Smith that Lieutenant Ennis said he had meant this time turned out to be "this man in the courtroom here." Having realized what he said, the prison officer blurted an addendum that this time took the defense counsel by surprise: "If disciplinary action was recommended up against the wall, then it was carried out under *my* orders."

Lieutenant Johnson rose to defend his witness, who would himself be facing charges: "I request that the court inform this witness of his rights in regard to answering questions that might tend to incriminate him."

Major Hopper delivered a rather legalistic speech during which he read a previous court interpretation of Article of War 24, defining its intent as being broader than merely protection against self-incrimination: "No witness or deponent need answer any question not material to the issue when such answer might tend to degrade him. This privilege applies only to matters not material, i.e., relevant to the issue, whereas the privilege against self-incrimination covers *all* matters whatsoever."

Having experienced his first strike leading to the possibility of catching bigger fish than Provost Sergeant Smith, the assistant prosecutor was not about to let go. He did not ingratiate himself with the court when he broke into the law member's lecture.

"It seems to me that this is a little late in these proceedings," Carroll argued. "This witness came to the witness stand and volunteered to testify."

Obviously irritated, Major Hopper finished advising the witness of his rights, but he did not respond to Carroll.

The assistant TJA picked up where he had left off, concentrating on what appeared to be Ennis's fabrication of the additional Sergeant Smith.

"You distinctly remember this other Sergeant Smith?"

"Yes, sir."

"Can you describe him to the court?"

Lieutenant Ennis proceeded to detail the height, weight, and hair color of the "other" Sergeant Smith. Captain Carroll then requested the accused Sergeant Smith to stand and asked the witness to describe him. The hapless Ennis, repeating the same height and weight estimates and even matching hair color, was forced to admit that the description of the other sergeant he had provided for the record would also fit the accused, Judson Smith.

Carroll refused to let it go at that. He took Ennis through the rest of his own sworn statement to the IG investigator, line by line, asking him each time which Sergeant Smith he was talking about. Finally, Major Hopper interrupted:

"If the witness feels that his answer to any question is ambiguous, he may explain it. We will permit that to be done."

The law member's intervention produced another surprising statement volunteered by the prison officer.

"I would like to explain to the court before I go any further that when I was giving testimony to the IG in France I was under a nervous breakdown. I was sent home two days later. I was sent to the States as a psycho-neurotic, and some of these questions that have been referred to were rather shot at me. I told the colonel, when he was interviewing me, that I was sick, and he kept pushing me on those questions. Some of them are incoherent."

Captain Carroll was unmoved.

"When we come to one that is incoherent, you tell the court about it. We will have it in the record for your benefit." The assistant TJA then read a segment of Ennis's sworn statement to Colonel Swope that seemed to contradict Colonel Kilian's earlier testimony:

"Question: 'Was the Provost Sergeant authorized to place men in the hole overnight without getting the permission of the Prison Officer and Post Commander?' Answer: 'I know it was required in No. 1 Guardhouse, but not through my orders. I know they were held over twenty-four hours.'"

Lieutenant Ennis acknowledged that his statement to Colonel Swope was true. Carroll then got him to admit that, thus far in the document under question, there was really only one time in the lengthy deposition when he was referring to the mysterious Technical Sergeant Smith instead of Sergeant Judson Smith, and further, that Ennis had made no effort to explain the distinction to Colonel Swope.

Major Hopper obviously thought the witness was being abused. Breaking in, he instructed the court to "disregard the witness's inconsistent statements except for needed clarification of his sworn statement."

Captain Carroll obviously disagreed.

"That, of course, goes right to the heart of the matter," he protested, "as to whether or not this accused is responsible for this act, or whether someone of higher authority is responsible for it. It is directly in issue. If this punishment was administered by the accused upon the authority of this officer; and this officer, in turn, administered it upon the authority of a higher authority, it goes directly to the issues in this case."

Carroll had revealed both his personal motivation and the strategy that would govern his subsequent conduct of the case.

Lieutenant Cassidy rose to object.

"I think the prosecution is confused. The issue is whether this accused is guilty of the offense or not guilty."

The law member agreed with the assistant defense counsel, sustaining his objection.

But Carroll continued to bore in.

"Did you ever discipline Sergeant Smith for having a fight with a prisoner?"

"No, sir."

The assistant prosecutor now continued his reading from the Swope deposition:

"Question: 'Did you ever have occasion to discipline the Provost Sergeant, Sergeant Smith?' [Your] Answer: 'Yes, sir.'"

Lieutenant Johnson interrupted.

"I would like the court to reflect that the prosecution is going ahead with exactly what the prosecution has been directed by the law member to refrain from doing."

That was sufficient to motivate the law member.

"Rather than go into that, we will go back and strike the [Swope] statement from the record," Major Hopper declared.

Carroll couldn't believe it.

"Can the court go back and strike testimony from the record of its own motion?"

"The court *has*," Hopper shot back.

Carroll sighed.

"Then those are all the questions that I can ask," he said quietly. And the assistant TJA sat down.

Major Smith took over the questioning briefly. But the atmosphere in the courtroom was so charged that the witness was twice asked to leave the courtroom while arguments raged over the admissibility of his testimony. The court eventually excused the audience, meeting in closed session to shield the gallery from the acrimony.

When the court reconvened, Major Hopper had reversed his ruling. He now permitted Captain Carroll to put into the record the entire pretrial statement by Lieutenant Ennis, which statement the officer had made during April and May of 1945, to Colonel John G. Swope, Assistant Inspector General, European Theater of Operations. The reason for the reversal became clear when it was revealed that Colonel Swope's investigation had been conducted at the personal request of General Dwight D. Eisenhower.

The document included Ennis's sworn statement that he had disciplined Provost Sergeant Smith, restricting him for seven days, "when he had a fight with the colored boy." When examined on the point, Ennis now claimed that his discipline had not been directed against Sergeant Smith, but against the elusive Technical Sergeant Smith.

The stormy session was finally adjourned at noon on Saturday, December 8th. But before the members left their chairs, Lieutenant Johnson told the court that he could not proceed with his defense without "a determination on whether Major Bluhm will be available for us." (Major Bluhm had been post inspector of the Lichfield depot.)

"We do not have any more witnesses until we make a determination with regard to Major Bluhm," he declared.

The announcement precipitated a sensational headline in the Tuesday issue of *The Stars and Stripes:*

LICHFIELD DEFENSE WITNESS DISAPPEARS
By Ed Rosenthal

LONDON, Dec. 11—A mysterious disappearance of a key defense witness in the trial of Sergeant Judson H. Smith, former 10th Reinforcement Depot guard, accused of brutally mistreating prisoners in the Lichfield depot last winter, may delay his general court-martial, which is now entering its second week here.

Major Herbert W. Bluhm, former inspecting officer of the Lichfield prison, who was ordered on November 20 to proceed by air from the U.S. to London, still has not reported to the UK Base Judge Advocate's Office.

Major Richard D. Kearney, staff judge advocate, members of the defense, and prosecution officers all declared the witness's whereabouts were a mystery.

Colonel James A. Kilian, former Lichfield CO who was listed on the same movement orders, and subsequently testified at the London hearing, declared he had last seen Bluhm in a Chicago railway station, and that the major had remarked then that he was either going to or coming back from a military hospital.[4]

8

THE ACCUSED TAKES THE STAND

Despite his protest on Saturday morning, Lieutenant Johnson was ready to put additional defense witnesses on the stand when the trial resumed on Monday, December 10th. His first witness, Technician 5th Grade Ellis D. Adcock, a prison guard against whom charges had already been filed, delivered essentially negative testimony: Since he had filled the role of duty sergeant in the guardhouse, Adcock said he would have known if Sergeant Smith struck anyone, and since he had never heard of such a thing it must not have happened. Or, rather, that is what the defense lawyers had wanted him to testify to. But Adcock got rattled on the witness stand. Under cross-examination, he essentially nullified his testimony by admitting that he had discussed what he was going to say with Sergeant Smith before the trial, as well as with the two defense counsels.[1]

After other indicted jailers, Sergeant Robert E. Scott and Staff Sergeant James M. Jones did no better, Lieutenant Johnson decided to put the accused on the witness stand.

Sergeant Smith was asked to stand. Major Hopper explained his rights to him: The accused could, he said, take the stand as a witness in his own behalf, be sworn, and testify under oath. But, if he did so, he would be subject to cross-examination. Alternatively, he could make an unsworn statement—in writing, if he wished. Or he could simply remain silent.

Sergeant Smith elected to make an oral sworn statement—to testify under oath. The oath was administered, and Lieutenant Cassidy addressed the charges against him at once.

Under direct examination by the assistant defense counsel, the accused seemed quite forthcoming. As to alleged disciplinary measures, Smith passed the buck upward. Asked by counsel what form of discipline was authorized if a prisoner did something wrong (e.g., infringing the no-smoking rule or acting rowdy in ranks), Smith stated that the man would be taken to see the prison officer, and that *only* the prison officer could authorize disciplinary action—especially the much-discussed business of standing against the wall.

When asked about putting a soldier in solitary confinement, Sergeant Smith essentially parroted the testimony of Colonel Kilian:

"The actual procedure was that the lieutenant recommended through the commanding officer. That was the only way that a man should be placed in solitary confinement."

Lieutenant Cassidy then asked about the incident involving Private William Sims. In characteristically short, simple sentences, the accused presented his version of what happened. It seemed innocuous enough:

"One morning on the block, Lieutenant Ennis was observing an exercise. He called the prisoner Sims over. He ordered him to double-time. Sims walked over. He wouldn't double-time. So he taken [sic] Sims inside to talk to him. He sent for me to go in there with him. I followed Lieutenant Ennis and the prisoner inside. We got on the inside. Lieutenant Ennis started talking to this prisoner, Sims, telling him the way he had been behaving out there in the ranks and Sims would just stand around and he wouldn't take the exercises.

"So he ordered Sims to double-time. Sims refused. He ordered him to double-time again. He refused. He told me to turn the man around to face the wall, and I did so, sir. Lieutenant Ennis went out of the office. I had prisoner Sims go back out in the ranks."

Lieutenant Cassidy asked Sergeant Smith about his authorization to carry a billy club and what it had been for. Smith responded that "the billy club was carried for the protection of yourself in case of a riot or something."

This led directly to the Richey incident. During his testimony, the defendant stated three times that Richey had just returned from the hospital, thus contradicting the testimony of Lieutenant Cubage, who had claimed that Richey was being returned to the stockade after having escaped.

The diversity of conflicting stories told by witnesses about the clubbing of Private Aubrey Richey was reminiscent of the Japanese movie, *Rashomon*—except that in Kurosawa's 1951 classic there were only four variations of what happened during the violent event the film is about. Smith's testimony was the seventh version of the Richey incident heard by the court; and it would not be the last.

"One morning we got a call from the dispensary," Sergeant Smith began. "Lieutenant Cubage was in the office when that call came through. The man [Richey] was getting out of the hospital.

"He [Cubage] said: 'As soon as that man comes I want to see him.' And so we had to send a guard up to get him. Lieutenant Cubage was in the office and I was in the office at the same time. He told me to go out in the hall and bring this man in. I went out of the office and told the jailer to open the gate and let the prisoner Richey come after. Prisoner Richey walked over to the door. He got over there and I told Richey to go in. He wouldn't go in.

"I brought Richey to this door and I told Richey to go on in. Richey didn't move. He just kept standing there. I told Richey to go in again and he stood there, so he didn't take my command. So I gave him a shove and he went in and I came in and closed the door. Immediately I closed the door the prisoner Richey hit me on the side of the face and in the mouth and I fell back on the coal bin. He knocked me back, and then this prisoner jumped on top of me. We had orders that when a man did that, we couldn't hit a man with our fist. That was the order that was laid down. The reason I hit the man was in my own self-protection."

"What did you hit him with?" Cassidy asked.

"I hit him with a billy club. The first time I hit him, I hit him a light blow and the next blow was a little harder."

"What happened then?"

"Prisoner Sims—"

"Do you mean Richey?" Cassidy interrupted.

"Prisoner *Richey* rolled over and I got up by myself. I got another guard. I think it was the same guard as the one who brought him from the hospital—and carried him upstairs and I sent for an officer." Smith apparently had forgotten his earlier statement that Lieutenant Cubage was present during the altercation. The defendant offered no explanation of how Richey ended up in solitary.

"Did you remain with Richey?" Cassidy asked.

"Not all the time. No, sir."

As to other abused prisoners, Sergeant Smith denied even knowing any of the nine alleged victims of his brutality as listed in the charge sheets. For the record, the defense also had him deny ever having pushed any prisoner's head into a wall.

Lieutenant Johnson asked Sergeant Smith why he thought prisoners had testified that they had been mistreated. Smith suggested that this was due to their discomfort caused by overcrowded conditions in the prison.

That ended the defense's direct examination of the defendant. When the prosecution took over, Smith had been on the witness stand for less than thirty minutes. But he would spend the next eight hours in cross-examination.

As tough as he had been on other witnesses, Captain Carroll's initial questioning of the accused seemed perfunctory. The assistant TJA spent some time on details of the prison organization and its reporting relationships, thus inviting the accused to again pass the buck upward, all the way, once again, to the commandant, Colonel James A. Kilian—whose name Carroll repeatedly offered the defendant for confirmation as the ultimate authority in matters of prison policy. Smith readily admitted that, as he was in charge of approximately 120 guards and jailers, he was responsible for their actions, but he denied any mistreatment of prisoners by his men or by anyone associated with the prison. Ed Rosenthal summarized Smith's testimony in *The Stars and Stripes* the next day:

Smith painted a picture of comparative tranquility at the Lichfield guardhouses, telling the court that he got along well with most of the 700 to 1,000 prisoners, and that in most cases it was not even necessary for him to carry a billy club. He said he did not punish prisoners.

Smith maintained that he had not struck any prisoners except in one "rare" instance, and that no prisoner to his knowledge bore any animosity toward him. Asked how the prisoners felt about their treatment, Smith replied: "I've heard men say they'd just as soon be in the Lichfield guardhouse as on the front line."[2]

Considering the magnitude of the investigation that had resulted in his trial, the defendant's categorical denials were difficult for the court to accept. Smith claimed he had never witnessed any fights or altercations between guards and prisoners, that he never had seen a guard strike a prisoner or a prisoner strike a guard during his entire period of service at Lichfield, from August, 1944, until he left Lichfield on March 7th, 1945.

The only prisoner complaints he knew about, the defendant testified, had to do with obtaining toilet articles or articles of clothing. Some men were distressed by personal problems, he said, and they requested an opportunity to see the prison officer for counseling. Some, he was embarrassed to admit to the court ("because there is a nurse present"), had gotten local girls pregnant—except the term he used was "fixed up."

Smith was also quick to substantiate Lieutenant Ennis's testimony that there had been *two* other Sergeant Smiths in the prison cadre—one a technical sergeant. But he didn't know what they looked like, nor could he remember their first names. When asked to identify some of the other 120 guards and jailers who worked for him, Smith could name only two, and then he forgot the two Sergeant Smiths.

The assistant prosecutor attempted to pin down the daily calisthenics schedule as he had with Major Lo Buono. While Lo Buono had been merely evasive, Smith's answers have a vague, surreal quality about them. The following (condensed) court record provides some insight into the defendant's thought processes.

Captain Carroll began by asking about issuance of a printed daily schedule:

"From where did you get this program for the routine of the prison?"

"The detail sergeant made it up."

"Who made up the schedule for the people who stayed in the prison?"

"The guards had to stay there."

"Did you have some kind of a daily schedule that you were administering so far as prisoners who were not sent out on detail were concerned?"

"If we had a guard, yes, sir."

"Did you have some kind of written schedule given to you which told you what you were to do during the day with the prisoners who remained in the guardhouse during the daytime?"

"The officer told me what to do."

"Did you have a *written* schedule?"

"I didn't see it."

"You never saw a written schedule which said that starting at eight o'clock in the morning you were to do certain exercises or certain drill and that then at nine o'clock you would do something else—a schedule of that nature?"

"The prison officer explained that to me."

"I am asking you now, did you ever see such a schedule?"

"No, sir."

"From where did you receive your orders as to what you were to do with the prisoners who remained in the guardhouse?"

"Through the prison officer."

"Did he tell you when the calisthenics were to start?"

"In the morning."

"Did he tell you what time in the morning?"

"As the work details got out."

"What time would that be, usually?"

"Last winter I can't explain whether we had run forward or run backwards."

The defendant's last answer was left unexplained. Smith seemed unable to quantify anything, even though he had sat through detailed testimony by others on the same subjects.

"What was the seating capacity of the mess hall?" Carroll asked.

"I never counted."

"Can you estimate it?"

"I couldn't estimate it. If I'd counted, I could estimate it."

"If you had 800 prisoners there, approximately what percentage of them could be seated at one time?"

"I couldn't say, sir."

"Could half of them be seated at one time?"

"Let me think. Will it be all right?"

Colonel Leone interrupted in an effort to help the befuddled defendant.

"You are going to be on the stand a long time," the president of the court counseled. His tone was kindly, almost paternal. "Any time you want to take time to answer questions, you take time for it."

"I want time to count," Smith pleaded.

The president nodded, smiling a little.

"If any question is confusing to you," he added," you just take all the time you want to to answer it. If you want a question repeated, it will be repeated."

"I was trying to think how many rows of tables were in our mess hall," Smith explained.

"You can draw a picture of it if you want to," Colonel Leone offered, "if that will give you an accurate answer to the prosecution. You take your time and give the answer."

"Yes, sir."

The assistant prosecutor took the cue.

"We are in no hurry to get an answer," he conceded, literally backing away from the witness.

But the defendant found it impossible to estimate how many prisoners could eat in the prison mess hall at one time.

So Carroll tried another tack.

"How *long* did it take to feed 800 prisoners, if you recall?"

"I know that we had a schedule there to feed the prisoners and also the guards," Smith allowed. "We tried to follow that schedule as best we could. Sometimes it would run over."

The assistant TJA had no more success when he tried to inquire into the sergeant's personal daily routine:

"In a normal day when you were on duty, how much time did you spend out in the yard?"

"It was always an estimated time."

"*About* how much time?"

"I couldn't say."

"Would you spend an hour or two in the yard?"

"No, sir."

"You would spend less than that?"

"Yes, sir."

"You might spend thirty minutes or an hour a day?"

"Or I might spend ten minutes out in the yard."

"What did you do with the rest of the day?"

"I went to work at eight o'clock in the morning."

At times Smith's slow-wittedness became comedy relief. The defense, for example, entered an objection to the prosecution's bringing in the names of other guards, fearing that Carroll would make unfair use of the defendant's answers.

"The prosecution has asked the witness whether he knows Nunes, Wilkins, Adcock, and Cappello," Lieutenant Johnson protested. "Do they intend to use that on the same basis as this other evidence that was admitted earlier?"

"No," Carroll responded. "Of course, if he knew Sergeant Wilkins, and Sergeant Wilkins was his roommate for several years, and he told us that he never knew him, that would be one thing. But that isn't my purpose. I have to find out who he knew and who he didn't know."

Sergeant Smith interrupted.

"Sir, may I ask a question?"

"Yes," the law member responded.

"He said that Sergeant Wilkins was my roommate for two years?" Smith sounded incredulous.

Major Hopper gently explained that "the assistant trial judge advocate was stating a hypothetical situation in his argument with Lieutenant Johnson." The explanation was lost on the defendant.

By late afternoon, Carroll had lost his paternal manner. He began to tighten the screws.

"Staff Sergeant Newlands was the [temporary] guard who testified that he saw a prisoner selected from a formation by you and told to stand up against a wall with his nose and toes to the wall and to start double-timing; and when he didn't double-time fast enough, you pushed his nose and face into the wall. Do you remember that incident?"

Not only did Sergeant Smith deny remembering such an incident, but he also had no recollection of Sergeant Newlands ever having been a guard at the Lichfield prison.

The assistant prosecutor then cited the testimony of other witnesses. Did the defendant remember threatening his prisoners before a visit from the Inspector General's office, saying "it would not be healthy to make any complaints?" Did he remember "an occasion when one or more prisoners were wrapped in a blanket and then clubbed by one or more jailers?" Did he remember "when several prisoners, including Mike Koblinski, Jr., were taken down into a latrine in Guardhouse No. 1 and then beaten until they fell to the floor, and then had cold water poured on them?" Did he remember striking Daniel MacMillan with a club one night after he had escaped from prison? Did he remember when the jailer called "Missouri" took Daniel MacMillan down into the latrine on his orders, and, together with another guard, administered a beating to him? Did he remember personally "tearing all the clothes off a soldier, forcing him down on the floor and throwing a blanket over the prisoner and beating him with a rubber hose?"

The accused denied remembering any of these things (and, indeed, he may not have). There was a strategy behind Carroll's haranguing of the defendant. Now that Smith had denied each of the incidents, the assistant prosecutor would call no less than two dozen rebuttal witnesses to provide the ugly details of each offense denied by the defendant. Carroll sought not only to impeach the veracity of the accused, but also, by the repetition of these atrocities, to predispose the court to a finding of guilty.

By midafternoon, Judson Smith began to modify his adamant position. He acknowledged that the double-timing in a circle had taken place, but he claimed that men volunteered for this activity in order to get warmed up in the morning—and then it was for only for five minutes or so. And, yes, some men *had* been ordered to stand up against the wall. But this was for their own safety when coal trucks came in, so they wouldn't be in the way of the vehicles. They were never placed against the wall as punishment.

But then Carroll pulled out the Swope depositions, springing the same trap in which Lieutenant Ennis had become ensnared.

"Did inspectors come to the prison?"

"They came there quite often; yes."

"Would they ask you if certain prisoners had been mistreated?"

"Yes, sir."

"They called you in and asked you in generalities as to certain acts of mistreatment; is that correct?"

"That's correct, sir."

"So that when you told this court earlier in this cross-examination that you never heard of any complaints being made in this prison, that wasn't exactly true?"

"You didn't bring out the IG inspectors," the defendant argued.

"The IG told you that there had been complaints made?"

"That's right, sir."

"So when you told the court that you didn't know of any complaints having been made in this prison, that wasn't exactly true?"

"You didn't bring out the IGs," Smith repeated.

"I have to bring out who made the complaints in order for you to answer the question, have I?"

"That's what I don't understand." The defendant sounded genuinely confused. But reference to the Swope report seemed to abruptly alter his responses. He began eliminating his categorical denials.

"Wasn't it customary to administer the punishment of standing up against the wall for not doing what they were supposed to do?" Carroll asked.

"It wasn't a regular *routine* thing," the accused corrected, waffling.

"It wasn't part of the routine, but it was a *customary* method of punishment that was used?"

"That was one method used."

"What were some of the other methods?"

"Solitary confinement."

It was now on the record.

"With regard to the standing of these men up against the wall, some of them were stood with their faces towards the wall, were they not?"

"Sometimes they were."

Suddenly realizing his damaging admissions, Sergeant Smith tried to backpedal, passing the buck up the chain of command. The only time any punishment of any kind was administered, he insisted, was upon the order of an officer. While he admitted having taken prisoners out of line himself, all he ever did was "give them a good talking to and put them back in line."

At this point, at 4:58 P.M., court was adjourned. When it reconvened at 9:30 A.M. the following morning, Carroll resumed as if there had been no break.

"Would you say, Sergeant, to this court under oath, that you had never ordered any man to stand up against a brick wall?"

"Yes, sir; I would say that under oath."

"As a matter of fact, Sergeant, at almost any hour of the day you were to walk around this prison yard you would see anywhere from one to seven men standing with their nose against the wall, with their feet about two feet away and leaning against that wall on their nose or forehead, wouldn't you?"

As he said the words, Carroll demonstrated the position, walking over to the wall of the courtroom, leaning his own head against it and stepping backward, his body poised at the awkward angle.

"No." It was a curt, categorical denial.

The assistant prosecutor returned to the Swope deposition.

"What were some of the complaints that had been lodged against you at that time?"

"There were no complaints at all." The defendant had returned to his earlier position, perhaps on the advice of counsel the night before.

"Weren't you asked questions as to how you treated the prisoners?"

"That's right."

"And you were asked whether or not you struck prisoners?"

"That's right."

"So complaints *were* lodged against you?"

"That's right."

"[So] when you told this court that you never received any complaints or any notice of any complaints during the time you were the provost sergeant from August through to the day you left in March, 1945, that wasn't true, was it?"

"You never said the IG."

The court was getting very tired of this routine, but Carroll kept at it throughout the morning and well into the afternoon. By then Sergeant Smith had begun to create conflicts with his previous testimony. The longer he testified, the deeper he became mired. Having denied at least thirty times that he ever ordered men against the wall, "except when the coal trucks would come in and we would have the men stand over at the side out of the way," the bewildered Smith began to reverse himself.

"I don't mean that [the coal trucks]," Carroll challenged. "I mean facing the wall as a form of punishment. You never saw a man who was facing the wall doing double-time?"

"It was an order by the prison officer."

Carroll brightened.

"You *did* see men?"

"No, I didn't."

The assistant prosecutor shifted gears.

"Did you ever know of or hear of any man who had been sent to the *hospital,* or who went to the hospital immediately after receiving this punishment facing the wall?"

"No, sir."

The assistant TJA pulled out one of the Inspector General's report pages. The witness blanched.

"I wasn't there," he pleaded. "I don't know what happened." Then suddenly he blurted, "*I* sent men to the hospital."

"*You* sent men to the hospital?"

"I called an ambulance, yes."

"After they received the punishment of standing before a wall?"

"I don't know what the punishment was."

The incident Carroll was about to introduce would figure prominently in the prosecution's planned rebuttal testimony, when the court would learn how two prisoners, Wright and Alford, had been so severely beaten by guards that they both suffered massive internal injuries and were vomiting blood. Sending them to the hospital may have been a panic move on Smith's part at the time to avoid having them die in the guardhouse.

"Who were the men you sent to the hospital?"

"I don't recall their names."

"Do you remember whether they were white or colored prisoners?"

"I believe there was one white and one colored."

"How did these prisoners come to your attention to have to go to the hospital?"

"I got a call from No. 3 Guardhouse, I went down there and they had a man on the floor laying on a blanket. I asked them what was the matter."

"Who did you ask what was the matter?"

"The jailers. I asked had they called an ambulance. They said they hadn't; so I called an ambulance and the man went to the hospital."

"When you asked the jailer what was the matter, did he reply?"

"No, sir, he didn't."

"He just stood and looked at you?"

"He didn't tell me."

"You didn't pursue the matter any further?"

"I come back to the guardhouse and reported to Lieutenant Cubage."

"Could you tell from looking at this man what appeared to be wrong with him?"

"No, sir, I couldn't."

"Were there any marks on his face?"

Smith's answer was another of his non sequiturs:

"He didn't have his clothes off."

"He was just reposing peacefully on a blanket?"

"I believe he was coughing up blood."

"When was this episode?"

It was a question the defendant couldn't answer. He seemed to have no sense of time. He couldn't remember whether it was in the summer of 1944, or whether it was after Christmas that year, or maybe in early 1945.

"What is your best recollection?" Carroll finally inquired.

"To the best of my recollection I couldn't say." But it must have been while he was working there, Smith allowed.

"Where did you see the other one, the colored fellow?" Carroll asked, trying to get back to the sergeant's narrative.

"Half an hour to an hour later. After I come back to the guardhouse, I got another telephone call down from Guardhouse No. 3."

"The same guardhouse?"

"That's right. I don't think at that time Lieutenant Cubage was with me. I wouldn't say for sure on that. I went down there. In the back room, where the biggest room was, laying on the bed, was this other fellow."

"What was he doing? Was he coughing up a little blood, too?"

"Yes, sir."

"When you got there and saw this boy on the bed, what was said when you entered the room, and who said it?"

"I asked them [the jailers] what was the matter."

"Did anybody reply?"

"The jailers didn't tell me anything. So I told them I would ask them to call an ambulance."

"They didn't say what was the matter?"

"No."

"So you went out and called an ambulance?"

"I don't know whether I called an ambulance or not."

"Then what did you do?"

"After they taken the man to hospital, I went back and reported to Lieutenant Cubage."

"What did you report to him?"

"I told him another man went to the hospital."

"Did you tell him why the man went to hospital?"

"No, I didn't."

"So you, as sergeant in charge of the prison, never took it upon yourself in either instance to ask for an explanation of why these men were in that condition; is that right?"

"I tried to find out."

"You just said 'What's the matter with this fellow?' and nobody answered you, so you just went about your business; is that your testimony?"

"No. I went back and reported to Lieutenant Cubage."

"In other words, you just walked in, in one instance you saw a white boy lying on a blanket spitting up blood, you said 'What's the matter with this fellow?' Nobody answered you, so you went back and told Lieutenant Cubage 'I sent a boy to the hospital. He was lying on a bed and he was spitting up blood. I don't know why he was spitting up blood.'"

"I told him as best I could."

"Then, about thirty minutes later, you had this second instance. And when you went into the room and asked them why this boy was in this condition they didn't answer you and you just went back and told Lieutenant Cubage 'Another boy was sent to the hospital. He was spitting up blood, but I don't know what happened to him.' Is that right?"

"That's right."

"You didn't make any additional effort to find out what was wrong with these boys?"

"They wouldn't tell me why."

"When you testified to this court, both on direct examination and also on cross-examination a little earlier, you just forgot all about this incident, didn't you?"

"No, sir, I didn't."

"Didn't you tell this court that you never knew of any prisoners that were injured or any prisoners that had anything wrong with them or had to be sent to the hospital or any prisoners being hurt in this prison?"

"You said a man facing the wall."

"You have limited your answers that you have given me to prisoners that might have been hurt facing the wall. Is that right?"

"You said 'facing the wall.'"

Carroll went back to the subject of running men in a circle as punishment. Smith repeated his contention that the only time he had ever seen men doing that was when they wanted to get warm and did so voluntarily.

Carroll reminded the accused that he had told Colonel Swope that he had double-timed men as punishment "for twenty-five or thirty laps around the enclosure," adding, "that was routine." Carroll asked him whether that had been a true answer to the colonel's question.

Smith said yes, but *he* hadn't done it. An officer had. On second thought, he hadn't actually *seen* an officer administering double-time punishment; he had merely *heard* about it. From whom? From Lieutenant Cubage. So how did he know the number of laps—the agreed-upon prescribed number of laps that were administered depending on the offense?

The harried defendant stared at his feet.

The assistant prosecutor's last subject was the matter of shakedown inspections—during which discovery of any contraband articles (e.g., knives or cigarettes) was said to have resulted in immediate punishment.

The accused claimed that such immediate punishment would have been impossible, because these shakedown inspections were done when the barracks were empty—while the prisoners were out on detail, or while they were doing their calisthenics. And because of the crowded conditions in the prison, the cadre never knew whose contraband property they were confiscating during their inspections.

This was too much for some of the members of the court, who had, after all, been in the army themselves for some time.

CAPTAIN BLUM: Sergeant, if you found cigarettes in a locker or cupboard, were you required to take them away?

ACCUSED: Yes.

MAJOR PERS: When you made these inspections while prisoners were out, you went through everything thoroughly, and let us assume you found some cigarettes or you found a knife. To whom would you give the disciplinary action for finding that knife or cigarette?

ACCUSED: No one. You couldn't find out who it was.

MAJOR PERS: Then what was the purpose of these inspections?

ACCUSED: That was a standing order when I went to the guardhouse as jailer that jailers would shake down.

MAJOR PERS: Don't you think it would have been a better arrangement if you had everyone standing beside his bunk or his bed, and had him open up everything he had and look in things, so that if you did find something contrary to regulations you could very easily remedy it. Isn't that so?

ACCUSED: Yes.

MAJOR PERS: In other words, if you found a knife, cigarettes, or something that should not have been there, you just let it go by? What did you do? Was anyone punished for it?

ACCUSED: No, sir.

MAJOR PERS: It was just taken away?

ACCUSED: That's right.

Colonel Leone changed the subject. When he sought to confirm some of the defendant's personal statistics, the witness became very forthcoming, and easily remembered relevant dates and statistics. He was "going on" thirty-three years old, had an eighth grade education, and had accumulated a total of nine years and nine months of service in the army. He had joined the army on November 8, 1928, "right after graduating from grade school." He had been discharged on January 16th, 1935, and had worked in coal mines until his present hitch. His memory had improved.

Although Smith had been overseas since August 19, 1942, he explained, he had never been in combat, having spent nearly a year in an army hospital while the doctors worked on some torn cartilage in one of his knees—first performing surgery, then instituting physical therapy. After his release from the hospital, he had reported to the Lichfield replacement depot as a casual early in 1944. Of his forty months overseas, he had spent twenty-nine months as a casual. All of his service as provost sergeant of the prison had been temporary duty while awaiting assignment to a "package" for shipment to the Continent.

When the court ran out of questions, Lieutenant Johnson announced that "the defense rests," and Sergeant Smith returned to his seat at the defense table.

Major Smith rose and addressed the court.

"May it please the court, the prosecution will have some rebuttal witnesses. It will take a few minutes to check up on them and see in what order to call them; and I ask the court for a ten-minute recess. It may take a little longer."

The preparation took almost half an hour. And, as it turned out, the prosecution's parade of rebuttal witnessses would continue for many weeks.

9

REBUTTAL WITNESSES

Orchestrated by Earl Carroll, the testimony of the prosecution's rebuttal witnesses provided a daily tide of unsavory narrative that overflowed into the public press on both sides of the Atlantic Ocean. These unremitting descriptions of outrageous abuse were also serving to sweep away any doubts on the part of the court as to the defendant's guilt. As Captain Carroll declared on January 9, 1946, defending what the court was beginning to regard as an ordeal:

"Rebuttal testimony is not limited to impeachment. Rebuttal testimony may prove motive; it may prove intent; it may prove scheme and design; it may prove, circumstantially, the *case.*"[1]

Thirty minutes after Sergeant Smith left the witness stand, the first rebuttal witness was sworn in. General Prisoner Lester J. Chaves had languished in the guardhouse for seven months awaiting his court-martial, giving him ample time to observe conditions there. Although he had volunteered for combat duty, he had actually been turned down because he had not completed his prison term—a decision obviously at odds with the mission of the reinforcement depot. Neither could time served before trial be credited against his sentence.

Ed Rosenthal summarized Chaves's testimony in a lengthy *Stars and Stripes* news item:

LONDON, December 12—A former prisoner at the 10th Reinforcement Depot who testified yesterday that he had been punished for possessing a copy of *The*

Stars and Stripes, said today that 'no reading material whatsoever' was allowed in the Lichfield guardhouses last winter.

Lester J. Chaves told the general court-martial court that, with the exception of the Bible and personal correspondence, prisoners were forbidden to read any printed matter.

Colonel Louis P. Leone, president of the court, asked Chaves: 'Did you hear about the Battle of the Bulge, which Americans were mixed up in?'

"No, sir," the witness replied.

"When did you hear about it?" asked the colonel, a former regimental commander in the Armored Division.

"When I got to France, sir," Chaves replied.

The witness offered a startling description of mess hall mistreatment. Prisoners slow in sitting down or rising, he said, were ordered to move up and down 600 times at their mess hall bench and then double-time back to the guardhouse.

When Chaves and another prisoner went up for seconds, according to his testimony, a guard ordered Chaves' tray filled to a height of four inches with beans [the food trays were twelve by eighteen inches], and he was given three minutes to consume the beans and a helping of bread.

"I ate 'em," Chaves told the court.

Cigarettes were as dangerous to have as reading matter in the prison, the witness said. One man who confessed to possessing cigarettes was forced to eat them and then stand with nose and toes touching the wall.

Chaves then offered a full description of prison calisthenics, which, he said, extended for over three solid hours without a break in the morning and more than three hours without a break in the afternoon.

In regard to sanitation, Chaves said that, although prisoners scrubbed the hallways as daily punishment, there were no urinals and only one commode in each wing, and prisoners often relieved themselves on the floor.

Chaves testified that he did not make complaints of abuses because prisoners who did so were found with bleeding face bruises.[2]

On the witness stand, Chaves provided considerably more detail about the time Sergeant Smith sent two men to the hospital. They were being punished for something that had occurred during calisthenics, he said.

"Sergeant Jones came down to the guardhouse and called out Alford. He had him in the hallway, which was near the latrine in No. 3 Guardhouse, and he started beating him on the chest and stomach and chin with his fist. I was approximately four feet away in a cell with the door open.

"Alford told him he had been wounded in the chest and did not want to be hit there. Sergeant Jones told him he didn't give a damn where he had been wounded. Sergeant Jones evidently tried to knock him out, but he couldn't. He left and sent down to No. 2 Guardhouse for Pfc Gheens. Gheens came down and they took [Alford] out the back of No. 3 Guardhouse—a little courtyard. Sergeant Jones held one arm of Alford and Corporal Robson held the other arm. Gheens started hitting him in the stomach and chin.

"Alford had his head down and [Gheens] kept hitting him. Then he backed off and he kicked him in the stomach three or four times. Then they carried Alford in and laid him on the hallway.

"He was bleeding internally through the mouth and nose. He was unconscious. We told Loveless and Corporal Robson to call the ambulance. They didn't want to call it. We kept talking to them, the prisoners and myself, and they finally called the ambulance."

Chaves said he had tried to revive the unconscious man and later helped carry him out to the ambulance on blankets. He had also witnessed the beating of Wright in the courtyard by jailer Loveless.

"Afterward the jailers carried him to his bunk. He was bleeding through his mouth and nose. He stayed there approximately half an hour before we talked Loveless again into getting the ambulance to take Wright to the hospital, as he couldn't walk. He kept mumbling, pointing to his chest and stomach, and he was bleeding through his mouth."

Later testimony would reveal that Alford's and Wright's injuries would be listed by Medical Corps doctors as *"self-inflicted."*

While he waited to see IG inspector Swope, Chaves said, Sergeant Smith made him stand nose and toes from 8:00 A.M. until 5:00 P.M., with a single break of thirty minutes for lunch. In his cross-examination, Lieutenant Johnson tried to impeach Chaves's testimony using a Carroll technique. Reading from Chaves's deposition in the Inspector General report, the defense counsel demanded to know why he couldn't find statements that matched his testimony. The witness embarrassed Johnson by pointing out that the defense counsel needed to read a little farther into the document he held in his hand.

Day after day, rebuttal testimony ground on, until the stories of more than two dozen witnesses had been heard. Items reported by the witnesses included:

• Prisoners were made to stand nose and toes for ten hours after being clubbed by Sergeant Smith.

• Pfc Thomas P. Cappello was deprived of food for twenty-four hours—after which he was overfed, then dosed with castor oil, and finally put on "swing shift," a KP function lasting from supper until 3:00 or 4:00 A.M.

• Swing shift workers were required to get up with everyone else at 5:30 A.M, with no difference in their daytime schedules—forcing them to survive on less than two hours sleep per day.

• A Sergeant Nunes took pleasure in making prisoners eat spoiled vegetables, fat that had been cut from meat, and other kitchen garbage.

• Sergeant Nunes and Sergeant Adcock put pistols to the heads of two Negro prisoners, forcing them to dig "graves" for themselves, having the men occasionally lie down in them for "measurement."

• When General Prisoner Albert Beach mouthed off to a guard who was a former boxer, his upper dental plate was broken by a right to the jaw. The same guard drove another prisoner's teeth through his lower lip with his billy club.

• Some guards ordered prisoners to fight each other. Others demanded that men run across the room and repeatedly slam their recently wounded bodies into the wall.

• During calisthenics, Lieutenant Ennis kneed one soldier in the groin for failing to keep his eyes front. When Ennis challenged anyone to come out of ranks and fight him, twice he had takers.

• The broken glass in the windows and the holes in Lichfield ceilings were not due to German air raids. Perimeter guards had orders to shoot at any prisoners looking out the windows. One guard was restricted for three days for not having a bullet in the chamber of his rifle (a dangerous practice, normally forbidden except in combat).

• Numerous examples were presented alleging that Lichfield medical officers were a part of the conspiracy to make life miserable for the prisoners. Captain Warnecke sent Thomas Cappello back to duty with a fever of 104 degrees.

• When Charles McGinnis went on sick call with scabies, the medical officer gave him some salve and told him to spread it on his skin and not to wash it off. His dirty neck got him into trouble with Sergeant Smith, since McGinnis worked on the coal truck. Smith, McGinnis said, worked him over; and his scabies got worse.[3]

This last story got the attention of the court's senior medical officer, Major Pers. The doctor broke in with his own questions and seemed relieved to hear that McGinnis's problem was cleared up in a matter of days after he was transferred out of Lichfield and received proper medical treatment.

The litany of abuses at Lichfield was interrupted when Private Joseph M. Mallory was called to the witness stand. His testimony revealed that a few weeks earlier during the current court-martial, he had been dragged out of a London pub near the witnesses' barracks on Green Street and beaten up by two Lichfield guards, Corporal Louis L. Robson and staff Sergeant James M. Jones, both of whom were already facing charges of brutality.

Mallory drew a knife, stabbed Jones in the shoulder, and cut Robson on the neck. Asked why he drew the knife, Mallory said, "I thought they might have killed me. Dead men don't talk."

Afraid to go back to his quarters, Mallory had spent the rest of the night at the Red Cross. When he returned, he was arrested and shipped to the guardhouse to await court-martial.

Mallory said he was never interviewed by anyone before his trial. His required charge sheet was delivered by "some lieutenant. I don't know who he was. He handed it through a little hole in the cell and told me I would be tried the next day. When I looked at it he was gone."

Mallory was convicted along with twenty-three other defendants in a series of rapid-fire hearings lasting a total of forty minutes. The guards who had assaulted him were not charged in the incident.

Mallory's story was featured in the Saturday morning, December 15th issue of *The Stars and Stripes*.[4]

The week of rebuttal testimony ended with Prisoner Mike Koblinski's recounting of how his stint in solitary coincided with several days of Richey's confinement in the hole. They were grateful, he said, for the loose brick whose existence had been denied by Cubage, Ennis, and Smith. The secret slot not only permitted communication with other prisoners, but, like Richey, netted them an occasional supplement to their diet of bread and water.

A severely wounded (Armored Corps) combat veteran who had been refused a furlough before returning to his unit, Koblinski had gone AWOL twice. Upon his return the second time, because he was a "repeater" he had been beaten for several hours in one of the latrines by two guards (who wore gloves so they wouldn't hurt their hands). When his face hit one of the sinks, his front teeth had been chipped. He showed them to the court.

"I went to get them fixed but the dentist said he couldn't when he found out I was at Lichfield. 'As soon as the trial is over,' he said, 'you come over here and I'll fix them—because I don't want to get in on that trial.'"

It was the defense counsel who inadvertently brought out an unexpected little patriotic speech by the witness.

"You felt pretty strongly about the way you were treated at the 10th depot?" Lieutenant Johnson asked him.

"I *joined* the United States Army and took an oath that I would fight for my country and go through anything in the world for my country. [Koblinski had volunteered when he was sixteen, lying about his age.] Then I got in there. . . . Beating American soldiers around is a crime. You *know* better, because *you* were in that depot," he challenged.

Johnson, who had, indeed, been stationed at Lichfield, ignored the speech, saying only, "Now let us continue your testimony. . . ."

In a characteristically theatrical gesture, Captain Carroll called the court's attention to the probability that Sergeant Smith, who had never seen combat as Koblinski had, was wearing an unauthorized ribbon—the army's pre-Pearl Harbor Ribbon. Smith apparently thought his earlier 1928 to 1935 service qualified him to wear it. But Carroll read aloud the salient paragraph from Army Regulation 635, paragraph 68, which stated that "only those persons in service during the period of 1939 through December 7, 1941 are permitted to wear that ribbon."

Colonel Leone, an Armored Corps combat veteran himself, ordered the accused to remove the ribbon from his blouse. Smith unpinned the ribbon and put it in his pocket.

Guardhouse No. 1 at Whittington Barracks, Lichfield, also used during American occupation of the facility as offices for the provost marshal and for temporary detention of new prisoners. (Photograph by the author, 1978)

Guardhouse No. 2 at Lichfield. (Courtesy of the U.S. Army Judiciary)

Guardhouse stairway on which prisoners were required to "double-time," sometimes being struck with clubs if they did not move fast enough. (Courtesy of the U.S. Army Judiciary)

Latrine in Guardhouse No. 2, with one broken toilet for hundreds of prisoners. Some of the cold-water sinks drained directly onto the floor. (Courtesy of the U.S. Army Judiciary)

Interior of "the hole," the solitary cell in Guardhouse No. 2. The infamous "loose brick" is visible in the rear wall. (Courtesy of the U.S. Army Judiciary)

Close-up of the "loose brick" (after mortar repair by the British garrison). Through this opening, prisoners in solitary confinement communicated with other prisoners and received contraband food. (Courtesy of the U.S. Army Judiciary)

Interior of guardhouse: hallway into wings, where "nose and toes" punishment was inflicted. (Courtesy of the U.S. Army Judiciary)

Courtyard behind Guardhouse No. 2, where punitive "calisthenics" were ordered by prison cadre. (Courtesy of the U.S. Army Judiciary)

Courtyard where prisoners were "braced" at attention while waiting to enter mess hall at left. (Courtesy of the U.S. Army Judiciary)

Bullet hole from armed perimeter guards firing at prisoners who violated orders by looking out the window. (Courtesy of the U.S. Army Judiciary)

10

THE COURT VS THE PRESS

With their daily dispatches in *The Stars and Stripes,* Rosenthal, White, and other writers were turning the trial into a political event. After a week of rebuttal testimony, the Saturday morning edition of the paper embarrassed the army by publishing evidence of a coverup:

LONDON, December 15—S/Sgt. James B. Gallardy, former 10th Reinforcement Depot prisoner, testified yesterday that the depot executive officer offered to remit his sentence and restore his staff sergeant's rating if he would "forget about" mistreatment of prisoners at the Lichfield stockade.

Lt. Col. Robert Norton, deputy for Colonel James A. Kilian, CO, called Gallardy to his office last winter, according to the witness, and when Gallardy described prison beating Norton declared, "The best thing to do is forget about it, and we will get you out of here."

A week later, Gallardy testified, he was returned to his unit, the 29th Infantry Division, with his rating restored, his sentence remitted, and full back pay granted.

The witness, who wears the Bronze Star and the Purple Heart, said he had been confined to Lichfield for being five or six hours late on a pass. The colonel had called him to the office and made the agreement, he said, because he had an excellent military record prior to his AWOL sentence.[1]

Reading these daily accounts in the GI newspaper, an American MP stationed in the French port of Le Havre went to his commanding officer and offered to swear an affidavit about conditions at Lichfield. Pfc John P. Buckmaster complained that *The Stars and Stripes* stories were watered down, and he wanted to see justice done. Instead of accepting his affidavit or taking his deposition, his CO issued travel orders to permit Buckmaster to testify in person.

Buckmaster had been a bazooka man with the 90th Infantry Division who had landed in one of the D-Day waves at Normandy. Seventy-eight days later he was wounded at the Falaise Pocket. After six weeks in the hospital, he began convalescing at Pheasey Farm, which was adjacent to, and under the jurisdiction of, the 10th Reinforcement Depot at Lichfield. One of his last nights at the facility, with oral permission from his platoon sergeant but without a pass, he had left the post with hospital buddies for about four hours to go to a farewell party for one of their number at a local pub two miles away. When Buckmaster returned at 11:30 P.M., he was arrested, sent to the guardhouse, and subsequently sentenced by the Lichfield assembly-line special court to six months in the stockade and forfeiture of two-thirds of his pay—and he was not permitted to return to his unit.

Enjoying its own journalistic impact, *The Stars and Stripes* ran the story the next day. The article included some new material:

Staff Sergeant Ashur Baizer, a former Lichfield jailer, told the court that 1st Lieutenant Leonard W. Ennis, a prison officer, called all of the guards to a meeting one day, and ordered them to be rough with prisoners, or the guards themselves would be put behind bars.

Two guards on temporary duty, who gave cigarettes to inmates, were imprisoned, Baizer said, and the guards complained to their officer, 2nd Lieutenant Andrew J. Caffrey, who said he would take their complaint to Colonel James A. Kilian, post CO. When defense counsel objected to the line of questioning, subsequent testimony concerning the incident was stricken from the record.

Last week Kilian denied he had ever received complaints of prison mistreatment.

Earlier today, Pfc. Henry Petras, a former prisoner, testified that an inmate had spent 33 days in solitary confinement, and emerged with four front teeth missing, hollow cheeks, smashed eyeglasses, and 30 pounds under his normal weight.[2]

On Tuesday morning, December 18th, the front page of *The Stars and Stripes* brought down the wrath of army brass:

LICHFIELD MURDER SUSPECTED
Probe Opens in G.I. Death

The banner headline would nearly cause a mistrial. It would also change the rules in the *Stars and Stripes* newspaper office, limiting the freedom of GI journalists. On orders from European Headquarters, the headline was toned down in later editions, but Ed Rosenthal's story remained unaltered:

DEATH LAID TO BEATING AT LICHFIELD

LONDON, December 17—An investigation into the possible murder of a Negro prisoner through brutal beatings at the 10th Reinforcement Depot last February was reopened today by Captain Earl J. Carroll, assistant prosecutor in the Lichfield trials, who submitted two I.G. reports of the death. Private Eril L. Bolton of the 3433rd Trucking Company died March 15 on the way from Lichfield to the Continent from "a massive intercerebral hemorrhage," possibly caused by having his head rammed against a cement wall, according to the I.G. report.

Although the cause of Bolton's death was diagnosed March 19 as a malignant brain tumor, General Eisenhower ordered an investigation three days later, and the autopsy report found that external blows could have caused the death. Microscopic examination of the brain tumor revealed that there was "no evidence of malignancy."

In the I.G. report of April 17, Lt. Col. Lawrence W. Varner stated Bolton's name was not entered on the stockade sick book.[3]

The bomb had been quietly delivered by Earl Carroll. At the end of the day, he had submitted two hitherto secret Inspector General reports, asking that they be marked as prosecution exhibits to be offered into evidence at a later time.

When the court convened on the morning of December 19th, fireworks erupted. The defense entered a motion for a mistrial, claiming that the newspaper's account was prejudicial to the rights of the accused. The resulting flap occupied court proceedings for most of the morning. Then, in an unprecedented ritual for a court-martial, each member of the court, including the president and law member, was sworn in and examined on the witness stand. As *The Stars and Stripes* self-consciously recounted the drama the next day:

Flourishing a copy of the newspaper, Johnson asked members, "Have you read this story?" Five had, and they were challenged in turn. The court was closed each time while the remaining members voted on whether the challenged member had been prejudiced by reading the paper. Two members who said they had only glanced at the headlines were not challenged. In each case the court found that Johnson's challenge was not sustained.

After the challenges were overruled, Major Walter E. Hopper, Jr. declared "for the record and for the benefit of the accused, the court wishes to state that the article in question in its principal tenor is entirely erroneous insofar as it stated things took place in this court which did not take place.

"*The Stars and Stripes* story was in error where it stated that the IG report was submitted to the court. It was not submitted. It was marked for identification only, and has not yet been admitted as evidence."[4]

Although *The Stars and Stripes'* sensationalism resulted in new rules being imposed at the newspaper, there was a loophole. One of the new guidelines was that the GI paper could print anything that had already appeared in the public press. This made it fairly easy for enterprising GI journalists who clandestinely passed on their stories to correspondent friends working for the Associated Press, *Time, Newsweek,* and news agencies, sometimes even passing along carbon copies of their already typed dispatches.[5]

When the courtroom finally settled down after Johnson's motion for a mistrial was denied, the 10th Reinforcement Depot's former provost marshal, Major Lo Buono was recalled. The major's memory seemed to be even worse than during his first appearance on the witness stand. And when Captain Carroll introduced the subject of the investigation of Private Bolton's death, Lo Buono seemed to panic. His voice dropped to an inaudible mumble. Instead of answering the assistant prosecutor's questions, he began shaking his head.

Major Smith told the witness that the court reporter had no way of recording nonverbal responses. Four times in the first twenty minutes of his testimony, Lo Buono was admonished by the president to speak louder and to face the members of the court so they could hear his answers.

Claiming he did not even recognize Eril L. Bolton's name, or remember any officer ever investigating the prisoner's death ("there were so many investigations"), the former provost marshal did identify his signature on a document which turned out to be his own report of his investigation of Bolton's death. But Lo Buono could not remember its content, and he now disagreed with facts presented in his own report. When confronted with his testimony during Colonel Varner's hearing on the matter, he doubted he had given the answers sworn to in the document.

When the questioning turned to the bullet holes in the guardhouse windows, the major didn't want to hear the answers he had given Colonel Varner. Instead of admitting they were caused by gunfire, as he had stated at the time, he now spoke of backfiring automobiles and a noisy bus that regularly stopped nearby. (He did not explain how this noise could have made the holes in the windows.)

Nearly an hour was spent splitting hairs about whether Lo Buono had control of the prison. He "had contact with the prisoners" but "was not in charge of them," he insisted. He had "responsibility" but not "control."

When Captain Carroll took over the questioning, he reminded the major of his earlier trial testimony that, "I was provost marshal during that period. I had charge of the interior guard, the guard pool, the military police detachment, and the prisoners. I was Sergeant Smith's commanding officer, and I know that Smith handled the prisoners in an excellent manner at all times."

Lo Buono claimed he had no memory of saying the word "prisoners" when he had testified earlier, and if he had said it, he had misspoken. Despite the many Inspector General investigations of conditions at the Lichfield prison, the witness asserted he had never heard of mistreatment of prisoners during his tenure as provost marshal.

But as the prosecution bored in, he admitted that maybe he had heard *rumors*—not rumors of mistreatment, of course, just *"general rumors"* about the post. Soldiers, he conceded, didn't like Lichfield and sometimes complained.

He had not *"removed* a psycho-neurotic officer for mistreatment of prisoners," he said, but had merely *recommended* to Colonel Kilian that the lieutenant be removed to avoid any possible incident in the *future* that might reflect unfavorably on the 10th Reinforcement Depot.

The fruitless interrogation continued until 5:07 P.M., when the court adjourned for the night and the witness stepped down. To the major's chagrin, he would run into Colonel Kilian in the officers' mess later that evening. The encounter would create turmoil in the courtroom the following day.

11

LO BUONO CRACKS

On Friday morning, December 21st, the court reconvened at 9:30 A.M. Major Richard Lo Buono resumed his place on the witness stand and was reminded that he was still under oath. Captain Carroll first explored the witness's remarkable record of promotions under Colonel Kilian. Major Lo Buono pleaded a poor memory on the subject. Earl Carroll asked for and was granted a brief recess to obtain the major's 66-1 personnel record, a copy of which would ultimately be entered as a prosecution exhibit by the assistant TJA.[1]

The record revealed that Richard Lo Buono had entered the army as a private in February of 1941, but was awarded a commission in August of 1942, having graduated from Officer Candidate School at Fort Sill, Oklahoma. He had arrived at the Lichfield depot in September as a newly commissioned second lieutenant. A few months later, in March of 1943, he was promoted to first lieutenant. In December of the same year, Colonel Kilian made him a captain. Only thirteen months later, in January of 1945, the commandant had promoted him to major.

Since during this period Lo Buono had received two efficiency ratings of "excellent" and no less than seven as "superior" from Kilian, Carroll asked the major why his efficiency rating had suddenly dropped two notches from "superior" under Colonel Kilian to "very satisfactory" under Kilian's successor, Major Free—the equivalent of going from an "A" to a "C." Lo Buono at first had no idea; but he tended to agree with the assistant prosecutor's suggestion that it might have had something to do with the visits from Colonel Swope and Colonel Pence of the Inspector General Department.

While being questioned on the subject of the IG investigation, Major Lo Buono mentioned that he had received a written reprimand after the inspectors left. Under the 104th Article of War, that constituted criminal punishment, and his acceptance of it (instead of exercising an officer's right to opt for a general court-martial) was tantamount to a plea of guilty. To the astonishment of the court, the former provost marshal stated that he did not know what the reprimand was for.

"It is the only reprimand that you have ever received in the whole of your army career," Carroll reminded the witness. "It occurred less than six months ago. You had it in your hand and you can't remember what it was about?"

"It was a long letter," pleaded Lo Buono. "I don't recall the letter. It was a long statement."

"And you didn't pay enough attention to it to find out what they were reprimanding you for?"

"I was very much disappointed in it." The answer was not responsive.

Realizing that his mentioning the reprimand had been a serious gaffe, the former provost marshal retreated to making vague, equivocal speeches instead of answering the prosecution's questions. He seemed to be trying to create the illusion of testifying while putting nothing concrete on the record. It was worse than his first appearance on the witness stand.

Dozens of pages of court record reflect Earl Carroll's simply trying to establish whose signature appeared on documents setting forth prison rules and regulations. Lo Buono thought one copy of such documents might sometimes have been signed by Lieutenant Cubage, as prison officer, *if* Colonel Kilian told him to do so. It was not clear whether Cubage had authority to institute and sign regulations on his own. In fact, Lo Buono thought, another copy of the same document might very well have been signed by Kilian's executive officer. There was never any mention of a probable signature by the post provost marshal.

Tension mounted in the courtroom as the witness parried one question after another, committing to nothing, leading Carroll finally to exclaim, "I am at a loss for words! You and I do not understand the meaning of words the same way. Listen to this: Did he [Cubage] have authority to write on a piece of paper rules and regulations for prisoners, put his name on the bottom, and then issue it out to some place where prisoners or guards could see it?"

The major's wary answer was typically noncommittal.

"Not particularly, no."

It began to drive the court up the wall. Major Hopper broke in repeatedly:

"Answer the question, please. . . . We do not want assumptions, but we want your own knowledge. . . . Keep to the point. . . . Answer the question. . . . Do you remember the discussion or not?"

At one point, the law member warned the former provost marshal in terms he might have addressed to a juvenile:

"You realize, major, that you are under oath and that you must give this court the truth. . . . If you do not know, you must tell us that you do not know. If you do know, you must tell us that you know. I will read to you a passage of the *Manual for Courts-Martial*, page 174: 'So, a witness may commit perjury in testifying falsely as to his belief, remembrance, or impression, or as to his judgment or opinion on matters of fact. Thus, where a witness swears that he does not remember certain facts when in fact he does, he commits perjury.'

"You must realize when you are testifying under oath to this court the seriousness of your answers. . . . Major, perjury is the willful and corrupt giving, upon a lawful oath . . . in a judicial proceeding or course of justice, of false testimony material to the issue or matter of inquiry."

When Carroll turned to Lichfield policy for handling soldiers who repeatedly jumped ship when their replacement packages sailed for the Continent, and what Lo Buono's recommendations for punishment had been, the major didn't remember his exact words. After Carroll asked him just to tell the court the substance of what he had said, the witness became uncertain about which of his many conversations with Colonel Kilian and Lieutenant Cubage the assistant prosecutor was asking about. Carroll told him it didn't matter. Any one would do. Whatever he remembered. "Do you recall *some* of the corrective measures that were discussed relative to that situation?"

The major thought there had been "something from higher headquarters. There was a top secret mounting plan on that."

"That is not an answer to the question," the frustrated law member declared, interrupting. "The assistant TJA asked you if *you* ever recommended to anybody what should be done with these package jumpers and other escaped prisoners. You can answer 'yes' or 'no,' and then explain. Did you tell anybody what you thought should be done with them?"

"No. I don't recall. I may have."

The major's multiple choice answer brought in the president of court.

"You still haven't answered the question. You have said 'yes,' and you have said 'no.' Just say *either* 'yes' or 'no.'"

The major decided he didn't remember for sure.

Captain Carroll simplified his question. Had Colonel Kilian given him any delegation of *any* authority making him, as provost marshal, responsible for the treatment of prisoners? What was his best recollection? Yes? Or no?

"He would occasionally just mention something about it, and I was usually at the meetings." The witness squirmed as he said it.

"Obviously, you are avoiding a direct answer to the question," Colonel Leone asserted. "The reporter will reread the question. Think what you're going to say, and then *say* it."

The question was repeated.

"No, sir; nothing definite, other than to escort the inspectors through."

"The answer is not responsive to the question," the law member declared. "You must answer the question. It is your duty not to evade an answer to these questions."

Next, nearly an hour was spent trying to get the major to decide whether he had ever had a conversation with the depot's commanding officer or his executive officer about establishing a policy for the treatment of combat-wounded soldiers apprehended after going AWOL. The witness's answers kept getting longer and longer. At first he denied that any convicted AWOLs were ever confined in the guardhouse, which was obviously untrue. Then he began to list "rare exceptions," such as men awaiting trial on another offense, or those shipped in from North Africa, or men with venereal disease.

"I don't care if they had *leprosy!*" Carroll shouted. "Were there *any?*"

When Major Hopper finally broke in this time, the exasperated law member's sarcasm sounded a little like that of Captain Carroll:

"Major Lo Buono, there is a misapprehension on your part about the answering of questions on the witness stand. When you are asked a question, answer it. Don't go into a long-winded explanation of everything you know that remotely pertains to the matter about which you are questioned. If you are asked, 'Do you own a dog?' simply say 'No.' Don't say, 'No, but ten years ago I owned an Airedale!'"

Captain Carroll reminded the witness once again that he was under oath. He then read him a passage from the *Manual for Courts-Martial:* "Where a witness swears that he does not remember certain facts when in fact he does, he commits perjury." Then the assistant prosecutor addressed the court:

"In fairness to this witness, I think that he should be told just what are the provisions with regard to committing perjury. I don't think that he realizes the seriousness of this at all. I would like the law member to direct the witness to the provisions."

Major Hopper complied, even though he had previously given the witness a similar lecture on his own. In an effort to move things along, the law member even offered Lo Buono the 24th Article of War, which gave him the privilege of refusing to answer if he feared self-incrimination. At that point, the witness was looking very pale, and his skin was clammy. Then, in full view of the spectators and the press, Richard Lo Buono cracked.

"I've been hounded for seven months!" he suddenly exclaimed, his color returning, his face reddening. "I can't think straight. I just want to give it. I want to give him what he wants, but now—I'm confused. I am under a mental strain at the present time—nothing to do with this—and I'm not thinking clearly. I know it."

"I'm not nervous," he added, sounding like television personality Don Knotts, who used the same line in his comic parody of nervousness.

Possibly contributing to the former provost marshal's demeanor that afternoon was his confrontation with Colonel James A. Kilian outside the building during the court's noon recess. That night, after the court adjourned, they would see each other yet again. Because he was staying at the Hotel Cumberland and dined at the London Officer's Club, Earl Carroll was keenly aware of this mounting intrigue; and he suspected who the "him" might be in the witness's last utterance about "giving *him* what he wants."

By the next morning, as Major Lo Buono's performance deteriorated even further, Captain Carroll interrupted his interrogation:

"I am going to say this much to the court: Either this witness is completely incompetent and unable to testify before a court of law, or he is here laying the foundation to get himself into very serious trouble for perjury. I don't want to take unfair advantage of him. I think that the court should take that under advisement at this time. Obviously, he is either hopelessly incompetent to testify before a court and the court should so find, or he is being compelled to lay the foundation for criminal action against himself at this time."

Major Hopper publicly reviewed the probable competence of Richard Lo Buono based on data provided to the court. Citing the fact that Lo Buono had earned a B.S. degree from Syracuse University, had completed a year and a half of graduate work toward an M.A.

degree in Romance languages, and had risen to field grade rank and been appointed provost marshal of the 10th Reinforcement Depot, the law member concluded that it was unlikely that the witness was incompetent.

The major suddenly seemed to sense a way out of his desperate situation. He made an effort to declare *himself* mentally incompetent— an assertion met with skepticism by the president.

For the next twenty minutes, the court actually turned into a sanity hearing. Colonel Leone asked the witness whether he could name his hometown. He inquired whether the major was married (Lo Buono had been married the day he shipped overseas). Lo Buono was asked what his wife's first name was, where he had landed in Europe when he arrived, and other questions on a similar level.

Major Pers's questions proved more medically professional as he inquired into the witness's emotional state. When the real truth finally came out, it made the headlines in *The Stars and Stripes* the next day:

CO THREATENED TO HANG HIM, MAJOR ASSERTS

LONDON, Dec. 22—Major Richard E. Lo Buono, a key defense witness in the Lichfield guardhouse trials, blurted out in court today that Colonel James A. Kilian, his former commanding officer, threatened to "hang" him for making such a poor impression on the witness stand.

Moreover, Lo Buono said he feared physical violence from 1st Lieutenant Leonard W. Ennis, former Lichfield prison officer, who is awaiting trial. He told the court that Kilian, former CO of the 10th Reinforcement Depot (Lichfield), threatened him last night in the London officers' mess. Kilian was not in court to hear the accusation.

Colonel Louis P. Leone, president of the court, assured Lo Buono he would be given "all the protection available," and Major Walter E. Hopper, Jr. the law member, urged him to "go ahead and tell everything you know, let the chips fall where they may."

Lo Buono, former 10th Reinforcement Depot provost marshal, said Kilian told him last night he had made a bad showing on the witness stand Thursday and warned: "I made you what you are today, and I'm going to hang you."

White and shaken after two days of grueling cross-examination by Captain Earl J. Carroll, during which he was warned three times against perjury, Lo

Buono announced his entire testimony at the trial had been made while under pressure from Kilian.

"He follows me everywhere," Lo Buono whispered. "If I go to the mess, he's there. Last night, I told him, 'I don't want to talk to you,' but it didn't do any good."

Asked whether Kilian threatened him when he testified for the first time at the trial on December 6, Lo Buono said: "He called me to his room and talked to me. I felt that he wasn't interested in me, but his desire was to protect himself."

He said Kilian exerted pressure on him and tried to influence his testimony even before the trial opened.

Protesting "I have no fear for myself; I have testified the best I can," Lo Buono said that for the last seven months his memory had been failing and he could not remember dates and incidents.[2]

During his interrogation, the major had volunteered that he thought his memory would improve significantly if the Kilian threats hanging over him were removed.

The Kilian bombshell completely disrupted court proceedings. The prosecution's interrogation ended abruptly. The witness was questioned by various members of the court, and there was open discussion between the members—much of it sympathetic to Lo Buono. Only once was the matter taken into closed session, and then for only five minutes. The president assured Major Lo Buono that "the court will assume responsibility for your protection."

When he asked whether either the defense or the prosecution had anything further, Captain Carroll made a recommendation to the president that seemed out of character after his singularly tough treatment of the witness:

"I would suggest, sir, that steps be taken immediately to arrange for rebilleting of Major Lo Buono, and that some arrangements be made that he dines at a different mess, or that Colonel Kilian messes somewhere else. In other words, so that there will be no contact between the witness and Colonel Kilian over this holiday period.

"I would also call the court's attention to the fact that Lieutenant Ennis is now in the 312th Station Hospital, and that he was admitted on the 17th of December. The diagnosis was 'upper respiratory infection, acute.' I would suggest that some steps be taken to see that *he* does not leave this hospital during this period of time, or, if he does, that he is placed under some kind of restraint that will prevent him from interfering with this witness during that period of time.

"It may not be necessary for us to immediately put this witness back on the stand. If the court feels so inclined, it might give this witness a little while to recall anything. We might go on with other witnesses, and hear him last, but I would suggest, sir, that you advise him to be available, at least within a few hours' call of the court."

"We can leave that to your discretion," Major Hopper replied for the court.

"The court is through with this witness," Colonel Leone declared. "When we reconvene after the holiday, he will be your first witness."

"I would suggest that he come here," Captain Carroll offered, "but if he doesn't feel inclined to testify on that particular day, we will postpone the continuance of his testimony until such a time as he feels so disposed."

It may have been the Christmas spirit that had mellowed the assistant trial judge advocate. When Carroll finished speaking, at 12:45 P.M. on December 22nd, the president adjourned the court until the following Thursday, December 27th.

12

KILIAN'S UBIQUITY

Major Lo Buono did not reappear on the morning of December 27th, so the prosecution called another rebuttal witness, Technician 5th Class Robert Henney, who had been assigned to temporary duty as a guard while he was billeted in Lichfield's "Tent City." Henney had been so appalled by what he saw of Sergeant Smith's brutality that, when he landed in the United States on a twenty-day furlough, he talked to a New York reporter and, later, to the newspaper in his Ohio hometown.[1]

"Somebody should investigate that place," he told reporters at the *Toledo Blade*. In addition to the brutality he had witnessed, he was disturbed by the prisoners' living conditions: "The guardhouse mess hall was filthy. It smelled so bad you had to hold on to keep from falling down." The resulting publicity led to his being interviewed by a captain in the Inspector General Department, and to his being subpoenaed as a witness in the Smith trial.

As a casual guard, T/5 Henney had personally seen "a soldier molesting another soldier. There were two soldiers taking the clothes off of this fellow. I stood there for ten minutes until they threw him to the floor with no clothes on—naked. One soldier was holding this soldier and other soldier [Sergeant Smith] was beating him—with a rubber hose about three feet long."

Questioned by assistant TJA Earl Carroll, Henney testified that the victim was white and about the same height as he was (five feet four inches), an example, he said, of the cadre's penchant for picking on little guys who couldn't defend themselves.

"Would you like to see Colonel Kilian get court-martialed?"

Surprisingly, it was the defense who asked the question.

There was no doubt in Henney's mind.

"If he's responsible for this, I would."

When Colonel Leone picked up the questioning, he uncovered something new. The reason the witness had remembered Colonel Kilian's name as post commander was, Henney said, that "I was there when he was beat up."

"Colonel Kilian beat up?" The president didn't understand.

Henney explained that, while the colonel was in town, he had taken it on himself personally to arrest two paratroopers.

"He picked them up and brought them back to camp one night, and they were drunk and they beat him up."

Later inquiry would reveal that the two men were each sentenced to twenty years in prison.

Lieutenant Johnson announced that the elusive Major Herbert W. Bluhm, Lichfield's post inspector, was now present. Johnson had him sworn in as a defense witness. When asked if he could identify the accused, Bluhm stated that *he did not know who was on trial.*

Initial questioning of Major Bluhm was polite and uneventful. He outlined his former duties, explaining that, in order to inspect Lichfield's sixteen mess halls and the three guardhouses two or three times a week, he rode a bicycle over the expansive two and three-quarter square miles of the post, in which twenty thousand troops were billeted. The only complaints he ever received from the prisoners were about their lack of toilet articles, he said. His inspections included the solitary confinement cells, and he never found a prisoner whose confinement had not been properly authorized. He had never heard of a death of one of the prisoners during his tour of duty, and he did not recognize the name of Private Eril Bolton. He had never heard of guards shooting at prisoners looking out of windows, nor did he remember that this was one of the subjects investigated by Lieutenant Colonel Varner.

Under the prosecution's cross-examination, however, the major's list of prisoner complaints began to grow. He remembered that prisoners also complained about not having enough time to eat, not having sufficient clothing, and not having hot bath water or soap. He confirmed that there was only one toilet per wing, and that these were often very dirty and were sometimes not even in operating condition—in which case, he "always reported the deficiency to the post utility officer."

But these were not the issues that interested Captain Carroll at the moment. Although the major had claimed in earlier testimony that he didn't know what the current trial was about, why he had been summoned to testify, or even who the defendant was, the assistant TJA's questioning revealed that the witness had met with Colonel Kilian the night before. At first, the major declared that they had spent only a few minutes together in the lobby of the Cumberland Hotel. But when Carroll asked the major to account for two missing hours in his schedule the night before, the meeting with Kilian grew to an hour—or maybe it was more than an hour: "I didn't pay much attention to the time."

Major Bluhm finally admitted to an hour and a half. Further questioning revealed that he had also seen Colonel Kilian before his testimony that morning. In fact, they had had breakfast together. They hadn't discussed the case, of course.

"He asked me what was new in the States. We talked about the devaluation of the franc and some of the general situation, and world conditions, too."

Carroll eyed him suspiciously.

"I want to know what you talked about." The assistant prosecutor spoke the words slowly, with deliberation. "Did you talk about this case?"

Well, actually, Colonel Kilian had shown him copies of *The Stars and Stripes* articles about the trial and had indicated his displeasure at

Major Lo Buono's "going to pieces a little" on the witness stand. And "we talked about the whole course of the case; I don't remember specifically just what."

But he did recall that Kilian told him nine men and two officers were to be tried. And, as to the current case, "he said it was the trial of Sergeant Smith, and that it hadn't been concluded yet."

"But you told this court, major, that you didn't know who was on trial. When you told the court that you were not telling the truth, were you?"

Carroll sat down without waiting for a response. Major Leland Smith now picked up the questioning. The trial judge advocate seemed to possess some direct knowledge of the breakfast conversation between the two officers:

"As a matter of fact, Major, Colonel Kilian mentioned Captain Carroll to you, did he not?"

"Yes." The witness said the word in two syllables—the second one slurring downward half an octave. "As being the *prosecutor*, he did."

"He said, *'You want to watch that son of a bitch,'* didn't he?"

The witness denied it.

Before the end of the day, Captain Carroll had earned whatever pejorative epithet Colonel Kilian might have bestowed on him. Using simple arithmetic, Carroll got the former post inspector to admit that it was impossible for prisoners at the end of a line of two hundred to five hundred men to have had even ten minutes in which to eat when the mess hall time for the entire group was limited to thirty minutes. Reluctantly, Bluhm conceded that he had doubled the allotted time from thirty minutes to a full hour after Colonel Varner's IG inspection. He also admitted publishing the prison rules, including the infamous Rule 14, which stated that "food wastage will bring about severe punishment," but insisted he didn't remember stipulating "severe."

Grudgingly, Major Bluhm abandoned his claim that he knew nothing about beatings in the guardhouse, and admitted that he realized they had been the specific focus of one of Lieutenant Colonel Varner's IG visits to Lichfield. But he made no investigation of his own at the time, he said, because it was something that "apparently had occurred in the past." There were a great many things the major had no information about. Conduct of the prison, he insisted, had been the line responsibility of the provost marshal, Major Lo Buono.

The court's senior medical officer was particularly interested in the fact that there were no urinals in Guardhouse No. 2 and only one toilet per wing. What had the post inspector done about that?

"We talked about that," the witness said. "There was no way of doing anything. We couldn't get together with the British on it."

Captain Carroll eventually got around to the witness's unexplained protracted absence. Major Bluhm himself had, in a sense, been AWOL from the court. Bluhm's response made *The Stars and Stripes* the next morning:

LICHFIELD MAJOR DENIES HIDING

LONDON, Dec. 28—A prosecution allegation that he entered the Vaughn General Hospital at Hines, Illinois, last month to avoid testifying at the Lichfield trial was hotly denied today by Major Herbert W. Bluhm, former inspecting officer at the 10th Reinforcement Depot.

Bluhm maintained he was under orders to enter Vaughn on November 20, and said it was pure coincidence that he received a letter on that date informing him he was to be called to testify.[2]

When Captain Carroll inquired as to the nature of his ailment, it turned out that the major had suffered from "migraine headaches and a cold." He had spent thirty-two days in the hospital having these two illnesses treated.

Back in the U.S., the print media were starting to take increased notice of the trial. In its "Army & Navy" section, *Time* devoted two columns to the subject in its December 31st, 1945, issue. Under the title, "Crime and Punishment," the magazine oriented its stateside readership:

In spite of its similarities, this [was] no Nazi concentration camp, but the prison stockade of the 10th Reinforcement Depot at Lichfield, in England's Midlands. The victims of these brutalities were U.S. soldiers—most of them AWOL (often by a technicality of having overstayed a pass by a few hours); only a small pro-portion of them were guilty of more serious crimes.

In the background of the whole trial was a fact which everyone recognized. During the invasion of Europe, General "Ike" Eisenhower's combat divisions had been hampered by the shortage of replacements. Gold-bricking was a threat to victory. Some of the GIs who landed in Lichfield as prisoners were suspected of trying to dodge combat. There was some reason for the Army to make Lichfield so tough that gold-brickers would prefer the front lines. Did that justify the kind of brutality that prosecution witnesses described? . . .

There were others besides Judson Smith facing trial—other enlisted men, some junior officers. The trail of trials might not stop there. The U.S. Army was on trial.[3]

While Major Bluhm was on the witness stand, Major Richard Lo Buono had entered the courtroom, and he was now recalled. Captain Carroll returned at once to the subject of Colonel Kilian's attempts to influence the former provost marshal's testimony. The officers fre-quently saw each other, Lo Buono said, since both were staying at London's Cumberland Hotel. The major claimed that Colonel Kilian now sought Lo Buono's sympathy for his personal predicament.

"He left me with the impression that somebody higher up was gunning for him," Lo Buono said. "In other words, they were trying to make an issue out of this case."[4]

Lo Buono now suggested it really wasn't all Colonel Kilian's fault. When Major General Albert E. Brown, the commanding general, Ground Forces Replacement Command, visited the facility (Lo Buono couldn't remember when it was), he had expressed his dis-pleasure with the way the guardhouse was being run.

"You're running a hotel here, Sergeant," the general told Judson Smith, and immediately ordered Major Bluhm to get rid of the mat-tresses on the beds ("they should have boards to sleep on") and tear out the stoves ("get all the fires out of here, and I'll be back"). Gener-al Brown gave the provost marshal thirty minutes to remove the stoves. Not long thereafter, a top secret GFRC directive ordered that all combat-wounded returnees who had gone AWOL at any time were to be put aboard their package ships to the Continent under armed guard.

Major Lo Buono said he had once interviewed sixteen or seventeen incoming prisoners waiting to be processed while they stood nose and toes against the wall. Convicted as a unit for being AWOL because they had missed a truck and were three hours late returning to the post, they were sentenced to serve six months in the stockade and forfeit two-thirds of their pay during their incarceration. Lo Buono said he had gone to Colonel Kilian about the matter, pleading that it was an injustice to the men, and that he felt their sentences should be remitted. As he remembered the incident, he had prevailed, and the men were shipped out on an early package after he pointed out that this would be more in keeping with the reinforcement depot's mission.

The former provost marshal said the commanding officer told him several times that he had to be rougher with the prisoners. On one occasion, having just returned from investigating an escape attempt, the major reported to the colonel during noon officers' mess that a guard had shot a prisoner through the knee.

"Well, make the guard a sergeant!" was the colonel's jolly reaction. The major did not (there was no unfilled NCO slot in the Table of Organization), and the guard complained about it later, having heard of the commandant's order through the Lichfield grapevine.

The rest of the former provost marshal's testimony was summarized in *The Stars and Stripes* the following morning:

MAJOR TELLS OF FEAR FOR LICHFIELD CO

LONDON, Jan. 3—Describing Colonel James A. Kilian, former 10th Reinforcement Depot commanding officer, as a man who "would stop at no means to get his end," Major Richard E. Lo Buono testified today that he believed Kilian had enough influence to carry out his threats "even after I'm out of the Army."

Two weeks ago, Lo Buono, former Lichfield provost marshal, startled the court trying Sergeant Judson H. Smith on charges of mistreating prisoners by announcing that Kilian had threatened him at the London officers' mess.

Asked today by the prosecution whether he feared for himself, Lo Buono answered, "not exactly."

Major Leland Smith, chief prosecutor, then asked whether he feared for his family because of Kilian's threat.

After a tense silence, Lo Buono replied: "He would stop at no means to get his end. Even after I'm out of the Army, no matter where I am, he could do something."

The prosecution asked Lo Buono whether he might have evaded telling all the things he knew about Lichfield.

"I've not had an occasion to tell all the things I know," he said.

The witness said that, in his conversations with Kilian during the trial, he had received the impression that Kilian "wanted this thing stopped before it got to him."[5]

On Friday morning, it developed that Colonel Kilian was not the only Lichfield principal the former provost marshal feared. Lo Buono was asked by Major Smith whether he thought there was a possibility that Lieutenant Ennis might harm him.

"If such articles appear in *The Stars and Stripes,* I can't see why he shouldn't," Lo Buono acknowledged. "I just knew that if I stated anything with reference to Lieutenant Ennis . . . I know he is not the type of person to take anything lightly. He's an ex-combat man; he's a psycho-neurotic; and that's what I was thinking of."

When Earl Carroll took over the questioning, he abruptly changed the subject. He seemed to be playing a wild card.

"I am going to ask you if you ever called any members of the defense 'sons of bitches?'"

The witness blinked.

"Never!" he exclaimed.

"Did you ever call any member of the prosecution in this case 'sons of bitches?'"

"No. I don't use that term."

"Did you ever call the *court* 'sons of bitches?'"

"No, I didn't."

"By the 'court,' I mean *this* court."

"No!"

"Isn't it a fact that a very few minutes after you left this witness stand on the 22nd of December, right in the anteroom out there where you hang your coat you made this statement: 'Those sons of bitches are not going to get me to help string those boys?'"

The witness's color changed. There was a long pause before he found any words:

"I didn't say it that way." Another pause. "Now, wait a minute—I'll give you the statement I made in the hall."

It was a tactical error.

"What statement you made in the hall?" Carroll asked. Having admitted he said it, Lo Buono had to decide who the son of a bitch was.

"I said it with reference to Colonel Kilian," he explained. "I made a statement as I went out of the door: 'That son of a bitch was not going to get me to string any boys.' I didn't use the words that you stated. I said, '*That* son of a bitch will not get me to string these boys.' That's all I said."

"You didn't say, '*Those* sons of bitches are not going to get me to string any boys?'"

"I didn't use the words you stated there. As I went out the door I said, 'That son of a bitch was not going to get me to string any boys.'"

But his explanation only got him deeper into confusion.

"So then you referred to Colonel Kilian as 'a son of a bitch?'"

"No, I didn't. I had nobody in mind when I said it. I just said it to myself." Beads of sweat were beginning to appear on the witness's forehead and upper lip. "I just muttered. I don't recall exactly what the reference was to. It wasn't to the court."

"But you have a good memory of the words you used?"

"I said something, yes, when I went out through the door."

"I want to know whether you used the words, '*Those* sons of bitches.' I am referring to the word 'those' in plural. '*Those* sons of bitches are not going to get me to help string those boys.' Did you use the words, '*those* sons of bitches?'"

"No; I don't recall using any plural in that connection."

"Is it your testimony then that you used the singular, 'son of a bitch?'"

It was getting a little silly. But no one smiled.

"I don't know whether I used the singular or the plural. I know I said something like that when I went out and I was muttering to myself."

Carroll sat down. At the defense table, Johnson and Cassidy exchanged glances. Neither picked up on the president's offer to ask questions in redirect examination.

Asking the court's indulgence, Captain Carroll now called a surprise witness from the spectators' gallery—Major John Shilling. He had been in the audience since December 22nd and was being called out of sequence to avoid missing his ship back to the U.S. Shilling had been a casual officer at the 10th Reinforcement Depot, hence his interest in the trial. And he had been in the cloak room "when Major Lo Buono came in and made a quick passing remark in my presence as I was getting my coat. The words that he said were, *'Those sons of bitches are not going to get me to help string those boys.'*"[6]

Major Shilling was quite sure of the plural reference because he had tried to analyze just what the major had meant as he returned to the Cumberland Hotel—where he had sought out Captain Carroll and reported the incident.

Unwilling to settle for ambiguity, Captain Carroll put another witness on the stand the next morning to verify the plurality of Major Lo Buono's expletive. First Lieutenant Albert B. Friedman, Signal Corps, another spectator who had departed through the cloak room, had, in fact, discussed Lo Buono's remark with Major Shilling as they walked back to the hotel for lunch.

"We didn't think he meant Colonel Kilian or Lieutenant Ennis. You see, he had been questioned by the *court* that day instead of by the prosecution, and we both felt that he was talking about the court—or the court and the prosecution combined—but not about Colonel Kilian."

Earl Carroll took his witnesses to lunch after they testified. There John Shilling told him that he was at first too frightened of what might happen if he reported his observations of what was going on behind Lichfield's barbed wire. But, finally, he decided to call U.K. Headquarters. However, written instructions had been posted stating that "no casual officer will call any higher headquarters or other headquarters without permission." Telling the local authorities that his reason for calling was to get the U.S. Strategic Bombing Survey to expedite his orders, Major Shilling said he had sought permission to use the telephone on three separate occasions and was turned down each time. Carroll had him repeat this part of his story in court for the record the next day.

While all of the "son of a bitch" testimony was kept out of *The Stars and Stripes,* a new issue had emerged, and was duly reported:

PERJURY TRIAL DEMANDED FOR MAJ. LO BUONO

LONDON, Jan. 4—The prosecution demanded today that Major Richard E. Lo Buono, former 10th Reinforcement Depot provost marshal, be tried for perjury in order to prevent "sinister or ulterior purpose" from influencing the testimony of witnesses appearing at the Lichfield general court martial.

Charging that Lo Buono deliberately falsified his testimony, Captain Earl J. Carroll, assistant prosecutor, asked the court to have Lo Buono arrested and take further action to impress upon future witnesses the necessity of telling the truth.

Carroll said "a party" whose name has appeared in testimony [obviously Kilian] was attempting to influence the testimony of witnesses because of the fear that a conviction of the defendant, Sergeant Judson H. Smith, "may result in the prosecution of this person himself."

The court requested the prosecution to draw up and submit specifications of perjury according to the 93rd Article of War. The court declared that it would consider the specifications, and if they were substantiated, would recommend that charges be preferred.[7]

13

THE LINEUP

The procession of rebuttal witnesses continued into the following week. The variety of reported outrages expanded. One witness revealed that prisoners were punished for not laughing at a guard's joke, while Private Philip Damon quoted a slogan used by the guards: "Your soul may belong to God, but your body belongs to me!"

General Prisoner Add Baker provided additional information on just how crowded Guardhouse No. 2 had been. Of the 100 or more prisoners in his wing of the building, twenty-five to thirty men had to sleep on the floor, he said, while four or five slept on top of lockers. He had been one of those without a bed. Although some of the cots were two feet apart (as Major Lo Buono had testified), there were "only a few inches" between others. At times, Baker said, the number of prisoners sleeping on the floor was fifty or more—many of of them lying between or under the cots. He also said that Sergeant Smith sometimes asked a prisoner where he had been wounded and then jabbed him in the spot with his billy club. When his own injured back would not permit him to stand up straight, Baker said he had been kicked in the back by Lieutenant Ennis.[1]

Baker said he once asked one of the guards, T/5 Ellis Adcock, "Why do you treat us so bad?"

"If we weren't rough on you guys, we'd be sent back to combat," Adcock had explained.

When Earl Carroll put Private Sam Holloway on the stand, the assistant prosecutor seemed to be fishing for further evidence to incriminate Major Lo Buono. Holloway was asked to describe a beating that was, according to the witness, "supervised by an officer." The victim, Private Theodore Taylor, "a Negro soldier," had been pulled from his bed during the night, dragged down the concrete steps of the guardhouse to the first floor, blindfolded by a blanket thrown over his head, and then beaten into unconsciousness by two guards—after which he had been thrown into solitary. Holloway had observed the incident from the second floor, and he could see that the officer was a captain, Lo Buono's rank at the time.

At the prosecution's request, a lineup of officers, including Major Lo Buono, was assembled in the courtroom in an identification parade. The president of the court even invited the witness to stand on a table if he wished, to observe the group from the same angle from which he had witnessed the beating. But to the prosecution's disappointment, Holloway could not identify the officer.

Then, at noon on Tuesday, January 8th, Carroll had a stroke of luck, when the victim of that beating, Private Theodore Taylor, showed up in the courtroom. On furlough from Southampton, he had come to Grosvenor Square to visit his friend Lewis King, who was scheduled to be a witness. Holloway immediately recognized him and persuaded him to go to Captain Carroll, who had him on the witness stand before the day was out.

Taylor testified that he was taken from his bunk by two guards (one of whom he identified as Private Arthur Duncan) and dragged downstairs to where Sergeant Smith, Lieutenant Cubage, and then-Captain Lo Buono, were waiting.

"Here's one of the guys who's been acting smart," one of the guards announced.

"Break that nigger's goddam neck," Smith had ordered.

Then, the witness said, Smith struck him on the head. A blanket was wrapped around his head, and he was beaten with a club for about fifteen minutes.

In his cross-examination, Lieutenant Johnson first tried to impeach

Taylor's testimony by attempting to prove that the witness "did take marijuana and that it affected his mind." But the law member interrupted to instruct the witness that he could refuse to answer a question that he considered might be self-incriminating. Johnson's crudeness in questioning Taylor made the *The Stars and Stripes'* daily account of the trial, and did the defense's public image little good:

When Johnson mentioned two names and asked the witness, "Do you know these two nigger boys?" Taylor reported heatedly, "I know two Negro soldiers by those names, not nigger boys."[2]

Obligingly, the court once more assembled an identification parade of officers for Private Taylor. But this time Major Lo Buono could not be located—to the embarrassment of the court and the annoyance of its president, although Taylor immediately picked out Lieutenant Cubage as one of the two officers who had been present at his beating.

Major Lo Buono had his turn the next day, when yet another lineup was assembled, this time including noncommissioned officers and other enlisted personnel who had been guards—five officers and sixteen enlisted men. At the invitation of the law member, Private Taylor marched up and down the line of men, peering into the faces of the former prison personnel.

The likelihood of the U.S. Army assembling the equivalent of a police lineup of officers through field grade, to be identified by a black private who had recently been released from an army prison, is so remote that no one acquainted with the military culture and social order of 1946 would have believed that anything like this could ever happen. Such a bizarre thing might have been depicted in a satirical skit at an enlisted men's company party, but was not to be expected in the real world. Yet it did occur in a U.S. Army general court-martial three times in two days, in the unique atmosphere of this first of the Lichfield trials. The unlikely events made headlines in the Army newspaper again the next morning:

EX PRISONER IDENTIFIES LO BUONO FROM LINEUP,
NAMES 4 IN COURTROOM AS BRUTALITY WITNESSES[3]

The prosecution, at last, rested its case.

14

RECANTATION

When the court reconvened at 9:30 A.M. on Friday, January 11th, the atmosphere was strained. Colonel Leone asked rather tentatively if the defense was ready to proceed, the prosecution having rested.[1]

"I would like the prosecution to explain the reason why the defense is *not* ready to proceed," Lieutenant Johnson responded.

It was Major Smith who spoke for the prosecution, but his language was oddly formal and obscure.

"With reference to the matter of these proceedings, matters have arisen on which it is necessary to consult the appointing authority [of the court], and the appointing authority is not immediately available. The staff judge advocate has been advised and is making every effort to reach the appointing authority. Until the appointing authority can be reached, neither the prosecution nor the defense is prepared to go ahead.

"While I am not at liberty to disclose to the court what the matter is, I should assure the court that the staff judge advocate has been advised fully, and that the staff judge advocate has told me that the only thing that can be done under the circumstances is to request that the court recess until the appointing authority can be reached."

With the court paralyzed, the president adjourned proceedings until after lunch, and at 1:30, he dismissed the court for the rest of the day. On Saturday morning, the suspense was broken when Major

Smith explained that Sergeant Smith, the accused, as well as witnesses Jones and Adcock had requested that they be permitted to return to the witness stand and tell the truth this time.

"In order that there should not be any question about their right to purge themselves of any perjury in this trial," the TJA explained, "I agreed that they could go back on the stand and say anything they wanted to without being faced with a charge of perjury. There is no immunity granted to these men *except* for perjury."

Explaining that "it will be necessary to change our entire plan of defense," Lieutenant Johnson obtained the law member's permission to excuse himself, and he turned over the conduct of the defense to his assistant defense counsel, Lieutenant Cassidy.

When court reconvened on Monday morning, January 14th, the defense recalled a rather nervous Lieutenant Granville Cubage. Sitting bolt upright, the former prison officer stated that he had volunteered to return to the witness stand, "because, when I testified before, there were facts that I knew about that I didn't think could be used at the time; but since several things have come up I believe these facts *can* be used."

What had changed, of course, was Major Bluhm's pending indictment for perjury and the exposure of Colonel Kilian's flagrant manipulation of witnesses. When the defense counsel, Lieutenant Johnson, questioned Lieutenant Cubage, the officer revealed that the night before he testified the first time, Colonel Kilian had summoned him to his room at the Cumberland Hotel and told him what he was to say, since "it was important that the matter stop with this case with Sergeant Smith and not to let it get any further."

Cubage's first reversal was to disclose an order, signed by Colonel Kilian, instructing guards to "discourage prisoners from loitering near the windows to prevent them from escaping." This had been "interpreted by the interior guard to mean to fire at the windows whenever prisoners were seen too close to the windows."

Before going into other details, the witness took the opportunity to distance himself from direct responsibility for the prison after October, 1944, testifying that"Colonel Kilian said to Colonel Aldridge, 'Aldridge, I want you to take charge of that guardhouse and ship those prisoners out of there.' Colonel Aldridge called me over to his quarters and told me that the 316th Replacement Company was taking over the guardhouse and that he wanted me to concentrate on the *packaging* of prisoners and to take as many parolees as I possibly could.

"[Thereafter] I considered my status as the supply officer and the parolee officer and packaging officer.

"Captain Robertson [company commander of the 316th Prison Company] called me into his office and said, 'I'm going to put Lieutenant Ennis in charge of the guardhouse, since he is the executive officer of the 316th. I want Lieutenant Ennis to take charge of the guardhouse because of his previous experience as a provost sergeant in Hawaii and because of his appearance. When Lieutenant Ennis gets out with those prisoners, they'll know exactly what he means.'

"At that time Lieutenant Ennis was a first lieutenant and I was a second lieutenant."

Lieutenant Cubage then moved his office out of the guardhouse, he said.

Having established where the responsibility lay, Cubage now readily admitted to his observing "unorthodox" calisthenics (often led by Lieutenant Ennis), including the frequent use of the now-familiar "nose and toes" punishment, double-timing against the wall, and physically forced double-timing (guards using their billy clubs) on the stairways "just as fast as they could come down the stairs." Many of the guards, he said, were illiterate. He demonstrated "nose and toes" against the wall of the courtroom, for the benefit of the court.

Lieutenant Cubage made it clear that, while Lieutenant Ennis habitually carried a club, he never did. "I didn't think an officer should carry a club," he declared. He also volunteered an anecdote about the new prison management:

"This was in the month of December. I was sitting in Captain Robertson's office. Lieutenant Ennis came in out of breath. Lieutenant Ennis seemed excited and he said to Captain Robertson, 'I just saw two lieutenant colonels and a casual officer on the post. They just stopped me and didn't like the manner in which I was giving calisthenics. I told them if they didn't like it they could go and see Colonel Kilian.'"

Captain Robertson, Cubage said, told Ennis that he had handled the matter properly.

When Captain Carroll took over for cross-examination, he established that Lieutenant Cubage was afraid of Lieutenant Ennis. "I certainly don't want to see too much of Lieutenant Ennis now," the worried Cubage declared. "Ennis is a tough man. Ennis's presence acts as a deterrent to giving testimony to this court."

"That is all I want to ask at this time," Carroll announced. "I want to bring this much to the court's attention: We have evidence in this court of a concerted plan to influence the testimony of witnesses. We have had witness after witness come in here to this court and tell us that they are afraid of Lieutenant Ennis. Nothing has been done so far as to keeping Lieutenant Ennis away from other witnesses.

"We have had Colonel Kilian who has been influencing witnesses. Last night Lieutenant Ennis and Colonel Kilian were together. If it please this court, admonition after admonition has been issued. These witnesses are obviously afraid to tell the truth, and nothing has been done about stopping this intimidation. Here is a witness who is an officer. How do we know how much this intimidation has permitted these men not to tell the truth upon the witness stand. Certainly I have never seen a case in which a court has been so flagrantly flaunted as it has been in this case. Something should be done about it or we shall not get the truth at this time."

Grimly, the president spoke five words: "The court will be closed."

It remained closed from 11:55 A.M. until 2:25 P.M., with its members foregoing lunch. When it reopened, Colonel Leone announced the result of the court's deliberations:

"After due consideration of the request of the trial judge advocate regarding Lieutenant Ennis, the court directs that the trial judge advocate convey to the appointing authority the recommendation of the court that Lieutenant Ennis be confined." He said nothing about limiting Colonel Kilian's activities.

With that directive in hand, Captain Carroll returned to examining the witness. Lieutenant Cubage acknowledged that there was a prevailing general rumor about prisoners being mistreated in the Lichfield prison. Indeed, it might have been considered by the Lichfield command to be a useful rumor.

The witness then revealed that, in "four or five conversations" with Colonel Kilian, the former Lichfield commandant had instructed him in detail, telling him "Now, this is what happened. . . ." And he expected the lieutenant to testify accordingly. The colonel had, in fact, insisted that Cubage take notes, and later met with Captain King, Captain Warnecke, and Lieutenant Cubage, "to reconcile the testimony of these men, so it would be similar on particular points."

The witness quoted Colonel Kilian as saying "I know they're out to get me." But Kilian had added that "he wasn't such a bad 'guardhouse lawyer' himself, and if he could get a mistrial in the Smith case it would help him." He then hypothesized five possible scenarios that could produce a mistrial.

The testimony precipitated another plea by Captain Carroll.

"If it please the court, it is obvious that we have in this case a situation that certainly is without parallel to my knowledge in any trial before a military court. We have a high-ranking officer in the army, a full colonel of the Regular Army, contacting witnesses, bringing them to his room, instructing those witnesses as to their testimony, checking up on what the witnesses have testified to, calling them back for criticism when the testimony does not agree with some prearranged idea of his own—a man who has admitted to these witnesses that he has a real interest in the case, that he is seeking to protect himself, and he is seeking to do it at the expense of defrauding a court of justice.

"So, I ask that this court take some appropriate action in connection with Colonel Kilian. We have evidence here of a prima facie case of perjury of the worst kind. If this were an ordinary court of justice, I would ask for a bench warrant and have him placed in arrest immediately. I ask that the court take some action—or this trial will never come to an end."

The president said nothing. The court seemed in shock. Attacking Lieutenant Ennis had been one thing, but the assistant TJA's new target made the court uneasy. When at last the law member spoke, the way Major Hopper phrased his question to the assistant prosecutor seemed designed to take the president off the hook: "What specific recommendation does the government wish to make?"

"I think Colonel Kilian should either be placed in custody," Carroll responded, "or placed in such a state of seclusion from the rest of these witnesses so that he has absolutely no physical contact with them. He should be removed entirely from the area of this trial and only called when he is needed as a witness; and he should be forbidden to have any type of contact, directly or indirectly, by telephone or through any other third person, with these witnesses."

Recovering, the president now addressed Lieutenant Johnson: "This man is a defense witness. Has the defense anything to say?"

Lieutenant Johnson obviously didn't care to get involved.

"The defense accepts no responsibility for anything any of its witnesses do in this court. I would make a suggestion. I don't know whether it would be appropriate to put it in the form of a suggestion. If the court would like to close, we might be able to handle the thing."

Major Hopper, whose attitude had been changing during the trial, displayed more courage than the defense counsel: "This is such an important matter that I think anything said concerning it should be a part of the record."

The defense counsel cautiously proceeded.

"I would suggest then," Johnson ventured, "that as long as the prosecution adopts this attitude—and I'm not going to say that *we* don't adopt it—maybe Colonel Kilian should be given a leave, and let him go somewhere out of the immediate area here, and remain there until either the prosecution, the defense, or the court would like to call him as a witness. I think that would be the best."

Johnson's offering would prove to be political mistake. The president, a Regular Army colonel who understood the system, anticipated the repercussions that could follow. Trying to head them off, he addressed Captain Carroll.

"The only evidence you've got in front of the court today is the evidence of a person who has changed his previous testimony. And you're asking to put an officer in restraint who is not in any position to defend himself."

But Carroll wouldn't give up.

"The prosecution is not basing it only on the testimony of this witness," Carroll argued. "We have evidence of the witness Major Bluhm, and we have the evidence of the witness Major Lo Buono. They are two field grade officers who have testified to the same effect. If it please the court, how many witnesses do we have to have to recognize that there has been some tinkering with witnesses, when men come back on the witness stand and say, 'we want to purge ourselves.'

"I say that either one of two things has to be done: If Colonel Kilian is going to stay here, he will have to be placed under some kind of restraint, so that he cannot contact these witnesses—or the suggestion of the defense should be followed out and he should be removed entirely from this area."

It was 5:15 in the afternoon. Colonel Leone adjourned the court for the day.

The president had obviously been thinking about matters overnight when he reconvened the court the next morning. Earl Carroll was to get considerably more than he had asked for:

"In answer to the prosecution's request," Colonel Leone announced, "the court instructs the prosecution to advise the appointing authority [the commanding general of the American forces in the United Kingdom] that it is the recommendation of the court, after due consideration of the evidence before it, that Colonel Kilian be removed from the London area, but remain within the United Kingdom, available for recall as a witness; and that the appointing authority directs that Colonel Kilian refrain from any further contact with witnesses before this court.

"The court further directs the prosecution to prepare for the consideration of the court *charges* against Colonel Kilian for subornation of perjury, intimidation of witnesses, conspiracy, dereliction of duty.

"This court is also desirous of knowing what progress has been made on our request regarding the drafting of charges of perjury against Major Lo Buono."

It was, of course, the headline in *The Stars and Stripes* the next morning:

COURT ORDERS CHARGE AGAINST LICHFIELD CO[2]

The events of the day would percolate up through the chain of command at the commanding general's office, United Kingdom Base. It would be a day or two before General Thiele could give them his personal attention.

15

INTRIGUE

The court's dramatic move, and especially the resulting headline in the GI newspaper, would be viewed as most unwelcome by the "appointing authority," Brigadier General Claude M. Thiele, UK Headquarters Commander in London. Accusing a full colonel in the Regular Army of subornation of perjury and dereliction of duty, especially in connection with such a sensational trial, was embarrassing to the army, as was citing two more field grade officers for perjury. A Regular Army colonel himself, Colonel Leone knew what he was getting into, but, having made his decision, he calmly ordered the prosecution to proceed.

Captain Carroll was not finished with Lieutenant Cubage. Warming to his new assignment by the court (of investigating Colonel Kilian's possible subornation of perjury), he began asking the witness about meetings with a Lieutenant Colonel William G. Hummell of the Inspector General Department, an officer said to be a lawyer who had an office next door to the courtroom at 47 Grosvenor Square.[1]

Cubage described a meeting he went to at that address when both Kilian and Hummell were present. At the meeting, Colonel Hummell had suggested possible defense counsel candidates for Cubage, since, as Colonel Kilian had pointed out to him, "If Smith is found guilty, *you* will probably be tried." Colonel Hummell had also presented some observations he had made about the present trial, Cubage said. Captain Carroll asked him what they were.

"The defense counsels in this case are exceptionally weak," the witness quoted Hummell as saying, "and Captain Carroll is constantly baiting and intimidating the defense counsels to the point that they are convinced that they have lost the case and are not putting forth the proper effort."

Cubage's testimony was delivered in open court in the presence of the embarrassed defense lawyers, Johnson and Cassidy. Hummell had also complained that "two trained professional prosecutors had been 'imported' for this case." There had been much talk during the meeting of deliberately producing a mistrial. The mistrial suggestion, Cubage said, had come from Colonel Kilian, who alleged that "the prosecution people talk and discuss the case with anyone around the Officers' Club, intimidating the defense counsels." There had also been discussion about an "organized defense," as Colonel Hummell had put it, "some kind of coordination between your [Cubage's] defense, Sergeant Smith's defense, Major Lo Buono's defense, and Colonel Kilian's defense."

"That's all [Kilian] talked about most of the time: *organized* defense," the witness declared. "He thought it should be a *common* defense."

It was not clear where the assistant TJA was going with his questions about this mysterious Colonel Hummell. But then, in a characteristically theatrical move, Captain Carroll had a woman brought into the courtroom and asked the witness to identify her. When she was recognized as Lucy O'Connell, Colonel Hummell's secretary, it seemed probable that Carroll had gained access to some of Hummell's documents.

When the court returned from its luncheon recess, the assistant TJA had another surprise for its members:

"May it please the court, at this time the prosecution requests that

Lieutenant Colonel Hummell be called as a witness. [But] it seems he has some objection to testifying. I would suggest, if the court would permit it, that the *court* should call Colonel Hummell and at least find out whether or not he is willing to testify before this court, and if not why not."

The president accepted the challenge:

"He will have no choice whatever in the matter. If he is called, he will testify to what he knows."

Lieutenant Colonel Hummell claimed his reluctance to be a witness was due to his position in the office of the Inspector General and the probable confidential nature of some of his knowledge. But when Carroll got him on the stand, he tried to show that Hummell, an agent for Kilian as well as the army, had set up shop next door to the courtroom as part of a conspiracy to disrupt the present trial, to quash further unfavorable publicity about Lichfield, and, in the process, to get Colonel Kilian off the hook.[2]

Carroll's very first question revealed how things were likely to go. The assistant prosecutor asked the witness when he had first met with Colonel Kilian.

"I don't remember," the colonel snapped. "That is the Inspector General's function, and I am not responsible to make a note or otherwise with regard to the exact discourse that took place. Any officer and any enlisted man is entitled to report any alleged injustice, miscarriage of justice or irregularity at any time." It was a pompous speech.

"We are not challenging your right to make the investigation, Colonel," Carroll replied in measured tones. "What we want to know is, do you remember when you had the first conversation with Colonel Kilian in regard to the conduct of the defense in this case?"

"It must have been at least three weeks ago" was the petulant response. He spoke the words rapidly, avoiding eye contact with his questioner. "I think the best indicator is that it was immediately on the day that *The Stars and Stripes* had such a strong article about Colonel Kilian in it [December 14, 1945]. There was an implication that Colonel Kilian was endeavoring to influence certain witnesses."

"When, in relationship to that conversation, did you have your next conversation?"

"I don't remember."

"How many conversations subsequent to that have you had?"

"Fifteen or twenty."

"When was that first conversation with Lieutenant Cubage in relationship to the 14th of December?"

"I can't see that that is relevant at all. I don't remember."

Twice more, in petulant tones, the witness told his interrogator that his questions were not relevant. His answers were ordered stricken as not responsive.

Rising to the challenge, Carroll set out to cut Hummell down to size.

"As I understand it, you are an attorney at law. Is that correct?"

"It is *not* correct" was the curt reply.

"Are you a graduate lawyer?"

"That is not material to the case."

"I am asking you, are you a graduate lawyer?" Carroll's voice grew louder.

"I am not."

"Did you ever study law?"

"Yes."

"Will you tell us where you studied law?"

"I can't see that that is material to the case."

Carroll now addressed the court, pointing out that the colonel was obviously a hostile witness. He asked for and received permission to examine him under the rules of cross-examination, and, with obvious relish, Earl Carroll proceeded to destroy Hummell's credibility as a legal adviser.

"You have told this court that you studied law. Where did you study law?"

"At the University of Alabama."

"How far did you get in the study of law?"

"I had a roommate who was a law student and I read his books occasionally."

"You never took a prescribed course in law?"

"I did not. I don't see that that is material to the case."

"You know, don't you, that it is the province of the court to determine the admissibility of evidence and whether it is relevant?"

"I am prepared to answer questions that are put to me that have a direct bearing on this case." The arrogance of the witness was getting thicker.

Captain Carroll requested and got a ruling that the court and not the witness would determine the relevancy of his testimony. He then offered the witness his privilege under the 24th Article of War to decline to answer any question that amounted to "compulsory self-incrimination."

The witness testily refused.

Left with no choice but to answer the assistant TJA's questions, Colonel Hummell revealed that Colonel Kilian had been incensed at the publicity in *The Stars and Stripes* and asked that Hummell make such publicity an official matter for the Inspector General Department to investigate. Kilian had also told Hummell that Carroll had baited him outside the courtroom, saying, "I am trying your proxy, but you are not in court to defend yourself," and that Kilian had responded, "That is exactly true. I feel that I am being actually tried—in public opinion and in *The Stars and Stripes*—and I don't even have defense counsel."

Kilian had even paid Carroll a grudging compliment according to the witness, saying that "it was evident that Captain Carroll was an outstanding prosecutor in a class by himself as compared with the defense attorneys. He felt that the lineup was unbalanced; that a highly trained lawyer of some years experience was pitted against a comparatively young and inexperienced defense counsel. In speaking about Captain Carroll he used the remark that 'he knows every trick in the bag.'

"He [Kilian] wanted official advice," Hummell explained, "of what recourse he had as an army officer who was up to this time only a witness. He asked for advice as to who he could turn to—to stop this public heckling in *The Stars and Stripes*. He stated that he felt his character was being maligned—"

"As a matter of fact, Colonel," Carroll interrupted, "didn't you *volunteer* to assist him in getting himself out of prosecution in this matter?"

The question produced a tirade on the part of the witness. The assistant prosecutor moved that Hummell's outburst be stricken from the record. It was. But each time Carroll repeated the question, the cycle was repeated: an angry speech by the witness; a prosecution motion that the witness's statement be stricken as unresponsive to the question; and a granting of the motion by the law member.

Finally, Carroll tried to bring things into focus:

"Let us understand one another—"

"Let us understand that *I* am not on trial," Hummell shouted. "I am a *witness!*"

"That's right," Carroll agreed.

"And I am giving you answers—answers that are *relevant.*"

The president of the court had had enough.

"The prosecution is here to present its case," Colonel Leone instructed, "and you are here to answer the questions."

"Yes, sir." There might have been a trace of humility in the witness's response.

"Any expression of opinion other than answering questions directly is not permitted," the president ruled.

"No, sir."

At this point, the court took the customary twelve-minute recess to permit those present to stretch their legs and to visit the rest room. During the break, Captain Carroll apparently had noticed a conversation between Lieutenant Colonel Hummell and Colonel Leone, president of the court—quite possibly in the men's room while the two men were standing at adjacent urinals and while the assistant prosecutor waited his turn. When the court reconvened, Carroll didn't let it pass:

"Did you ever discuss this case with any person other than Lieutenant Cubage and Colonel Kilian?"

"Not to my knowledge," Colonel Hummell replied. Then, after a pause, "You mean with people who were directly connected with the case?"

"Yes," Carroll confirmed, "either as a witness or as a member of the court, or as a member of the prosecution, or as a member of the defense."

"I think that I *have*—casually with the president of the court," said the somewhat nonplused witness, "*and* the law member.

"Nothing specific," he hastily added.

"Let us go to the president of the court," the assistant prosecutor suggested. "Where was that conversation?"

"I don't remember," Hummell claimed, adding, "because there was nothing pertinent in the conversation that would call for recollection."

And, indeed, the conversation was probably trivial, but, typically, Carroll wouldn't give up. Hummell finally gave in.

"Let us say that we discussed *The Stars and Stripes* report of the case," the witness responded, hoping to brush it aside.

"Let us not 'say' anything at all," Carroll warned. "Just answer the questions."

"Answer the questions," the president commanded, removing himself as a potential ally of the witness. Carroll pinned him down:

"When and where did this conversation take place?"

"The only one that I can report accurately is that five minutes ago the president of the court and I discussed *The Stars and Stripes* version of it, and I don't even remember exactly what we said."

"Five minutes ago you discussed *The Stars and Stripes* version with the president?"

"That's correct."

"What did you say?"

"It was not material," Hummell squirmed, "not that I even remember it; and I don't think he does either."

"So you can't remember a conversation that you had five minutes ago?"

"No, I can't. It wasn't that important." Then, after a pause, "Yes, I can. The president of the court said that I—"

Apparently Captain Carroll had turned away from the witness in his moment of confessional agony, and Hummell's temper flashed:

"ARE YOU INTERESTED IN THIS, CAPTAIN!?"

"Reply to the court," the president instructed, cutting him down.

It developed that the men's room conversation *had* been about *The Stars and Stripes'* accounts of the trial. And it quickly became apparent that Carroll's petty questions were a warm-up before making an attack with another piece of his gum-shoe knowledge:

"Let's see if you can remember the *previous* conversation with the president of the court. When and where was it?"

"In the officers' mess hall at dinner," the witness blurted. "We sat together one day—one evening."

"What was said and who said it?"

"I don't remember."

"Your mind is a complete blank on the subject?"

"My mind is not a complete blank, but I don't remember anything specific enough that would have a bearing on the case."

"I don't care whether you consider that it has a bearing on the case or not. I want to know if you can remember anything at all of what was said."

The next several pages of court transcript are a record of Carroll's merciless goading of the witness, inquiring how it was possible for a trained investigator, a graduate of the Corps of Military Police School and Inspector General for the United Kingdom Headquarters, to find it impossible to remember a single thing about a forty-minute conversation that had occurred only weeks ago.

Finally, Carroll got to the point. He suggested that the president of the court was not the only court officer Hummell had tried to influence. It developed that the assistant prosecutor had done some impressive detective work. After citing dates and places in the city of London, he got the IG inspector to confirm that he had driven his staff car to the Mount Royal Hotel for breakfast three weeks earlier. There Hummell had arranged an "accidental meeting" with the law member, Major Hopper, offering him a ride to Grosvenor Square—which the major accepted. Then Carroll closed in.

"As a matter of fact, Colonel, didn't you go to the law member and attempt to engage the law member in conversation with the intent of producing a prejudicial error in this case? Didn't you do that?"

"I absolutely deny it!" the witness blustered.

Carroll then asked Colonel Hummell about a conversation he had had about the trial with Major Richard D. Kearney, staff judge advocate of the London area office. Carroll reminded him that the conversation had taken place "at the officers' club about two weeks ago at night—upstairs in the supper room."

"I did at one time, I believe," the dumbfounded witness admitted, "but I don't remember what I said."

"Maybe we can remind you of what you said and that might help you to remember," Carroll offered, laying down his cards. "Isn't it a fact that these in substance were the words that you used to Major Kearney: 'You had better be careful when you handle this 10th Reinforcement Depot, or Lichfield trials, or you will find *yourself* in jail instead of the others.' Did you ever say that in substance?"

"Definitely no."

Hanging over the witness like a specter, however, was the unspoken threat to bring over Major Kearney from his London office and put him on the witness stand.

The witness now appealed directly to the president of the court, pleading that "the trial judge advocate is, in fact, investigating my official actions as IG. I am entitled to make up my own opinion at any time and forward it to the proper authorities when I see fit, which is what I did."

But the court did not respond.

The assistant TJA now switched his focus from the IG inspector's conversations with Colonel Kilian to the ones he had had with Lieutenant Cubage. Again, Colonel Hummell tried to get out of answering:

"That was included in the report I made to higher authority."

Captain Carroll, obviously familiar with the report, picked up a document from the defense table, and, as he began to read from the paper, the scope of Carroll's sources began to sink in.

"Your notes are all taken from the letter that I forwarded to higher authority," Hummell protested. "They are almost verbatim! I think that I am entitled to look at them in order to refresh my memory."

Carroll handed the witness a copy of his own letter and asked him a question about it. The witness boiled over:

"*I'm* not on trial. I am a *witness!* All the time that we've been in here you haven't once touched on a point which has a direct bearing on the alleged beatings of men at Lichfield! You have been working 'Kilian, Kilian, Kilian'—and it verifies many of the hearsay stories going around."

"I am asking not only that that statement be stricken," the assistant prosecutor calmly moved, "but that this witness be admonished." And the president obliged:

"That is an expression of opinion on your part in which the court is not interested, Colonel. It is needless to say that it is painful to have to remind you for the third time to answer questions to the best of your ability and to refrain from using any remark which is an indication of your personal feelings toward any member of this court."

"Yes, sir," said the deflated Hummell.

As the questioning progressed, Colonel Hummell began to take pieces of paper from his pockets, leading to another petty skirmish.

"The record will show that the witness has now put away the letter and that he is reading notes," Carroll dictated to the court reporter. Then, to the witness:

"May we see these notes before you start to read them?"

"I object." It was the witness who was objecting. "There is·a reference in the notes to another case. This is *official.*"

The tableau that followed might have been lifted from a silent slapstick comedy. The witness began slipping some of his papers into his pockets, pulling out others, then quickly putting selected ones away. Meanwhile, the prosecution sought to have *all* of the colonel's written material entered into the record.

Finally, Major Smith suggested a compromise:

"Let the record show that the witness is continuing to read his notes, or whatever it is that he is reading. We request the ruling of the court: Give them to the law member and see whether it is proper for them to be given to counsel now that they have been read."

At first, the witness balked. "I consider that my notes are an official matter." But the law member overruled him:

"There is no immunity for official matter before the highest military court in the United States."

Receiving the papers from the witness, Major Hopper confirmed that some, indeed, had nothing to do with the case before the court. But then the law member had an inspiration:

"Perhaps we ought to see what is written on the *back*. I will look at the back. I believe that the back portion of the notes *is* relevant. Counsel can look at the page without turning it over," he ruled, handing the papers back to the witness.

"In fairness to you," Carroll taunted the witness, "haven't you got those two papers mixed up? Isn't the one in your left hand the one that you made from Colonel Kilian, and the one in your right hand the one that you made from Lieutenant Cubage?"

"No!" snapped the witness.

"You had a document in your hand which has a '1' with a circle around it. It says: 'One Regular Army officer, president.'"

"No," the witness protested. "That part the law member gave me permission to withdraw."

"That has got something on it relative to this case, hasn't it?" the cunning prosecutor persisted. "If that has to do with this case, I want the law member to look at it."

"The law member *has* looked at it," Hummell argued, "and it has nothing to do with this case." It was a lie, and somehow Carroll knew it.

"Let the law member look at it again," Carroll ordered. The witness complied.

"There *is* one word which does pertain to this case," the law member ruled.

"What is that word?" Carroll asked.

Major Hopper hesitated, then handed it to Colonel Leone with what seemed to be some embarrassment. "I will let the president read it."

And he did:

"One Regular Army officer president," Leone read, "*[WEAK]."*

"Weak?" Carroll asked.

"Yes," the president confirmed, "in brackets."

"I can understand why that half was not produced," Carroll noted.

Line by line, the assistant prosecutor then sifted through the witness's notes, pointing out discrepancies. Notes which the witness had stated were written during a single meeting had annotations that, Carroll pointed out, were in inks of different colors. The acrimonious cross-examination continued until 5:45 P.M., when the president finally adjourned the court for the day.

Significantly, none of the above made its way into *The Stars and Stripes.* It seemed likely to Carroll that, given Lieutenant Colonel Hummell's position as assistant theater inspector general, United States forces, European Theater, his activities must have had the blessing of his commanding officer. Back in the U.S., an article in the wartime "Army & Navy" section of *Time* magazine on the news stands that week began:

The man on trial before a U.S. court-martial in London was Sergeant Judson H. Smith—one of twelve men charged with cruelty to G.I. prisoners in the guardhouse of the 10th Reinforcement Depot at Lichfield. But last week, as the story of brutalities continued to unfold, lowly Sergeant Smith became almost the forgotten man at his own trial. The accusing finger pointed higher and higher up the chain of command.[3]

Earl Carroll seemed to be achieving his objective.

16

REACTION

When the court reconvened on Wednesday morning, January 16th, it became apparent that Captain Carroll had taken on the deflation of Lieutenant Colonel Hummell's pomposity as his mission for the day. Despite his pleas to the court that the assistant prosecutor's questions were "not material to the case," William Hummell was forced to reveal that he had attended engineering school at the University of Alabama for a time, but dropped out in his junior year. After leaving college, he entered the Army Air Corps Flying Cadets program, but washed out.[1]

After that failure, he had "gone on vacation" for a while in Florida before finding a job with the American Brass Company as a "sales engineer." He made it sound like an important, highly technical assignment, "traveling throughout the Middle West and studying certain metallurgical problems with certain industries and applying the proper copper alloys to their uses."

Carroll's series of denigrating questions about the engineering aspects of the assignment eventually caused him explode, "All right, I was a salesman!"

Somehow, during this period, Hummell had received a reserve commission. Between 1931 and the outbreak of World War II, he had managed to work up to the reserve rank of captain and had preserved his rank upon coming into the wartime (AUS) army. His service record during the war included a string of undistinguished assignments: operations officer for a headquarters company; officer in charge of an ordinance warehouse in Chicago; inspector of a staging area at Fort Dix, New Jersey; commander of a small port at St. Vast, France; and plans and policy officer at another French port. None of these jobs lasted more than a few months. After being relieved of his last assignment, he wound up as a casual officer at Lichfield, where he awaited reassignment. While at the 10th Reinforcement Depot, he had received his high-level IG appointment, the assignment coming only four months ago.

Hummell had long been fascinated with military law. He had been one of three assistant defense counsels before a stateside military commission that tried a number of "Nazi saboteurs." (Six of his eight clients were electrocuted, and the remaining two, who turned state's evidence, got twenty-five years to life). Hummell had also attempted unsuccessfully to get himself assigned to the general court that was trying Sergeant Smith.

Although Carroll's cross-examination ground on until noon, exploring Hummell's lackluster service record, the revelations of his checkered military career produced no discernible effect on Hummell's self-esteem.

Under the leadership of Colonel Leone, members of the Smith court-martial had reason to believe they had been facing up to their responsibilities in this sensational case with integrity. But their appointing authority, Brigadier General Claude M. Thiele, commanding general, London area, obviously didn't see it that way. During the court's adjournment for lunch, a personal messenger brought Major Smith an answer to his letter of two days earlier, signed by the general's staff judge advocate, Major Richard D. Kearney. The general was furious because action had been requested against Colonel Kilian in open court. He would not be cheered by Colonel Leone's directing his trial judge advocate to read "the appointing authority's" response without first closing the court—thus exposing it to the press.[2]

The letter was extremely critical, advising the court that its actions were "highly irregular," and that "the preparation of charges against Colonel Kilian, Major Lo Buono, or any other witness appearing before the court is not in the scope of the court's function. . . . The court's function in any trial is limited to the determination of the guilt or innocence of the accused before it." If other matters came to light in the process, the letter made it clear, the "appointing authority" should be advised for "such action as may be deemed appropriate by him."

The Stars and Stripes would summarize the communique in its Thursday morning headline:

LICHFIELD COURT ADMONISHED ON BLAST AT KILIAN [3]

Only twelve minutes after the court had reconvened, at 1:42 P.M., the president closed the court. It remained closed for an hour and a half, during which time Major Smith apparently called the staff judge advocate, Major Kearney. When the court reopened, the TJA made his report:

"The staff judge advocate has advised that he does not believe that it would be proper for him to come into court and give oral advice— or be here. If any clarification of the letter is required, he would prefer to give that in writing in response to a [written] request of the court."

Although Major Kearney was wisely staying out of the fray, the defense counsel, Lieutenant Johnson, was undeterred. He believed the general's directive was prejudicial to his client, and, with remarkable courage, told the court (and the press) that "I think this is undue influence on the part of the appointing authority." Not surprisingly, Captain Carroll agreed with him.

Then, in defiance of the commanding general, the law member cited for the record paragraph 25, page 16, of the *Manual for Courts-Martial,* which stated that "*Any* person subject to military law may prefer charges." Major Hopper then ruled that the court would stand its ground:

"We will withdraw the request that we made that the staff judge advocate appear before the court at this time; but we have not as yet changed in any way our request to the government in connection with this matter."

When Lieutenant Colonel Hummell returned to the witness stand, it quickly developed that he had been a party to producing the general's blast, having written a report sympathetic to Colonel Kilian's complaints and very critical of the court. Then, instead of sending his report through normal channels to the Inspector General, he had addressed it to the Commanding General, London Area—to General Thiele himself. To the colonel's considerable chagrin, the prosecution revealed that it had obtained a copy of Hummell's report, and had entered it as a prosecution exhibit.

Defense counsel Johnson had the report in his hand when he took over the questioning of Colonel Hummell from Earl Carroll. Perhaps because he had been accused by the witness of being "inexperienced, extremely weak," and generally ineffectual, Johnson came on like a tiger. The record reads more like a typical Carroll interrogation:

"Were you required to send this letter to the commanding general?"

"No, I wasn't required to send it to the commanding general. By the same token, I might have been guilty of dereliction of duty had I not done so. It's six of one and half-a-dozen of the other."

"On what basis would you have given this information to the commanding general, London Office Area?"

"Observation and accumulation of hearsay stories."

"You would have based that opinion, as assistant inspector general to the commanding general, London area, on *hearsay* stories?"

"On the accumulation of them."

"Do you mean to tell this court, Colonel, when you hear one story and then hear two, it may be they are not good enough. But if you hear *enough* hearsay stories that is good enough for you to give the commanding general a report as assistant inspector general?"

The defense counsel sounded a little like army counsel Joseph Welch questioning Senator Joseph R. McCarthy two decades later.

"There were, in my opinion, sufficient allegations to warrant investigation," Hummell stated defensively.

"You didn't know *what* you were reporting to the commanding general," Johnson asserted. He opened the colonel's report to a pre-marked page.

"You didn't know enough facts in the case to make a report like this in paragraph 3, did you? [He read an allegation of "collusion" because the defense counsel had sought advice from a lawyer in the London judge advocate's office.] Did you know it is the custom between two lawyers to talk about a case in the same manner as it is the custom between two doctors to talk about an unusual case? Did you know that, Colonel?"

"No." The response was almost inaudible. Hummell was slumped in the witness chair.

"You're not a lawyer yourself, are you?"

"That is correct." Then, after a pause, sitting up straighter, Hummell continued: "There are additional points, however. Were I able to do a perfect job, Lieutenant, on every case, or any inspector general, we would be very unusual people. We make mistakes of omission in many cases—in many investigations."

Sitting at the prosecution table, the assistant TJA seemed to be enjoying the proceedings. He could never have squeezed such an admission out of Colonel Hummell.

But Lieutenant Johnson wasn't finished. Demonstrating the shallowness of Colonel Hummell's "investigation," he got the witness to admit that his report had been largely based on "remarks in the office." Hummell didn't even know that, as a result of Colonel Swope's investigation of the 10th Reinforcement Depot, the IG had recommended (1) that Sergeant Smith be tried by general court-martial, (2) that Lieutenant Cubage be similarly tried, and (3) that Colonel James A. Kilian be administratively admonished.

"You didn't discuss these things ever?" It was an embarrassing question.

"I never did. In fact, I knew so little about the case—"

"Just answer the question," the president interrupted irritably. It sounded like pretty sloppy work for the no. 2 inspector general of the United Kingdom.

Turning to another page in Colonel Hummell's letter, Lieutenant Johnson read what the witness had written to the general:

"'The law member of the court, Major Hopper, has the reputation of being prejudiced against the defendant, and is alleged to have expressed himself to that effect; in fact, he so indicated in a personal conversation to the undersigned.'"

When had that conversation taken place, Johnson demanded.

Hummell didn't remember. The best he could offer at the moment was "a number of hearsay stories."

"Will you enumerate them to the court, please?"

"I couldn't enumerate them. Anyone could stand around the officers' club any night in the week and hear this case tried over and over, and hear opinion after opinion expressed by officers in close proximity to the club."

Johnson found the response less than adequate.

"Do you mean to tell this court, Colonel, and to go on record as saying you made an allegation against the law member on a general court-martial on hearsay stories that you heard at the officers' club?"

"Yes; supplemented by the fact that it stuck in my mind that Major Hopper was prejudiced."

The witness by now had alienated the president of the court (whom he had called "weak"), the defense counsels ("inexperienced, extremely weak"), the assistant prosecutor (a "son of a bitch who knows every trick in the bag"), and the law member (who, he now claimed, was "prejudiced"). His documented remarks had all been made behind their backs. He was the loneliest man in the room.

Reluctant to interrupt, given the way things were going, Earl Carroll entered an objection to what "stuck in his mind."

"Are you requesting the court to admonish the witness?" Major Hopper asked Carroll. The law member had reason to want such an admonition.

"Yes," Carroll replied obligingly.

"Since this goes to the law member," Hopper said, "I will ask the president of the court to rule in this instance."

The president did so, telling Colonel Hummell to pay attention to the questions and think about them before he answered, and then to be as brief as possible. The defense counsel then warned the witness about the seriousness of his having made an allegation to the commanding general against the law member of a general court-martial based on "hearsay stories that you heard at the officers' club." He returned to "paragraph 5d" of the witness's letter to the general.

"'In fact, he so indicated in a personal conversation to the undersigned,'" Johnson read. "Will you tell the court *what* Major Hopper indicated to you that made this strong impression on your mind that he was prejudiced against the defendants?"

All the witness could muster was, "I don't remember."

"Did you remember at the time you made this report as assistant inspector general to the commanding general, London area office?"

"No," the witness admitted. As his now-famous letter to the general, initially submitted as prosecution exhibit 36, was reentered as defense exhibit "D," there seemed little doubt that Lieutenant Colonel Hummell had been operating on behalf of Colonel Kilian, and the suspicion remained that he had been put up to it by the army establishment.

17

THE COURT STANDS ITS GROUND

When the court reopened on Thursday morning, the president immediately ordered it closed. It remained closed for an hour and a half. Colonel Hummell's testimony of the previous day and the communication from the court's appointing authority had had their effect. When Colonel Leone finally reopened the court at 11:55 A.M., he spoke defiantly, on the record and in open court:

"The law member will read the action of the court in response to the letter from the staff judge advocate to the trial judge advocate."[1]

Addressing the TJA, Major Hopper complied.

"Major Smith, the court requests that you, as trial judge advocate, return this letter to the staff judge advocate and advise him as follows:

'The court has considered the letter from the staff judge advocate and notes that it cites no reference to the *Manual for Courts-Martial, United States Army,* the opinions of the judge advocate general of the army, or any decision of any court of the United States for the position stated. The court, therefore, does not feel it is able at this time to alter its actions.

'The court invites attention to an apparent misunderstanding on the part of the staff judge advocate. [He] has confused the action of the court in requesting the *drafting* of charges against various persons with the *preferring* of charges by the court as such. At no time has the court stated its intention of preferring charges as a court. But the members of the court know of no restriction on the right of any officer to prefer charges against anyone subject to military law when, either through personal knowledge or investigation, such officer believes an offense has been committed by a person subject to military law under the Articles of War.'"

The individual members of the court were thus threatening to make the equivalent of a citizen's arrest.

Lieutenant Colonel Hummell's return to the witness stand produced a surprise when Earl Carroll approached the witness chair. The assistant TJA was holding Hummell's document in his hand.

"Colonel," the assistant prosecutor asked, "have you had an opportunity to give some consideration since you last testified to the contents of this letter, and to some of the subject matters which we have been going over in this court?"

"Yes, I have." The truculence that had characterized all of the witness's previous testimony had disappeared.

"Is there anything that you would like to tell the court in connection with this letter?"

"I am convinced that I used poor judgment in believing that Major Hopper, the law member, was prejudiced," the witness stated. "I am convinced I was wrong in making that addition to the letter."

"In other words," Carroll asked, "as to this paragraph 5d: 'the law member of the court, Major Hopper, has the reputation of being prejudiced against the defendants and is alleged to have expressed himself to the effect,' it is now your testimony that the words 'in fact he so indicated in a personal conversation to the undersigned,' is an erroneous statement. Is that correct?"

"Yes," Hummell admitted. Then, perhaps in an effort to avoid being charged with perjury, he began to hedge, mumbling an explanation that included, "I should have phrased it better. I meant again that a number of people around the club had ventured the opinion that he was. That is what I should have actually put. I have already stated I feel the letter could have been composed better."

Lieutenant Johnson thought it was getting a bit thick.

"Before we proceed any further," the defense counsel interrupted, rising to his feet, "are we going to have the law member make a ruling as to whether this witness is still hostile or not? From indications, we are having a confessional hour here, and if we are going to do that it is necessary for the counsel questioning the witness to adhere strictly to the rules."

Johnson seemed to be gaining confidence as a lawyer.

Because the law member was himself now the subject of the interrogation, he demurred. The president declared there was no change in the status of the witness.

Under questioning by Carroll, Colonel Hummell now began expanding his previous testimony about relations with his "client," Colonel Kilian, indicating that his letter to the general had been written to appease Kilian.

"He stopped me in the club and asked me to come over to his hotel with him for the first meeting. I realized at my first meeting with Colonel Kilian that he was in a highly nervous condition and actually I didn't believe he was responsible for some of the statements he made. He was so highly excited that a serious doubt arose in my mind as to whether that man was mentally in possession of his faculties to the point where he should be making any statements to anybody.

"I felt a legal opinion should be rendered as to whether, under the existing army regulations, this particular officer—and Lieutenant Cubage—shouldn't have been subjected to psychiatric examination by a trained psychiatrist before they answered any more questions or made any more statements to me or anybody else."

Lieutenant Johnson took over the questioning.

"Don't you realize that you have been used as a tool in writing this letter to the commanding general? Don't you realize that someone has taken advantage of your official position to further their own ends?"

Colonel Hummell didn't like the word "tool." Before he had finished giving his extended, waffling answers, the court adjourned for lunch.

When the court reconvened, it was the law member and the president of the court who began interrogating the witness. Slowly reading Hummell's letter, line by line, and questioning its writer on the validity of its contents, the senior members of the court extracted a humiliating string of concessions from the witness. In sentence after sentence, Hummell acknowledged that the allegations in his letter were "unjustified," "without foundation," "erroneous," or "improper."

Major Pers joined in, asking for definitions of some of the IG inspector's expressions, including "wildly hearsay," "constantly raking up," and others. The medical officer's final question seemed to summarize his feelings about the actions of the IG inspector:

"And yet you formulated a letter which you admit was incomplete and full of many errors; you did not even read it over, and you forwarded *that* to the commanding general for investigation as to what appropriate action he should take. Is that correct?"

When Lieutenant Colonel Hummell was finally excused as a witness, Lieutenant Johnson addressed the court:

"This witness who has testified before the court today holds a responsible position in this command. . . . He is a lieutenant colonel, and he has been on the stand here for two days, and in his sworn testimony before this court he has admitted he made a false official statement; and this false official statement reflects on the dignity, the honesty, the intelligence, and the ability of the members of this court. . . . I am going to request that a copy of this witness's testimony be transmitted to the commanding general."

After discussion with the prosecution, the law member approved Lieutenant Johnson's motion and the court elected to send a copy of Colonel Hummell's testimony via the staff judge advocate to Commanding General Thiele. It was unlikely to have a favorable effect on Hummell's career, or to endear the court to General Thiele.

Lieutenant Cubage was recalled to the witness stand.

After once again confirming the truth of the Lichfield abuses he had previously denied, Cubage testified about discrepancies between the depot's official, posted rules and actual practice. The printed rules stated, for example, that each prisoner was entitled to allocate fifty cents per month for tobacco (which allowed a soldier to buy a carton of cigarettes at special army rates), but specified that "smoking will only be permitted between 1900 and 2100 hours." In actual practice, Cubage said, "smoking was not permitted," and any prisoner caught smoking was punished.[2]

Rule 24 stated that "Prisoners will not be double-timed for punishment." But they were. Rule 25 read, "Punishment will be awarded prisoners by the depot commander only," but it was routinely delegated all the way down to guards and jailers. Rule 27 specified "A maximum of one (1) hours [sic] calisthenics, not to exceed 1/2 hour during any one period, will be given prisoners daily."

"This was not in effect," the former prison officer said. There was no doubt in his mind that all of this had the tacit approval of Colonel Kilian. Cubage described a typical meeting with the depot commander, and how one dared not deviate from the post commander's undocumented regimen.

"When he called anyone in, no one ever told him *anything,* so long as they were standing. If he offered you a chair you might talk, but you did not *say* anything to him. You just told him it would not happen again.

"You couldn't reason with him at all. If you tried to explain anything he would say you were trying to change *his* orders.

"[Once] he walked into Guardhouse No. 1 and found cigarettes on the floor, and I thought he was going to have a hemorrhage." On another inspection tour, Kilian found some envelopes with British stamps on them, Cubage said.

"'Here is a letter that was going to be mailed in a British mailbox without being censored,' the colonel shouted. 'These prisoners will never receive any British stamps as long as they are in this guardhouse!' And so we cut off the British stamps until we thought he had forgotten about them, and then we started giving them back to the prisoners over a period of three or four months."

When Lieutenant Cubage was appalled by the beatings of Wright and Alford and began an investigation, he later heeded the advice of a veteran sergeant in the prison facility: "'I don't want to tell you what to do, Lieutenant, but don't you think it would be better if we wait and let a Line of Duty Board investigate this? I don't think Colonel Kilian would like it if you put charges on any guards for something like this.'"

Because of his previous experience with Colonel Kilian, Cubage testified, he thought the sergeant was giving prudent advice.

Captain Carroll asked about that previous experience.

"In September of 1944 I had a man that had given me more trouble than I could take care of." Cubage described the man as a six-foot-three-inch white prisoner by the name of King, who had long blond hair, and who had been in the guardhouse many times and refused to work.

"I had placed him in solitary confinement for fourteen days. I went to Colonel Kilian and asked him if I could send the man to a Disciplinary Training Center because I didn't have knowledge of handling a prisoner of this type."

"That prisoner won't be sent to the DTC," Kilian had said, "but he will be punished and punished severely in this guardhouse. We can be just as tough as any DTC."

"And then he began to tell me how they used to do it in the Cavalry," Cubage testified. The officer's quotation of his commandant's specific suggestion, in front of his executive officer, Colonel Aldridge, would make headlines on both sides of the Atlantic:

"'In a case like this I know what I would do. I would take that prisoner down to the rifle range and work him over; take him down where no one could see him—and *just don't break too many bones.'* Those are the exact words that Colonel Kilian said."

He had told Sergeant Smith about the colonel's instruction, Cubage added.

"What was his reaction?" Carroll inquired.

"He was just amazed like I was."

Lieutenant Cubage testified that he was frightened by the experience. If he complied, he was sure that both Kilian and Aldridge would deny the conversation had ever taken place. Instead of carrying out his commandant's order, Cubage said, he consulted the post psychiatrist, who suggested that the man be sent down to him for examination—which got Cubage off the hook, he said. Two days later the prisoner was shipped off to the 96th General Hospital, after which he was sent home and discharged.

Since other news media had the story, *The Stars and Stripes* got away with running a headline, albeit toned down, in the Saturday edition: "KILIAN ORDERED LICHFIELD BEATINGS, OFFICER TESTIFIES."[3]

18

PURGATORY

Lieutenant Granville Cubage returned to the witness stand the following day to further modify and correct what he had sworn to earlier. He acknowledged that clubbings by the guards were common, and he had tacitly approved of them "because of policies established by the commandant." Whenever an IG inspector was due, men with telltale marks of guard brutality were deliberately dispersed on work details, he said, so their injuries wouldn't be seen—a "standard operating procedure created by Provost Marshal Lo Buono."[1]

When Carroll reexamined the Richey episode, Cubage readily admitted that the man had been unconscious when carried to solitary confinement, but he said that Captain Robertson had refused to permit him to receive medical attention for his head injuries. Examined on the nearly fatal beatings of Wright and Alford, the former prison officer admitted that *he* had written the statement signed by jailer Robson for the Line of Duty Board. In the document, Robson had sworn that no guard had laid a hand on the prisoners, but that they had deliberately injured themselves.

"I saw Wright throwing his entire body against the wall of the cell room as he ran to and from one side of the room to the other," the document said. "Sergeant Loveless and I told him to stop or he would hurt himself." Alford, the statement claimed, had done essentially the same thing. Each prisoner later "complained of sickness," Alford's document concluded "and was immediately escorted to the post dispensary."

On Monday, it was Ellis Adcock's turn to purge himself.

"I want to get back on the stand again of my own free will to tell the truth and to accept responsibility—but not entire responsibility, because the things that were done were orders given to me by an officer," the former guard began.

Adcock described the first "orientation" conducted by Lieutenant Ennis.

"'I'm the new prison officer here,' he said. 'These men are going to snap shit. They're going to snap shit and you're going to make them. If these men sound off at you, rough 'em up and send them inside the guardhouse. Don't use your fists on these men.' And he grabbed an '03 [rifle] from one of the guards. He patted the butt with his hand and he said, 'You know what this is used for?' And he said, 'Let 'em have it,' and he demonstrated [a vertical butt stroke] in front of the guards. 'Don't mess up your hands.

"'I want these men to stand to attention at all times; and I mean they will stand to attention at *all* times. If you let one of these prisoners escape on you, *you* will serve his time! You're gonna be rough, or else.'" That night, Adcock testified, Ennis jailed one of the jailers.

Other directives issued by the officer, Adcock said, included "'These men are fuck-ups; they're no fuckin' good, and when they come in for the second time I want you to put 'em up against that wall and start double-timing them 'til they drop. By God, if a man comes in here for the second or *third* time, work him over and work his ass off on swing shift.'"

Adcock revealed a hitherto undisclosed punishment for repeaters, or for prisoners who "had done something the wrong way or messed something up, or had sounded off at a guard, or something of that nature. [They] put them on the 'brick pile;' that was at the back of Guardhouse No. 2. They had this pack. This pack weighed approximately twenty-five to thirty pounds, and it had bricks in it. They would send the man out with an English shovel; and he would have to shovel dirt and rocks from one place to another and then back again—all in a specified time for the workout."

The most bizarre testimony the witness delivered was written up in *The Stars and Stripes* on Tuesday morning:

LONDON, Jan. 21—The cries of a Negro prisoner being beaten in the Lichfield guardhouse and the noise of the blows were drowned out by a guard singing 'The Indian Love Call,' the guard, T/5 Ellis D. Adcock testified today.

Adcock, one of the defendants in the Lichfield trial, said other guards brought Private Joseph Mallory to his office for the beating. While the other guards beat Mallory, Adcock, who was duty sergeant, sang "The Indian Love Call" and two other songs to cover up the sound.[2]

It was a variation on what Jones and Gheens had done while beating Koblinski and another prisoner. They had ordered a whole wing of prisoners to shout "at ease" in unison for more than an hour to cover the cries of their victims—as Staff Sergeant James Jones admitted when he returned to the stand to purge himself.

Jones, a combat veteran who wore a Bronze Star for leadership during the Normandy landing, corroborated Adcock's testimony about instructions from Ennis and Cubage. He said he was told "the only way to teach prisoners is to beat them to the ground." After the visit by Colonel Varner, however, the policy on prisoner treatment changed abruptly. Prisoners no longer were to be beaten. "It was the difference between night and day."

When the current trial began, Jones said, Lieutenant Cubage and Major Lo Buono had called the guards into Sergeant Smith's office and instructed them to declare that the allegations against them and the Lichfield establishment were untrue. "Stick to your same testimony," Cubage had told them. "It's only the prisoners' word against yours. You have the whole post behind you."

"I'm with you 100 percent," Major Lo Buono had added.

But in meetings among themselves, some of the guards were unconvinced—particularly when their protectors began to disappear. Lieutenant Ennis, with his "nervous breakdown," was the first to be returned to the United States. It was Colonel Kilian's return to London from the U.S. to serve as a character witness for Sergeant Smith that finally made up their minds.

"We read a piece in the paper that said that Colonel Kilian had stated to the press he never ordered anything like that done, and if it had been done he would have known about it."

But then Colonel Kilian called his former cadre together in London and reassured them.

"He told me personally," Jones testified, "'Don't worry about it—we'll get this thing over and get you home.'" After Major Lo Buono met with and counseled the guards, they agreed to perjure themselves. It was actually Sergeant Smith who led the current move to tell the truth.

Although by now it was only Thursday afternoon, Lieutenant Johnson requested adjournment until the following Monday to complete the defense's preparation.

Monday morning, January 28th, was the fortieth day of the trial.[3]

"The accused, Sergeant Smith, desires to take the witness stand," Lieutenant Johnson announced.

Major Smith rose to remind the witness that he was still under oath. But the TJA was also concerned about the possibility of Sergeant Smith incriminating himself, and he asked the law member to explain the defendant's rights to him under the 24th Article of War.

"Your situation in taking the stand as the accused in the case, Smith, *is* a little different from that of the other witnesses who have come on the stand," Major Hopper told him. "When an accused in a case takes the stand in his own behalf . . . he cannot avail himself of the privilege against self-incrimination to escape proper cross-examination." After the law member read him several relevant passages from the *Manual for Courts-Martial* and "Training Manual 27/255," Earl Carroll pointed out that the accused could "limit his testimony to any particular specification."

None of it seemed to matter to Judson Smith. When his defense counsel took over, Smith seemed to welcome the opportunity to pour out his heart, explaining that he wanted to return "to tell the truth—to explain to the court who I got my orders from. This has been on my head since last November," he pleaded. "I never had been in trouble in my life until this thing come up."

Smith now readily admitted to the allegations of brutality against him, explaining that he was following orders from Lieutenants Ennis and Cubage. And, of course, prisoners were kept in solitary longer than the twenty-four-hour limit prescribed by the rules; and no written record was kept on such confinement. When asked how long men were actually kept in the hole, he said he could hardly recall any prisoner who had spent less than fourteen days in solitary confinement. He related one incident that had bothered him.

"There was a prisoner by the name of William Berry in solitary. The man had been shot in the leg and wanted medical attention. Colonel Kilian come in the guardhouse and I reported to him. He went through the guardhouse, coming into this wing, and this prisoner in solitary confinement hollered out to the colonel and said, 'Sir, can I talk to you for a few minutes?' And the colonel said he didn't want to see the prisoner." So the wounded man had remained confined to the hole, Smith said, where "he may get a loaf of bread or he may not."

The former provost sergeant's comments about medical treatment of the prisoners were written up in *The Stars and Stripes* the next day:

The witness asserted that although it was usual to tell medics who inquired about prisoners' injuries that they had "fallen downstairs," Captain Rudolf E. Warnecke of the Lichfield medical staff "must have known" that it was not the truth.

Smith agreed with the prosecution that the story was concocted in order to keep the camp records clean. "The doctors knew as well as anyone else that the men didn't receive their injuries that way," he added.[4]

Before concluding his testimony, Sergeant Smith had also implicated Lichfield Commandant Kilian, Provost Marshal Lo Buono, Post Inspector Bluhm, Prison Company CO Robertson, Sanitation Officer King, Prison Officer Ennis, and Prison Officer Cubage.

Stepping down from the witness stand for the last time, Sergeant

Smith had left the impression he would have chosen, despite his fractured syntax and less than brilliant performance—that of a sincere, uncomplicated, loyal soldier who did what he was told and felt he had been let down by the army.

When Captain Joseph A. Robertson, MP, former commanding officer of the 316th Prison Company was recalled to the witness stand, the court ceased being a purgatorium. As a defense witness recalled by the prosecution to face new testimony delivered by men he had commanded, he was declared a hostile witness and was examined under the rules for cross-examination. Unlike the others, he had not volunteered and had no immunity. Robertson insisted he had previously told the truth in claiming he had never heard of any mistreatment in the Lichfield guardhouses. Although he had seen men facing the wall, he had never seen them "touching it nose and toes."[5]

The roughest guards, especially one called "Nunes" (whose real name was Menunes), were selected for guardhouse cadre by higher authority over his objection, he said. Nunes in particular was unfit for such duty "because he couldn't handle troops."

When Carroll asked the witness if he thought Nunes was a "psycho," Robertson said, "It would be kind to call him a psycho."

Asked the same question earlier, guards Adcock and Jones had offered the opinion, "No. He was just plain crazy!" It was Menunes who had allegedly killed Private Eril Bolton, producing the GI newspaper's "MURDER" headline.

The assistant prosecutor then asked Robertson, "If Lieutenant Cubage came in here and told the court that he had actually had discussions with you about the beating of prisoners, what would you say?"

"I would say he was a liar!" Robertson asserted. When Carroll repeated the question with regard to such a statement from the provost marshal, Major Lo Buono, the witness responded, "I would say the same thing about him; he was a liar."

"I told [the guards] there would be no rough stuff in there. We were going to run the guardhouse according to army regulations."

But Robertson's denials began to weaken the next day when he quoted Kilian's instruction, "You can be as tough as you like." And when Carroll asked him, he said he had known that his part of the Lichfield compound was called "Colonel Kilian's Navy" (the prisoners wore blue uniforms), and, indeed, that the 10th Reinforcement Depot guardhouse was also called "Colonel Kilian's Concentration Camp." He finally admitted that there were no limits:

"You could kill a man if that's what you liked to do."

That one made *The Stars and Stripes* headlines on February 3rd.

Robertson added the standard caveat: "I accept responsibility only as an intermediary. I did not have the command that was mine so I don't think that I had the responsibility." It sounded a lot like Nürnberg.

Before he left the stand, Captain Robertson revealed that Lieutenant Ennis constituted such a major problem in his command that he had attempted to get rid of him. Ennis drank a lot, the former prison company commander said, and sometimes disappeared for days.

"He generally had everyone in the outfit afraid of his doing physical violence to them." One night after the bar closed, Ennis went to Major Bluhm's room and threatened to kill him if he didn't make more beer available. And "on previous occasions [Ennis] had chased other officers through creeks and canals and up roads and threatened them with one thing and another."

The next witness to be recalled was Lieutenant Leonard Ennis. He had received orders three days earlier to be present when the court opened on Monday morning, but Ennis failed to show up. The court was adjourned until 2:35 P.M., when the officer finally arrived. There was no public explanation for his being late.

After he was sworn in, Ennis was tight-lipped and self-protective.

Like Captain Robertson, he had no immunity, and he knew it. While he acknowledged that the guardhouses were run by a tough cadre, he minimized the degree of roughness. But he quoted Colonel Kilian's telling him and his boss, Captain Robertson, "You can be as rough as you wish"—an order the commandant gave while giving a tea party, Ennis said.[6]

The witness said he felt that calisthenics, double-timing, the nose and toes routine, and "whacking men on the rump with a club" constituted "fair punishment." But he did not favor hitting men in the *head* with a club. The rump, he insisted, was the only part of the body the guards whacked. And treatment of second and third repeaters was no different from that of other prisoners, he insisted, claiming he never knew who they were.

Ennis expressed regret at the inadequate medical treatment given his charges, sixty percent of whom were combat wounded veterans. As *The Stars and Stripes* reported his testimony:

The burly ex-prison officer told the court that Captain Randolph [sic] E. Warnecke gave "really sick" ex-combat prisoners doses of castor oil and sent them back to duty at the stockade, where they were forced to undergo strenuous calisthenics.

"What could I do? I'm not a medical officer," Ennis said.[7]

As the prosecution reexamined many of the incidents in which Ennis had been accused of personal physical abuse, he denied them all. He never even confiscated "books that prisoners stashed under their mattresses."

If there was any physical mistreatment of prisoners, Ennis insisted, it was something that had been going on before he got there. He had no recollection of his demonstrating how to strike a man with a rifle butt. He had only demonstrated "how to prevent a prisoner from taking a rifle away from a guard." He never said, "By God, if a man comes in here for the second or third time, work him over and work his ass off on swing shift." He never put anyone on swing shift.

"I never used the phrase, 'work the man over,'" he declared. He himself "never laid a hand on anyone" (although he did admit to giving them an occasional whack on the rump with a club).

Then why, Captain Carroll asked, had other witnesses made accusations against him in their testimony?

"They got themselves into such a jam they don't know what they're talking about. Somebody has got to be the scapegoat, and I guess it's me." It was hardly an adequate explanation, but Carroll let it stand unchallenged on the record.

Near the end of the former prison officer's testimony, he was questioned by the president of the court. Colonel Leone asked about his conception of the role of "a tough company commander," a reference to the former prison officer's testimony. Ennis made an idealistic speech about the qualifications of his personal role model.

"As far as a tough company commander is concerned, he is a man who is strictly 'army,' who adheres to the army regulations," Ennis said. "And when you are on duty you are on duty twenty-four hours a day. And if you get off at five o'clock or 5:30, or whenever they have retreat, you go over to the club and you act as an officer and a gentleman. You remember you are an officer and a gentleman even when you are out to play. You are still on twenty-four hours a day."

It didn't sound like the officer who threatened to kill Major Bluhm if he didn't get him some more beer, or who "chased other officers through creeks and canals and up roads and threatened them with one thing and another."

Ennis, a provost sergeant before he received his commission, made it clear that *he* was unequivocally "army." He told Colonel Leone he didn't believe that a superior's order could be questioned under any circumstances. What made any directive a lawful order was simply that it came from his commanding officer.

"When I got the instruction from my captain, who was a senior officer to me and he said they were sent down from Colonel Kilian, and he said the policy must be rough and tough and later on he stated, 'Let them know you're the boss,' that was good enough for me."

"Supposing he had given you an order to shoot every tenth man there, would you have shot him?" the president asked.

"I *would,* sir. When I was at Fort Jay, I was ordered to shoot some prisoners making a break by the colonel, and I shot them."

Leone, a combat veteran, seemed shocked. Although it was probably out of order in the trial, Colonel Leone tried to straighten out the witness's thinking.

"Isn't an officer supposed to exercise discretion and understand whether an order is lawful or unlawful? To use their discretion insofar as their ability permits them?"

That seemed a new idea to Ennis:

"If the colonel gave me an order and I followed out the order, who would be to blame for it?"

"*You* would," Leone told him.

Ennis couldn't believe it.

"For following out a superior officer's order?"

"If it is not a *lawful* order," the president explained. "I'm trying to find out from you if you can differentiate between a lawful order as prescribed in Articles of War 64 and 65, and an unlawful order."

"The only thing I can say to you, Colonel, is I *thought* it was a lawful order because the post commanding officer being a colonel gave it to me and I followed out his instructions."

His answer left the room in silence. The court record concludes, "There being no further questions, the witness was excused and left the courtroom."

19

THE COMMANDANT RETURNS

On Wednesday morning, February 6th, after Colonel Leone called the court to order at 9:30 A.M., the court's first witness of the day charged into the courtroom in a towering rage—his green eyes flashing angrily behind the round, steel-rimmed lenses of his government-issue glasses. Gone was the smooth, self-confident, unflappable commandant who had charmed the press two months earlier. Colonel Kilian was not pleased to be recalled by the court. As *Time* magazine (19 February 1946) reported:

Half an hour late, in strode imperious Colonel James Alphonse Kilian, former commandant of the depot. In barrel-organ tones he demanded to see the order convening the court. The president banged his gavel to silence the belligerent witness. Kilian called for a comfortable chair—"one with arms on it if I have to sit here all day."

Fourteen times during five hours, the gavel was slammed to bring the witness to order. Once Kilian stretched, looked at the prosecutor and stuck out his tongue. Said a G.I. onlooker: "I'd like to see one of us act like that!"[1]

In his first two hours on the witness stand, Colonel Kilian would be warned no less than six times against continuing his "hostile and belligerent attitude" as a witness. Before stepping down from the witness stand he would be cited for contempt for refusing to answer a question.

Questioning got off to a rocky start. As soon as Colonel Kilian sat down in the witness chair, he assumed his accustomed command role. Having previously expressed his contempt for the president of the court, the colonel attempted to take charge. Before anyone spoke to him, he told the court he knew he was still under oath. And that wasn't all:

"With the pleasure of the court, before we proceed I would like to ask the court a question or two."

"I think any questions the witness may have are out of order," Colonel Leone told him.

"In view of the irregular proceedings that this court has been going through," Kilian countered, "I think I should be permitted to ask at least for a copy of the order convening the court."

Lieutenant Johnson was on his feet, objecting to the witness's characterizing the conduct of the court as "irregular proceedings," and to having that statement be made a part of the court record. The law member ordered the witness's remark stricken from the record and directed him to answer questions put to him.

As Carroll approached the witness chair on behalf of the prosecution, his opening statement foretold the turbulence to follow:

"I think at this time the court might well advise the witness as to his rights under the 24th Article of War with regard to self-incrimination."

Major Hopper complied, explaining to the witness that "if the answer to any question might tend to incriminate you, you can state that as a reason for failure to answer."

Conscious of the stigma associated with such a plea, the former commandant asked if there was any other reason he could refuse to answer a question.

"Yes," the law member told him. "If the matter is not material *and* if the answer will tend to degrade you. I must remind you that the privilege is a personal one. Neither the trial judge advocate, nor the defense counsel, nor the court will point out to you that an answer may tend to incriminate or degrade you. That is up to you."

Kilian continued asking questions, demanding to know whether he was still a defense witness or if he had been recalled by the prosecution. He was advised that the latter was the case. The law member tried to move things along.

"The court has given the prosecution permission to reopen your cross-examination," Major Hopper indicated, turning to Carroll.

But it was the witness who spoke again, as the assistant TJA stood by.

"I am to understand that the cross-examination is to take place only on that testimony which I gave before this court, and that no new matter can be introduced under those circumstances." That was enough for Carroll.

"I am going to submit that we don't care what this witness understands," the assistant prosecutor declared. "If it please the court, we are concerned with the rules and regulations and the laws which govern trial by court-martial. We do not propose to be bound by his understanding. As matters come up, the *court* will rule as to whether or not they are proper or improper."

"If it is necessary," Major Hopper added, "the *court itself* at any time can call you as a witness."

In less than five minutes, the witness had alienated the president of the court, the law member, the defense, and the prosecution—and vice versa.

For all the preliminary theatrics, Carroll's first question seemed innocuous enough.

"Colonel, the last time you testified before this court, you gave us the chain of command at the post itself in connection with the operation of the depot. I would like you to give that to the court again."

"That is a matter of record," the witness snapped.

"The answer will be stricken as not responsive," the law member responded without being asked. "The witness will please answer the question."

"The chain of command at the depot was myself as depot commander. There was a deputy commander. There was an adjutant. There was a coordinating officer, and there were battalion commanders."

"For the purpose of clarifying this matter now before court," said the assistant TJA with exaggerated politeness, ignoring the intransigence of the witness, "let us get the *names* of the men that were in that chain of command." He offered to let the colonel draw a diagram of his table of organization.

The witness said he would "prefer to answer your questions," an invitation that fit with Carroll's agenda.

"Let us start with the chain of command from the very top," the assistant prosecutor directed, "the source from which *you* directly received *your* orders in connection with the operation of the guardhouse. We want you to proceed from your higher authority right down to the person who ultimately received the orders."

He asked whether the witness understood.

"That's clear." The colonel mumbled it so rapidly it sounded like a single word.

When Carroll asked if the former commandant ever received any instructions about the treatment of prisoners at Lichfield other than those in army regulations, Kilian smiled.

"I'm not going to pass the ball to higher headquarters, because it doesn't belong there," the witness responded smugly.

The law member ordered the answer stricken from the record.

"You will answer questions in the proper manner," Leone ordered.

"Who was your immediate superior officer?" the assistant TJA asked.

"Up until the time of his death, General Layman."

Carroll asked how the name was spelled.

"L-a-y-m-a-n," the colonel offered, but he wasn't sure. "There were two or three Laymans," he said. "*Walter* Layman," he added.

"General Walter Layman," Carroll mused. "Will you spell it again."

"It is a matter of record in the *Army Directory.*" It was a haughty response.

The interchange was getting increasingly petty.

"Do you *know* how to spell it for us?" Carroll asked.

"I told you once."

There would be many Kilian outbursts as Carroll's questioning continued, including, "I refuse to answer the question," "The trial judge advocate is trying to embarrass me," and, ultimately, "I don't know. You talk so much I can't keep track."

When the witness uttered the last remark, the president told him that it was "absolutely uncalled for," and admonished him yet again.

Before Carroll could ask his next question, Lieutenant Johnson broke in. He accused the commandant of being "dilatory and evasive," pointing out that "it is in the interest of Sergeant Smith to get the testimony of this witness." The defense counsel requested that the court instruct Kilian "that if he says he does not know the answer to a question when he does, it constitutes perjury as much as if he gave a wrong answer to a question." Once again, Johnson seemed to be learning courtroom techniques from Carroll.

But for all the sound and fury, nothing significant was produced during the entire first day the commandant spent on the witness stand. The assistant TJA continued to trace the table of organization of the Lichfield depot—who reported to whom, when various officers and cadre personnel served there, and how records were kept. To Carroll's surprise, Kilian denied ever having given Ennis *any* orders directly, and said he "had no recollection at this time" of any conversations with the prison officer. But he refused to "deny" they had taken place, insisting that in order to deny anything he first had to recollect it.

This kind of quibbling characterized most of Kilian's answers, and it got nastier as the day wore on. The prosecution began a series of questions delving into the commandant's military career. He balked at answering them, claiming it was "embarrassing."

Kilian's reluctance may have stemmed from the fact that he knew his name was on a War Department list of 349 Regular Army officers to be promoted from lieutenant colonel to full colonel—a list the Senate had just approved. The silver eagles he was wearing were a temporary rank in the wartime Army of the United States, but with demobilization under way, he would soon have been pinning his silver oak leaves back on and taking a cut in pay.

Kilian's concern proved to be justified. Before he left the witness stand, Senator Elbert Thomas of Utah got his fellow lawmakers to recall the list. The trial publicity had, in fact, delayed all 349 army promotions. On February 13th, Senator Edwin Johnson of Colorado, chairman of the Military Affairs Committee, asked the army for a detailed report on Colonel Kilian.

His line of questioning upheld by the court, Carroll went on, asking where the witness's Cavalry experience had been. He received a smart answer.

"I would like to ask the question if the trial judge advocate is starting out on impeachment proceedings," the colonel ventured glibly.

"That will be stricken from the record as not responsive to the question," the law member interjected. "The credibility of any witness is always at issue before any court."

Red-faced, the colonel boiled over.

"Then I request the court that I will not answer any more questions on this line until I have the benefit and advice of counsel. I object to being browbeaten and humiliated by being asked such fooling questions. I object to them as being immaterial and irrelevant."

The law member told him that as a witness he was not entitled to counsel. The president told him had better be careful about calling the court's interrogation "fooling questions."

That made the morning paper the next day, when the same issue arose. The colonel began pulling British newspapers from his pockets, saying, "At this time I want to state that in view of the published facts in the press, and in view of the hostility of the prosecution and the defense, I refuse to testify further until I have the benefit of the advice of counsel." *The Stars and Stripes* banner headlines read:

KILIAN IS ORDERED TO TALK AFTER HE BALKS ON STAND
LICHFIELD CO FLARES UP AT QUESTIONING[2]

Amidst the tense atmosphere created by the appearance of that headline, Carroll raised the emotional pitch of his interrogation by introducing documents that detailed prison rules forbidding the use of tobacco, requiring "silent mess," and specifying other limitations on prisoner privileges. Kilian denied being the author of them—or even knowing about them.

At this point, the assistant prosecutor placed into evidence a lengthy statement sworn to by prisoner William C. Berry, which Carroll asked the witness to read. The colonel's color darkened further as he reluctantly complied. The document described Berry's removal from the solitary cell by two guards who took him down to the obstacle course where, the statement said, one of the guards hit him and the other shot him through the leg, after which he was returned to solitary. It was the incident that Sergeant Smith had testified about when he returned to the witness chair—when Kilian purportedly refused to speak to Berry after the man called out to him from "the hole" seeking medical attention.

Asked why he never investigated the matter after receiving the report, the colonel reverted to endless quibbling, arguing that it wasn't a report, it was a "statement." And since the guards had been cleared by the Line of Duty Board, the incident had, in effect, never happened. Thus it wasn't even a statement any more, but merely "a rumor," and he never received rumors. In any case, he had no recollection of the guardhouse incident described by Sergeant Smith.

Carroll then asked the colonel whether he still felt that Sergeant Smith was "one of the finest noncommissioned officers he had ever met—better than ninety percent of the lieutenants who had served under him." Kilian quibbled that he thought he had said seventy percent. Pressed, he explained that "that was my opinion when he was at the Lichfield guardhouse. Sergeant Smith has considerably changed at the present time and I don't think that Sergeant Smith is his correct self."

Kilian went on to diagnose the defendant as "physically and mentally sick." When Carroll asked if the colonel's opinion of Sergeant Smith had changed "because Smith's new testimony is unfavorable to you," the witness's histrionic reaction was described the next morning in *The Stars and Stripes:*

Kilian leaped to his feet, smacked his right fist into his left palm, and shouted: "Am I the defendant here?"

Kilian sat down quickly after his outburst and the president of the court told him "that was a menacing gesture you made, and I hope we don't have any repetition of it."[3]

On Friday morning, February 8th, fireworks had erupted by 9:32 A.M. Carroll's question had sounded innocuous enough: "At those times when no prison officer had been appointed, did the colonel's adjutant, Lieutenant Colonel Norton, act as prison officer?"

"I refuse to answer the question," the former commandant intoned. "May it please the court, I should like at this time to stand on my constitutional rights as a citizen of the United States."

It didn't please the court, and a great deal of time was spent trying to fathom the colonel's basis for his refusal. Major Hopper wanted to know whether his objection was made under the 24th Article of War, which permits a witness to avoid self-incrimination in his testimony. If so, he didn't see how answering the prosecution's question could possibly incriminate him, so what was this about? The witness continued to puzzle the court:

"My objection is as stated, as a citizen of the United States."

The law member speculated aloud as to whether the witness's strange position referred to the U.S. Constitution's 5th Amendment. If so, he said, the 24th Article of War provides exactly the same protection for a witness. He almost pleaded with the commandant to let the trial get back on track as he counseled the witness that "it is no confession of guilt, or anything else, to invoke the 24th Article of War, but we must have an objection under the Articles of War, since those are the laws under which we are functioning. Is your objection under the 24th Article of War?"

"My objection is based upon my constitutional rights as a citizen of the United States," Colonel Kilian repeated. The court's frustration mounted.

"Will you answer the question, please," the president ordered.

"I refuse to answer."

That brought it to a head.

"Is your objection based on the 24th Article of War, or not?"

"I refuse to answer." That was enough for Major Hopper.

"I move the witness be held in contempt of court."

Colonel Leone tried to save it.

"Just before we act on that, if you fail to answer my question, then you become liable for contempt of court, don't you?"

"Yes, sir."

"In view of that, do you intend to change your answer?"

"I do not."

"You still refuse to answer both the question of the law member and the question put to you by the prosecution?"

"I do."

The court was closed at once. It was only 9:40 A.M.

When the court reconvened, having looked up some precedent in military law, Major Hopper made a lengthy statement doubting the legal correctness of charging Colonel Kilian specifically with contempt. Instead, the members of the court had decided to charge him under the 96th Article of War—"all disorders and neglects to the prejudice of good order and military discipline, all conduct of a nature to bring discredit upon the military service," etc.

Sounding almost paternal, Major Hopper tried to make it clear to the colonel that "courts-martial are courts of limited jurisdiction" and "operate under special rules set forth in the Articles of War." Since this court did not have the latitude of a civilian court, he explained, if a witness wouldn't invoke the 24th Article of War in refusing to answer, he was in violation of the 96th Article of War.

"Has the witness anything to say?" the president asked.

"I should like to have the court take a recess, please." It was another surprise.

"You have no basis for any such request," Leone ruled.

Major Smith tried to help, suggesting that Kilian might logically want to consult legal counsel, and if so he would have no objection to it.

"Do you desire to consult counsel?" asked the law member. "Is that the basis for your request?

"You continue by asking me questions, to force me. I have made a request for a recess."

"You must have a *basis* for it," the president explained.

"I wish to consult counsel," Kilian said, capitulating.

The president polled both the prosecution and the defense for any objection. Even Carroll, noting that the witness was not entitled to counsel, was nevertheless willing to go along. The president, "to assure the witness of the fair-mindedness of this court," declared a recess of one hour.

When he returned an hour later, Colonel Kilian told the court he had not meant to be evasive, and the answer to Major Hopper's question was "no." But it took several minutes of tedious argument to reduce his prolixity to that single word.

The colonel's verbose nit-picking continued to be a problem, even though the commandant had indicated he would now cooperate with the court. He was told dozens of times to give direct answers—to first say "yes" or "no," in answer to a question, and then explain. Instead, no matter what he was asked, however inconsequential the subject, he would make a diversionary speech, in the manner of Major Lo Buono's testimony. A typical exchange follows:

PROSECUTION (Captain Carroll): Lieutenant Colonel Norton was the adjutant during the period of time we have just referred to, was he not?

WITNESS: Colonel Norton was adjutant during that time. He was absent from the post for a period of time which I don't recollect without reference to the record.

PROSECUTION: Was he there as the duly appointed adjutant during that period of time?

WITNESS: He was a lieutenant colonel during that period of time, and the MOS [Military Occupational Specialty] I believe said he was the adjutant.

PROSECUTION: I move to strike that as not responsive.

LAW MEMBER: The proper answer when that question is asked is simply "yes." And it would save us time and confusion, and a great deal of difficulty—

WITNESS [interrupting]: Well, as far as that, he was adjutant, but he had gone at a particular time.

PROSECUTION: You weren't asked whether or not he was present.

WITNESS: There was an acting adjutant, and the way the trial judge advocate has been splitting hairs, it is necessary for me to be specific.

PROSECUTION: You can be specific by answering "yes" or "no."
WITNESS: He [Carroll] admitted he himself violated it in cross-questioning me, and I had to check him on that.
LAW MEMBER [wearily]: The court reporter will please read the question.
[The court reporter read the question.]
WITNESS: To the best of my recollection, yes. I haven't the order here which appointed him.
PROSECUTION: I move to strike the last part of that answer as not responsive to the question. We don't care about the order.
LAW MEMBER: That is sustained.

The technical quibbling went on and on. When Carroll asked him whether anyone was in the prison yard when he made his inspections, the colonel grumped, "There was no prison yard." When Carroll switched to calling the area "prison *grounds*," he answered the question.

Two hours later, apparently having forgotten his position, Colonel Kilian spoke of "the yard behind Guardhouse No. 3," distinguishing it from "other yards," including the "yard of Guardhouse No. 1," etc. Perhaps just to annoy the court and to slight Carroll, he seemed to avoid using the word "yes" even when giving direct affirmative answers, substituting "I did," "I had," "I think I was," "that is correct," or, usually, much longer speeches. And he probably got away with it because the court didn't want to take the additional time to argue with him.

Playing to beat Kilian at his own game, the assistant TJA's sarcasm offered a bit of comic relief when he asked the witness simply to identify his own initials on a document promoting then-second lieutenant Lo Buono to first lieutenant:

PROSECUTION: Are they your initials?
WITNESS: They appear to be mine.
PROSECUTION: Did you make them?
WITNESS: It is very similar to mine. I'm not a handwriting expert.
PROSECUTION: But to your best information and belief, and your best knowledge having to do with your lifelong experience with your own handwriting, you would say they were yours, would you not?
WITNESS: Yes, I'll accept that. [It was a rare "yes."]

PROSECUTION: Who was responsible for that promotion?
WITNESS: The depot commander was accountable for that.
PROSECUTION: And who was the depot commander?
WITNESS: I was.

But the humor was lost when Carroll asked the next question.

"So you were responsible for him being promoted from 2nd lieutenant to 1st lieutenant. Is that right?"

"Wrong."

Some members of the court groaned as they faced yet another technical debate—this one about whether a promotion was actually consummated at Lichfield, or whether it became effective after approval by the next higher headquarters, or the one above that, or in the U.S. Congress, or in the White House or wherever. Kilian may have have guessed that Carroll was leading up to inquiring about his famous warning to Lo Buono when he was coaching the provost marshal about his testimony: "I made you a major, and I'll hang you."

When the assistant prosecutor got into the subject of calisthenics, the colonel's memory seemed to fade abruptly. The conclusion of *Stars and Stripes* staff writer Ed Rosenthal's daily piece on the trial summarized the afternoon:

Throughout the day's session, Kilian stubbornly parried Carroll's relentless flow of questions, on several occasions making objections to giving replies.

Although testifying he had visited the prison at least 20 times from August 1, 1944 to January 18, 1945, Kilian claimed no knowledge of prison mistreatment.

The colonel had no explanation for testimony from both prosecution and defense witnesses, including the former post provost marshal and prison officers who had testified that their CO had ordered "rough treatment."

"We had no 'get rough' policy and I don't ever remember discussing a 'get rough' policy with anyone," Kilian said. He added that he had no recollection officially or unofficially about reports concerning beatings or allegations of beatings.[4]

Saturday was no better. The former commandant was questioned about his delegation of authority to Major Lo Buono and/or Captain Robertson, as Carroll sought to determine who had the authority to appoint a provost sergeant. The colonel wouldn't even admit that Sergeant Smith had been provost sergeant.

Carroll earned an admonition himself for badgering the witness and calling him names when he declared in exasperation, "This is the most dilatory witness who ever appeared before any court, and he is making a farce out of this trial by being deliberately evasive in his answers."

It may have been true, but the assistant trial judge advocate should not have said it on the record.

20

KILIAN BENDS

A breakthrough of sorts occurred on Monday, February 11th, when the commandant admitted that he had received an administrative reprimand after Colonel Swope's visit "in regard to the mistreatment of prisoners at the 10th Reinforcement Depot." The witness was asked to produce a copy of the document, and he promised to look for it, suggesting he might have have left it in the United States during his recent trip.[1]

Carroll questioned Kilian about his meetings at the Cumberland Hotel with various witnesses during the trial. Although the colonel didn't deny the meetings, he hedged about where they had taken place, avoiding an admission that they been in his room. Casting himself in the role of a fatherly adviser, he even admitted dictating some "suggestions" to Lieutenant Cubage, whom, he said, he had previously counseled to "just get on the witness stand and tell the truth."

"Lieutenant Cubage was so afraid of his shadow that after those things were written down, he tore them out of the little tablet and handed them to me. 'Here, keep this on your person. Don't even let it be around your room. Don't leave them laying around where anyone could get ahold of them.'" It was a somewhat different story than Cubage had told.

When Carroll asked why Cubage, Lo Buono, and others had returned to the witness stand and dramatically changed their stories under immunity from perjury, Kilian admitted:

"I am firmly convinced that the thing that had Lieutenant Cubage change his story was a little incident that occurred at the officers' club, where I am alleged to have threatened Major Lo Buono. And the next morning, Lieutenant Cubage appeared in my room at the Cumberland Hotel in a very excited condition. And his first remark to me was, 'My God, Colonel, why did you do it? Why did you do it? You spoiled everything.' And he went on along that line. He said, 'You never should have done it.'"

Focusing on the assistant prosecutor's question, the colonel made a statement that was received with skepticism by the audience in the courtroom—particularly by *Stars and Stripes* reporter Art White:

"My opinion at this time," Kilian announced, "is that there must have been something wrong at Lichfield that was definitely concealed from me, and when their hair began getting short, the people began to try to alibi. And you yourself have told me time after time they have passed the ball to the old man." The statement provided *The Stars and Stripes'* headline over Art White's column the next morning:

PRISON STAFF DUPED HIM, KILIAN SAYS[2]

Carroll then turned his attention to the personnel operating the guardhouses, asking if Lieutenant Cubage hadn't complained about being assigned personnel who were classified as "limited service because of their psycho-neurotic medical records."

Kilian granted that there had been some general discussions along that line, but because they had to send all "general service" personnel to combat units, the Manpower Board said "it was just too bad, because that's all we've got."

Carroll, leading up to an inquiry about Lieutenant Ennis, asked the colonel what he thought about Ennis's mental state: "He was not considered to be an exactly rational individual, was he?"

When Lieutenant Johnson objected on the grounds that Colonel Kilian was not an expert in mental health, and was sustained by the law member, the assistant TJA reworded his question:

"Let's put it like this: Didn't officers from time to time come to you and seek protection from threats by Lieutenant Ennis?"

A voice rang out from the spectators' gallery.

"If it please the court, I am not in this case, but I am here as counsel for Lieutenant Ennis in a case in which he is being charged, and I object to this question as not being proper or material in this case."

Astonished, Carroll turned around and looked out into the audience. A full colonel was on his feet in the midst of the spectators.

"This is not only an unusual procedure, but I think, in view of the colonel's statement, he should not even be in this courtroom," Carroll observed.

The president, caught off balance, finally managed to say, "I don't know the colonel."

Major Hopper addressed the new issue.

"An objection by a spectator to a question put by the prosecution is new to the experience of this court, and I think that it is so irregular and so entirely out of the way as to verge almost on contempt of court; and I will ask the president to request this particular spectator to withdraw."

The officer (Colonel Edward Chayes of the Antwerp Port Quartermaster Corps) sidled between the rows of chairs and left the courtroom. Recalled the next day and fined $100 for contempt of court, Hayes would be instructed by Colonel Leone "to absent yourself from the sittings of this court while it is still in force."

The sideshow allowed Colonel Kilian plenty of time to frame an answer to the assistant TJA's question. He readily admitted that Major Bluhm had complained about Ennis's threats and that, shortly afterward, Ennis was relieved of his duties as prison officer and left Lichfield.

Later in the day, Carroll asked the colonel about his calling the depot's unit battalion commanders together and telling them, "Any man missing the last roll call before a package shipment will be tried for desertion under the 58th Article of War," adding, "If I have to try these men by special court, they will get the maximum sentence of six full months."

To no one's surprise, Kilian denied making any such statement. But the question put the witness back on his guard and his quibble shield went up once again. The proceedings became an extended series of picky, inconsequential arguments over semantic nuances. As the colonel continued to squirm under Carroll's relentless cross-examination, he began to show the stress he was under. Beads of perspiration dotted his flushed face.

When Colonel Leone finally called for the court's afternoon recess, he permitted it to last more than half an hour to let the witness calm down. But when the session resumed at 4:30 P.M., Captain Carroll showed no mercy. Inquiring about some of the uglier accusations that had been made against the commandant in earlier testimony by Lieutenant Cubage, the assistant prosecutor asked about General Prisoner Joseph Brett being shot in the leg by guards near the rifle range. The colonel was obviously familiar with Cubage's testimony about the incident, and he attempted to parry the question.

"I don't know *where* it was. I know that a statement was made that a man was shot through the leg, and that I am supposed to have made the remark, 'Make that man a sergeant.'"

"Directing your attention to the rifle range," Carroll requested, "we'll see if there isn't another little episode in connection with that on which we can refresh your memory."

He went on to describe "a six foot three inch blond prisoner by the name of King that Lieutenant Cubage wished to send to a Disciplinary Training Center because he didn't have sufficient personnel to be able to give him proper discipline. "Reading from Cubage's testimony, Carroll asked if the colonel remembered replying, "'Well, that prisoner will not be sent to a DTC. He will be punished, and punished severely in this guardhouse. We can be just as tough as any DTC.'

"Do you remember that conversation?"

"I do not." The witness was tight-lipped.

"Do you you remember saying, 'In a case like this, I know what I would do. I would take him down where no one could see him,' and

Colonel Aldridge joining in and saying, 'That's right, where no one could see him,' and then your saying, 'And *just don't break too many bones.'* Do you remember that conversation?"

The witness's beet-red countenance darkened to purple as Carroll put his own dramatic inflection on the words. Veins stood out in the colonel's forehead as his blood pressure mounted.

"I do not," he gasped.

"Do you remember saying anything like that to Lieutenant Cubage?"

"I don't remember that conversation." Kilian's voice was hoarse.

"In other words, you *might* have had that conversation, and it just slipped your memory; is that right?"

"No! I don't agree with you on that. I don't remember that conversation."

Carroll refused to let it go, forcing the witness to deny the words again and again, then switching to an incident "when a prisoner was shot at [through a window] and got some glass in his eye." The colonel didn't remember that one either. But how, Carroll asked, could he not remember it? Hadn't an IG inspector been sent to Lichfield to investigate the incident? The colonel trapped himself with a quibbling answer.

"He wasn't an IG inspector," Kilian corrected. "His name was Rudelius; and Colonel Rudelius was from the Ground Force Replacement Center in Cheltenham."

Well, then, the commandant should remember calling Major Lo Buono and going upstairs inside Guardhouse No. 2 with the provost marshal, Captain Allen, and Lieutenant Cubage, to escort Colonel Rudelius around while he made his investigation of the incident. But the witness didn't remember, he said.

Carroll bore down. Did Kilian remember asking Colonel Rudelius whether this was an "official visit," and being relieved to hear him say, "This is unofficial"? Did he remember asking Captain Allen or Major Lo Buono what the marksman's rank was, and saying, "Make that man a corporal"? He did not.

"Do you remember his [Rudelius's] saying, 'If it had been official I would have brought my stenographer with me,' and then both of you laughed? Do you remember that?"

He didn't remember that, the witness said, but he did "remember that Rudelius came up to the depot, made an investigation, went back to Cheltenham, and that later a report came up."

Carroll's detective work had obviously been wide and deep in its scope. He forced the colonel to deny that a General Matchett had criticized his policy of keeping men in the guardhouse for several months awaiting court-martial under the 58th Article of War. But then the colonel had to admit that he had changed the policy after the general's visit. The change in policy had taken place all right, he said, but it had nothing to do with the general's visit.

Carroll then returned to the notes made by Lieutenant Cubage—notes which the prison officer had entrusted to Kilian for safekeeping.

"You have a piece of paper in your own possession upon which Lieutenant Cubage wrote, have you not?" It was the same device with which Carroll had ensnared Lieutenant Colonel Hummell.

"I have some of them," the colonel admitted.

"Have you got some with you now? Will you look in your pocket and see whether you have?"

The witness sat there, looking trapped.

"I will reserve that right," he finally said. "I will go outside and look them over and I will tell you that."

Carroll turned toward the long table with the row of officers sitting behind it. "I want the court to ask this witness whether or not he has in his possession any papers on which Lieutenant Cubage wrote down notes."

"If you have them," Major Hopper told the colonel, "they would be subject to the government through subpoena. It shouldn't be necessary to issue a subpoena. The request would be that you should lend them."

Ignoring Carroll, the colonel spoke to the law member directly. "I think that I have in my pocket a few notes that Lieutenant Cubage made, yes." The assistant prosecutor broke in:

"Those were notes put down in Lieutenant Cubage's own hand-writing?"

"That is correct."

"May I see them?"

"Is it necessary for me to turn my personal notes over?" the colonel asked plaintively. "I haven't attempted to use them in any way in this court to refresh my memory or anything else. They are *personal* records."

"They are available to the government if they are material to the issue" was Carroll's unrelenting response.

The witness gave in. With great reluctance, he withdrew several pieces of paper from the breast pocket of his blouse. He handed two of them to Captain Carroll after arguing successfully that only the two notes he handed to the assistant prosecutor were in Lieutenant Cubage's handwriting. The one he retained was in his own handwriting.

Carroll had the small pieces of paper marked for identification as prosecution exhibits 48A and 48B. They had been written by Cubage in his room at the Cumberland, Kilian eventually disclosed, and he had dictated them. Carroll read them into the court record. Several were quotations (with dates noted) of intemperate remarks Carroll had made at the London Officers' Club, including "I am getting out of practice. It used to take me two hours to break a fellow, and now it takes two days. In another day or two I will have Lo Buono where I want him. That Lo Buono will say anything I want him to." And, taunting Kilian, "You are certainly in a unique position. I am trying you, yet you are not present in court and cannot defend yourself."

Other items were examples of what the colonel believed were at-tempts to "get" him. One seemed a little silly:

"Girl was eavesdropping in a room next to Colonel Kilian's room, being Carroll's room. Girl was fully dressed without shoes." [Those familiar with Earl Carroll's reputation would not have drawn the same conclusion about why the girl was in the assistant prosecutor's room.]

While Carroll questioned the embarrassed Kilian about each note before going on to the next, the last one caused a stir in the court-room:

"The president and the law member were in consultation with the staff judge advocate for thirty minutes before this court convened. The staff judge advocate has been in frequent consultation with the trial judge advocate and various members of the court."

This last entry, Colonel Kilian said, had been "a rumor." He gave a number of awkward answers to Carroll's hounding him about why he would have a "rumor" reduced to writing by Lieutenant Cubage.

In conclusion, Carroll asked the former commandant several times whether his notes did not in fact indicate that he was bent on accumulating evidence to produce a mistrial. It was a motive that Colonial Kilian repeatedly denied.

21

FINAL SHOTS

Wednesday, February 13th, 1946, was the last day of testimony by former Lichfield commandant, Colonel James A. Kilian, and the last day of the trial, except for summations by the prosecution and the defense, and deliberation by the court.

Captain Carroll asked the witness if his "mutual defense" strategy was motivated by his hoping to reduce the possibility of his being tried himself.

"I *was* in the frame of mind that I might some time be a defendant, yes," the colonel admitted. "If these men were all found guilty, there was no question about it.

"I recall a statement to the effect that the prosecution would have to take each hurdle as they came to it," the witness added. "That way there are going to be separate trials. Like in the football season, the prosecution would have to take every hurdle as they came to it."[1]

Kilian's line kindled the showman in Carroll, who, as he asked his next question, idly grabbed a handful of pencils off the prosecution counsels' table that he and Major Smith shared.

"You told Lieutenant Cubage that the prosecution would have to take each hurdle as they came to it. Is that it?"

As he said the words, Carroll was laying down the pencils on a small table adjacent to the witness chair, creating a series of miniature parallel hurdles.

"I did," the witness answered, with obvious disdain for the visual aid illustrating the assistant prosecutor's question.

"Of course," Carroll continued, "if the prosecution stumbled on any of the hurdles along the line, that would protect the last fellow at the end of the hurdles." As he said it, Carroll laid a bright red pencil at the end of the row. The visual pun was not lost on the audience, since the color of the colonel's face was a close match.

"No," the witness answered, looking away from the interrogator's array and suddenly facing Carroll with just the hint of a smile.

"But it had a good chance, didn't it?"

The defiant smile vanished as Kilian thoughtfully regarded Carroll's hurdles.

"Regardless of whether these men be acquitted or not," the colonel observed, "I think there is still a strong possibility that I will have to stand trial."

"I am going to enter an objection to this opinion coming in," Lieutenant Johnson interrupted, "as to whether, if Sergeant Smith is acquitted, or if he is found guilty, Colonel Kilian or anybody else is going to be tried at the end of this. I think it borders on an attempt, whether it is intentional or not, to influence the court in a certain manner, and I object to it."

The objection precipitated a lengthy legal wrangle between the prosecution, the defense, and the law member. Joining in the discussion, Colonel Kilian made a statement that pointed up the increasing politicization of the trial:

"In my opinion, the result of this trial, or whether or not any of these men are tried, *doesn't* affect the fact of whether or not I might have to stand trial. As you [Carroll] yourself have said, this case cannot possibly help but be investigated by Congress—"

Carroll interrupted, having invited a comment he didn't want the court—or the court reporter or the newsmen in the audience—to hear, and he moved to have Kilian's statement stricken. But the law member overruled him and invited the witness to complete his statement.

"This case cannot possibly help but be investigated by Congress," the former commandant continued. "In fact, you [Carroll] told me that there was a separate record being prepared in this case for Congress."

The colonel was quoted the next day in *The Stars and Stripes:* "I'm not kidding myself. If Sergeant Smith is found guilty, I expect to be tried."[2]

For the next several hours, Carroll seemed to be conducting his own trial of Colonel Kilian, charging him not only with deliberately creating the climate that led to the mistreatment of prisoners at Lichfield, but also with mounting an elaborate scheme to create a mistrial in the case of Sergeant Judson Smith. His mock trial exhausted everyone, leading to frequent objections by the defense and admonitions by the court.

When the other members of the court finally took over the questioning, the commandant offered an interesting statistic as he sought to describe the stress imposed on the Lichfield cadre who operated the guardhouses after D-Day. They had received, he said, no less than two thousand replacements from the United States "who were the refuse sweepings from all the guardhouses on the Atlantic Coast," and at one time "the total number of people absent without leave in the [European] theater constituted almost a division."

Nevertheless, the colonel refused to admit he had ever instructed Lieutenant Ennis or Captain Robertson or anyone else that they "could get as rough as you want" with guardhouse prisoners.

Well, almost never. Actually, it was possible, he said, that at "some social event" in speaking with Captain Robertson he might have said something that could have been "misinterpreted." There was, Kilian admitted, "the possibility of a chance remark.

"Yes, I'll say that. I'll go all the way and get it over quick and say it is possible I made a remark to that effect. I wouldn't think he would approach me on such a subject under these conditions. I know I wouldn't. I would have thought 'Who the devil is this Robertson coming to me at a *tea party'*—or luncheon or whatever it was. I must have had something particular in mind and he may have said something. Maybe he didn't explain to me such as he would under normal conditions, and maybe I said 'yes.'"

Following the confused statement, which sounded like an acknowledgement of culpability, when Carroll pursued the possibility that something similar might have happened in a conversation with Major Lo Buono, the colonel seemed even more forthcoming:

"Yes, that might be true. Major Lo Buono might have been talking with me about someone in the guardhouse. Major Lo Buono had a big job there as military police officer and provost marshal of the surrounding towns; and we might have been talking about the men in town or somewhere or other, and I might have made the remark, 'We'll just have to tighten up,' or words to that effect."

"You might have said in connection with that particular thing the words 'tougher,' or 'rougher'? Isn't that correct?"

"Yes, there is a possibility."

At last, after the members of the court had their turn, Colonel Leone polled the defense and the prosecution to inquire if they had any final questions before dismissing the witness.

"No, I think that's about all," Carroll said with a twinkle in his eye. Fifty-five days had elapsed since the trial began on December 3rd, 1945—more than a year after the first accusing letters had been published in the "B-Bag" column of *The Stars and Stripes.* The trial by now had accumulated fourteen volumes of exhibits and testimony—nearly four thousand pages of court reporters' transcriptions containing more than 2.5 million words for the court to consult during its deliberations.

22

SUMMATIONS

On Thursday morning, February 14, Major Smith's summation for the prosecution lasted about an hour. After noting the dramatic change in the testimony of various witnesses after the truth emerged, the prosecutor dutifully called attention to specific pieces of evidence produced during trial testimony—evidence which he believed was sufficient to prove most of the charges and specifications of record against the accused. But then he treated what he believed was the bigger issue raised by this trial:[1]

"If men are to be acquitted because they were given orders, then we are entitled to know what the orders were, who issued them, and what was their source. Each witness as he took the stand has been willing at some time to say what others did, but with the exception of Lieutenant Ennis and Sergeant Smith, none has ever been willing to say what he did himself, either when it came to issuing orders or doing anything with reference to the mistreatment of prisoners.

"They have hidden that right from the start, and I think that that matter of hiding, scheming, designing and deceiving the IG investigators and other courts has a bearing here upon the question of whether the accused was openly and in a straightforward manner [merely] following orders."

Major Smith said he had been giving a lot of thought to the familiar Nürnberg defense, and he had done considerable research on the subject, but he had not found the standard writings on military law very helpful.

The section in Winthrop's *Military Law and Precedents* entitled "Obedience to Orders," for example, stated, on the one hand, "To constitute a defense, an order must be a legal one . . . must emanate from a proper officer, a superior authorized to give it, and it must command a thing not in itself unlawful or prohibited by law."

On the other hand, the same book said, "Obedience by inferiors is the fundamental principle of the military service." And, indeed, "For the inferior to assume to determine the question of the lawfulness of an order given him by a superior would, of itself, as a general rule, amount to insubordination, and such an assumption carried into practice would subvert military discipline."

"You can search through as many authorities as you please," Smith said, "and you won't find any satisfactory cut-and-dried decision saying, 'Well, if you get an order and you follow it, that's a good defense.'"

But the TJA believed he had sorted it out. He declared that the *circumstances under which an order is given* make all the difference.

"It depends on who is giving the order, and what the circumstances are—what is the degree of emergency, and all those things. If you are in the front line or in a great emergency and someone gives an order, 'Shoot that man,' and the man shoots him, there is no time for consideration; there is no time for thought; there is a very apparent emergency, and undoubtedly it would constitute a good defense even though the order might be absolutely illegal, and the act absolutely illegal. It would depend on the circumstances."

Such was not the case in the performance of those illegal acts which were committed at Lichfield, Smith declared.

"It bears on the matter of good faith. We have to admit that if an order was given to whip and beat these men it was an illegal order." And the officers and NCOs to whom it was issued obviously knew it was illegal, he said.

"The attempt to hide and conceal—hiding witnesses from the IGs, whipping men at night (and in semiprivate places like latrines), using the term, 'don't let anyone see you,' speaking of the affairs after they had happened as 'parties' ('they had a *"party"* last night')—there was nothing straightforward or honest about that. I submit to the court that everything about it indicates to me that everyone who had anything to do with these transactions knew that they were acting illegally. And while the surrounding circumstances and attitude of those in authority condoned it, everyone knew, I submit, that it was wrong. And, under those circumstances at least, you can't protect yourself by saying, 'I did it on orders.'"

Indeed, Smith said, the conspiracy of the witnesses to lie during the first part of the trial reinforced his argument. But then he added, "With the emergency that existed in the army in December, 1944, it is easy for me to see how Sergeant Smith could do these things and how the other guards would do them, and if they were done as I believe they were, under these circumstances, then they constitute *circumstances of extenuation* of the very highest order.

"There is a difference between extenuation and defense, and that is the point I want to make. The court should consider it is one thing to vote a man guilty or not guilty, and it is another thing when it comes to deciding what the penalty should be.

"But, in conclusion, I think not only is there sufficient evidence to support conviction, but it is clear and convincing and constitutes proof beyond all reasonable doubt."

It was a persuasive summation.

After the court took its morning recess, Major Smith asked the court's indulgence to read into the record a precedent from the *Digest of Opinions of the Judge Advocate General of the Army,* Volume 1912–40: "An officer of the guard who permits and encourages unlawful striking and beating of prisoners in the guardhouse is not relieved from responsibility by the fact that he committed and authorized such acts under the direction of his superior officers, since his orders to enforce prison discipline by beating prisoners were clearly in violation of the law and usages of military service (Court-Martial 118428, 1918)."

In his defense summation, Lieutenant Johnson found substantial precedent on the other side. He also read from the Winthrop reference, then quoted Secretary of War Conrad:

"An inferior should act upon the reasonable presumption that his superior was authorized to issue an order which he *might* be authorized to issue. If he acts otherwise, he does so at his peril, and subjects himself to the risk of being punished for disobedience of orders." And again, from the same reference: "For the inferior to assume to determine the question of the lawfulness of an order given him by a superior would of itself, as a general rule, amount to insubordination and an assumption that, carried into practice, would subvert military discipline."

Johnson then quoted the United States Attorney General in a similar case: "It is not for the subordinate officer who receives it to judge the fitness or legality of such order."

Perhaps the defense counsel's most persuasive citation came from a justice of the United States Supreme Court reviewing the case of a navy man. It highlighted the issue that would become the compelling theme of two popular plays written a few years after World War II, *The Caine Mutiny* and *The Caine Mutiny Court-Martial:*

"There would be an end of all discipline if the seamen and marines on board a ship of war on a distant service were permitted to act upon their own opinion of their rights, and to throw off the authority of the commander whenever they supposed it to be unlawfully exercised."

Johnson added a brief quotation directed toward the branch of service conducting this trial: "'That his command must be lawful and *reasonable* could scarcely be accepted as good law for the army.'"

Moving beyond legal considerations, the defense counsel asked the court to examine the reasonable expectation that Sergeant Smith could have been expected to thoughtfully refuse to carry out the orders he received. Here was a man, he said, deliberately chosen by the Lichfield command for his guardhouse assignment because of his limited education and limited intelligence—a loyal NCO with ten years of Regular Army service who could be expected to carry out orders to the letter. Was it reasonable to expect that he would have risked court-martial by refusing to obey his officers after evaluating their orders?

More to the point, could he be expected to refuse a man of Ennis's temperament after, for example, the officer had ordered him *twice* to work Sims over?

The defense counsel concluded his summation with a personal appeal. He asked the court to just *look* at the accused to see the physical and mental strain he has been under.

"If there are not three members of this court who will enter a finding of 'not guilty' in respect to these charges, I, like the sergeant who said he had lost his faith in the army by the refusal of his officers to come forward, will lose my faith in human nature."

Lieutenant Johnson seemed to have grown from his trial experience.

Colonel Leone, president of the court, then asked if Captain Carroll had "anything further in final argument to present to the court."

"Yes, sir, I have," Carroll responded. Initially he wanted to clear up such housekeeping items as whether the transcribed trial record, unchecked for errors at this time, could be available during deliberation by the court. But then he turned to more substantive matters. Using the time that would usually have been reserved to rebut the defense's summation, he began a speech that showed sensitivity to the predicament of an accused trapped in the web of a chain of command that denied its responsibility. Carroll then addressed what he believed was the deep-rooted malignancy that infected Lichfield.

"I think that not only was there a condition existing at Lichfield wherein this accused, Sergeant Smith, was given orders that certainly went to the mistreatment of prisoners, but I think it should be clear to this court that there was a deliberate attempt upon the part of officers . . . who were responsible for this condition to perpetrate a fraud upon this court. I think that by the fact that they attempted to perpetrate that fraud in what has developed into one of the worst cases of mass perjury that I believe has ever been committed before any court, they have thereby verified that *they* were responsible parties for that system of mistreatment of American troops who passed through this 10th Reinforcement Depot.

"I believe that this court, after it has concluded with Sergeant Smith's case, should give serious consideration to notifying the proper authorities as to the extent of the guilt and the extent of the participation of these high ranking officers. . . . We know that both civilian law and the military law in the form of army regulations imposes the responsibility for this mistreatment upon the commanding officer, Colonel Kilian." He added parenthetically that "a major part of that responsibility" should be born by the commandant's adjutants, whom, he told his audience, should have been brought before the court as witnesses.

Then, in his own distinctive style, Carroll presented a bill of particulars that went well beyond the case of Sergeant Smith.

"Major Lo Buono," he said, "came before this court. . . . [He] was given awards of promotion that raised him from a second lieutenant to a major. . . . Major Lo Buono, despite his own characterization of himself as some sort of glorified guide, was in truth and in fact the provost marshal. He had a very direct responsibility. In his attempts to evade that responsibility by evasive testimony, I think he only succeeded in more clearly affirming his guilt and his knowledge of the mistreatment of prisoners. . . .

"Then there is Major Bluhm. Major Bluhm [post inspector] has attempted to portray himself before this court as some sort of an innocent six-day bicycle rider. Actually, Major Bluhm could not have ridden his bicycle in the places in which he said that he rode at the times when he said that he rode there without being knocked over by the very acts of mistreatment which have been testified to by witness after witness before this court. Bluhm was the eyes and ears of Colonel Kilian. . . . There is the testimony (and, incidentally, it is the only uncontradicted testimony in this case) that he participated in the systematic scheme of falsification of testimony ever since some time in 1944 . . .

"I now come to Captain Robertson. Captain Robertson has come before the court and he has attempted to tell us he occupied a paper position as the commanding officer of 316th Prison Company. We would have to be gullible indeed to believe that Captain Robertson was not himself part and parcel of the entire system to get rough with American troops, and those boys who were unfortunate enough to have landed in the prison stockade at the 10th Replacement Depot. . . .

"There are two other officers of lesser grade to whom Sergeant Smith had to look directly for authorization of his acts. Let me deal with Lieutenant Cubage first. That Lieutenant Cubage was the police and prison officer in charge of the guardhouse [for over a year] is his own testimony, and it is the testimony of every witness without exception before this court—save that of the commanding officer, Colonel Kilian. The one man who is charged with the responsibility of knowing who the prison officer was does not know who he was.

"It is quite obvious why he doesn't want to know who the prison officer was. The motive, the reason, the bias, or the prejudice of Colonel Kilian is apparent, because we have a prison officer who has testified that he gave direct orders to the accused, Sergeant Smith, and that he received those orders from Colonel Kilian."

If this seemed a mild reproof of Lieutenant Cubage, one that seemed to ricochet off him to indict Colonel Kilian, Carroll's final particular, actually in support of the least likely officer in the Lichfield chain of command, was even more surprising.

"Now I come to Lieutenant Ennis. Lieutenant Ennis is, I think, the finest example of what happened when the 316th Prison Company took over. I think that we have embodied in witness Ennis everything that was embodied in the type of man and the character of the men who were placed in that guardhouse at some time around the middle of October, 1944.

"Lieutenant Ennis admitted that he handled prisoners roughly. I believe that Lieutenant Ennis lied when he said that he did not directly beat prisoners. That is my own personal belief. But I also believe that he "lied like a general," if there is such a phrase. I think he can be forgiven for that, because, after all, Lieutenant Ennis did not have to testify to things that would incriminate himself. But he certainly did not lie when he assumed the responsibility—and he was the *only* officer who *did* assume responsibility—of giving Sergeant Smith a direct order to beat these prisoners with a club, or to strike them. He is the only officer who has had the courage to say, 'Yes, I told Sergeant Smith to do it!'

"The government started to impeach Sergeant Smith on a little issue of whether or not a brick was loose. That loose brick and the falsification of that one small item, that one chink in the wall that had been built up of perjury and falsification and deceit—that entire wall crumbled. It was the responsibility of Colonel Kilian, Major Bluhm, Major Lo Buono, and Captain Robertson for [erecting] that wall of deceit."

Finally, turning toward Judson Smith as he spoke, Captain Carroll told the court, "It certainly is our duty as officers, and certainly our duty as American citizens, to give this boy a fair trial. In awarding punishment or in judging, we certainly ought to take into consideration just how much of this responsibility is on his shoulders."

His accusations against the Lichfield officers, Carroll told the court, "should not receive consideration in your determination of the guilt or innocence of Sergeant Smith as to the commission of the acts with which he stands charged. . . . But it has a great deal to do with what kind of *sentence* you propose to place upon Sergeant Smith's shoulders if you do find him guilty."

Earl Carroll couldn't let it go at that without setting in motion the series of events that would occupy the army for months to come:

"We also want this court to know that it has the right to recommend that the people who are properly responsible for these acts shall be brought to justice. It is the position of the prosecution that there is no better body of men more able to make that recommendation, based on their own personal knowledge, than the members of this court. And so, in your final deliberations, the prosecution asks you, when you have concluded with the case of Sergeant Smith, to make what recommendations you deem fit and proper in connection with those men who have been responsible for creating this unprecedented condition that confronted you in the trial of this case of Sergeant Smith."

The court was closed for its deliberations.

23

FINDINGS

Sergeant Smith would spend two restless nights in his cell awaiting the verdict. The court was closed all day Friday. On Saturday, February 16th, Colonel Leone announced that it had reached a verdict after nine hours of deliberation. Actually, the court had reached a series of verdicts. Smith was found guilty on almost half of the counts in the charges and specifications. (Detailed findings are listed in Appendix A.) *Stars and Stripes* staff writer Art Smith simplified the findings for the Sunday edition of the newspaper:

Smith was convicted of felonious assault and striking prisoners, but the court found that "in all the assault cases except one, Smith acted in accordance with orders on an established policy from his superior officers, and this was considered in mitigation."

Moreover, the president of the court, Colonel Louis P. Leone, announced that Smith was found not guilty on five specific counts, including making men stand with nose and toes against the wall and double-timing prisoners "because he acted in accordance with orders apparently regular and lawful on their face and was, according to their terms, entitled to obey them."[1]

Despite the court's recognition of the extenuating circumstances in the case, the punishment it specified was not lenient. Smith was sentenced to three years of hard labor, forfeiting all pay and allowances; and, after completing his prison term, he was to be dishonorably discharged from the army.

When reviewed by the London area commander, who by this time had reverted to his prewar permanent rank, now-Colonel Claude M. Thiele disapproved and vacated the court's guilty finding on several of the charges and specifications, but he let Smith's sentence stand and designated the Würzburg (Germany) Disciplinary Training Center as his place of confinement. Ironically, this DTC was exactly the kind of facility to which Lieutenant Cubage had wanted to send his incorrigible prisoner, King.

During his review of the case, Thiele also approved the sentence of Colonel Edward Chayes, who had received a reprimand for contempt after interrupting the court with an "objection" from the gallery, but remitted his fine. Ennis's counsel got his $100 back.

In his official actions, Colonel Thiele had followed the recommendations of his London area staff judge advocate, Major Richard D. Kearney, to the letter. In his twenty-nine-page review of the case, Kearney made some remarkably candid observations, concluding with "the alleged machinations of one Colonel James A. Kilian":

Oftimes the best view is obtained by those at a distance, and so it may have been in the trial of accused, Sgt. Judson H. Smith. Perhaps it was that "lowly Sergeant Smith became almost a forgotten man at his own trial," (*Time* 13 January 1946, pp. 7–8) for "there were others besides Judson Smith facing trial. The U.S. Army was on trial." (*Time* 31 December 1945, pp. 8–9).

The proceedings were more than a trial: they were proceedings wherein the prosecution became investigators and the court became a grand jury. Under the guise of impeachment and whatnot, it would appear that every phase of and every incident occurring at or in the vicinity of the 10th Replacement Depot was probed. . . .

Kilian's examination reflects little credit upon Kilian, the assistant trial judge advocate, or the court. Denied counsel and sometimes the right of objection, Kilian proved so recalcitrant a witness that it became necessary for the court to prefer contempt proceedings against him. By and large, his examination was little more than a feud between Kilian and the assistant trial judge advocate. At one point it became necessary for the defense counsel to observe that "It is up to some member of this court to preserve a sense of dignity and to keep the witness and the trial judge advocate from arguing with each other.". . .

The prosecution's conduct of the case was most unusual. Perhaps, as was charged, it used "every trick in the bag.". . . . [But] for much of what the prosecution did there was justification. The accused saw fit to have presented in his behalf a mass of perjured evidence. Sensing this, the prosecution staked its all on exposing the mass perjury. It probed, quilled, grilled, threatened, harangued, harassed, implied and impeached until, in the end, it prevailed and exposed the original defense evidence to have been, in the main, sheer fabrication designed not only to inure the benefit of the accused, but also to the benefit of other witnesses. Had it failed, any findings of guilty would have had to be disapproved.

But it did not fail. Instead it prevailed so completely that the accused changed his defense and adopted the prosecution's premise. . . . The defense repudiated its original contention that all was well at the 10th Reinforcement Depot prison, admitted that mistreatment was rampant and, in justification or mitigation, contended that any misconduct on the part of the accused was authorized by and done pursuant to the orders of the accused's superior officers. . . .

Certainly much inadmissible testimony was admitted. Too often the innocence or guilt of the accused became merely incidental. The conclusion is that the prosecution was laying the foundations for prosecutions to follow.[2]

On the final day of trial, Carroll confirmed that this had, indeed, been his objective. After the verdict and sentence were announced, he made one last appeal that the court recommend to its appointing authority that charges be prepared against the officers "properly responsible" for the acts of mistreatment at Lichfield.

Carroll got his way. Charges were recommended by the court and forwarded to the staff judge advocate, London area office, including a count of conspiracy.

One month later, on March 22nd, Major Richard Kearney announced that Colonel Kilian and five of his officers had been formally charged "jointly and in conjunction with various enlisted men who were formerly guards at the [Lichfield] depot guardhouses with having conspired to inflict cruel, unusual and unauthorized punishment on prisoners."

The other officers charged were Major Bluhm, Major Lo Buono, Captain Robertson, Lieutenant Ennis, and Lieutenant Cubage.

Major Kearney told *The Stars and Stripes* that an attempt was being made to locate former Lichfield executive officer Colonel Alfred

Aldridge (who had received a series of promotions from Kilian, going from second lieutenant to lieutenant colonel during his relatively brief term of office). Aldridge had returned to the United States, Kearney said, but the War Department "has been requested to determine whether he will be returned to this theater for trial with the other officers."[3]

As the army began scheduling multiple courts-martial, the press on both sides of the Atlantic was making plans to cover them—to the army's chagrin. The army would try to muzzle its own GI-edited *Stars and Stripes* and would attempt to escape the stateside press by moving the trials to the Continent. Tempers would flare and court members would resign in protest. It would be a long, hot summer.

AFTERMATH

The first week in April, 1946, Under Secretary of War Kenneth C. Royall, who had just returned from a personal inspection tour of the European theater, announced that "the required statutory investigation of [Lichfield] officers involved will be completed within 10 days."[1] Which officers would face charges had not yet been decided, however. Meanwhile, the court-martial of another former jailer, Staff Sergeant James M. Jones of Muskogee, Oklahoma, had already begun, in an annex of London's Selfridge department store. A *Newsweek* reporter found significance in a sign still attached to a rafter of the building: "EVERY HOUR ONE SEES SOMETHING NEW IN THIS SALES ROOM."[2]

Like Sergeant Smith before him, Staff Sergeant Jones soon began to slip into the background at his own trial. In what stateside media headlined as "LICHFIELD FIREWORKS," Earl Carroll asked to be relieved from further duty as assistant trial judge advocate, because of "flagrant mishandling of the trial." With his resignation, he also submitted a seven-page letter detailing his complaints. It was immediately classified.

Less than pleased with Carroll's turning the first trial inside out, the army's London Headquarters was delighted to comply with his request. In accepting his resignation, the army forbade him to discuss the trial with the press. Carroll's letter, however, was leaked at once.

It charged that higher echelons, "who wanted to whitewash the officers involved," had offered the enlisted men sentences from one year to a maximum of thirty months if they pleaded guilty.

Liberated from censorship by their publication in other media (but without a byline), *The Stars and Stripes* quoted other sensational items from the document "confirmed to be Carroll's by unquestionable sources." According to the published reports, the letter said that prosecution witnesses, mostly former occupants of the Lichfield guardhouses, had been kept locked up in an old London jail since December and paid irregularly or not at all. They were poorly fed, the document claimed, badly mistreated, and living from hand to mouth. Some had escaped, while the rest just "wanted to get out of the whole business." In addition, Carroll's letter said, "important witnesses were unavailable."[3]

Major Leland Smith, who had had no stomach for the first trial, thought Carroll had an excellent idea, and submitted his own resignation. It was rejected. He would stay on as trial judge advocate in the Jones trial. Hearing of the turmoil, five-star General Dwight D. Eisenhower, formerly supreme commander of Allied Expeditionary Forces in Europe and now army chief of staff, ordered an immediate investigation of Carroll's charges. The April 4th edition of *The Stars and Stripes* carried a banner headline: "IKE ORDERS LICHFIELD PROBE AS CARROLL QUITS."[4]

From his European Theater Headquarters in Frankfurt, Germany, General Joseph T. McNarney announced that he would comply with Ike's order at once, and also said that Carroll's resignation would not delay the remaining trials.

Meanwhile, Lieutenant Frank Johnson had become Sergeant Jones's defense counsel, with a new partner, 1st Lieutenant Morris Clinton McGee of Alabama—whom Jones had asked for and who was brought over from the Continent at the defendant's request. McGee and Carroll had earlier formed a popular defense team when they were without assignment after VE Day, volunteering their services to GIs serving in Europe who had gotten themselves into trouble. The team had won twenty-three acquittals. After Carroll announced his own departure, it was not difficult to guess where the suggestion of Jones's request for McGee came from.

The army structured this second court-martial much more carefully than it had the trial of Judson Smith. It had assigned a new president, Colonel Paul C. Cole, who had a reputation for being a tough chief justice. Using a peremptory challenge in a strategic move that may have been orchestrated by his former partner, McGee had Cole dismissed. The president was replaced by Colonel Buhl Moore.

The law member, Major Benito Gaguine, was challenged by Lieutenant Johnson on the second day of the trial. After a fractious morning, the defense counsel charged that "he has taken a pleasure and delight in overruling us without apparent deliberation." During questioning of the first witness, "the law member proved he is prejudiced and biased," Johnson claimed. While the defense was questioning Major Richard Kearney, London Area Staff Judge Advocate, Gaguine several times interrupted the interrogation and took over the questioning. Moreover, Johnson told the court that Gaguine, after overruling the defense lawyers, frequently looked over at them and "leered."

Johnson petitioned the court for Gaguine's removal, but Gaguine protested, claiming that he was not prejudiced toward the accused, that his rulings had been made to the best of his legal ability, and that his questions to Kearney were meant "to clarify points not brought out by the defense."

The court rejected Johnson's challenge of Gaguine.

Earlier in the day, there had been a confrontation between Major Gaguine and Lieutenant McGee. McGee had asked Kearney if he knew that, at the request of General Eisenhower, the army was investigating whether Lichfield officers were being protected by scheduling the trials of enlisted men first. Gaguine told the assistant defense counsel that his question was 'irrelevant.'

"Do not pursue that line of questioning," he commanded.

McGee protested the order.

"I have ruled!" Gaguine declared, interrupting the assistant defense counsel.

"I'll quit *now,*" said McGee, throwing up his hands. "You run the case." The exchange made *The Stars and Stripes.*[5]

Colonel Buhl Moore, president of the court, abruptly called a recess—after which McGee continued to present his case.

Having gained experience in the Smith trial, and now with Morris McGee as a partner, Frank Johnson began operating much like Earl Carroll. He challenged the jurisdiction of the court and said he believed that if Sergeant Jones' trial remained in London his client could not get a fair trial. He charged that a Major Scott Jordon, sent to London to "expedite" the proceedings, was offering the guards a deal to plead guilty.

Johnson wanted to subpoena no less an authority than Major General John T. Lewis, then commander of the Western Base Section, as a defense witness, as well as his staff judge advocate, Colonel C. E. Brand. The defense counsel alleged that General Lewis, while General Thiele's superior, had actively participated in the Smith trial, and had since dispatched Colonel Brand to offer "a proposition" to Jones if he would plead guilty.

Johnson's requests produced a major flap. On the witness stand, Major Kearney admitted he had told Lieutenant Johnson that it "would be unwise and dangerous" to bring General Lewis and other high-ranking officers into the case, but he denied that, as London area trial judge advocate, he had been instructed "to railroad the enlisted men" or "to whitewash the officers."

The defense's insistence on calling General Lewis deadlocked the court. Colonel Moore brought Lieutenant Johnson to his feet when he referred to "the apparent stubbornness of the defense." When Johnson protested the remark, the president warned the defense counsel about his conduct.

"You realize that if these witnesses are called and you fail to confirm your point about the order of testimony of the witnesses, you can be charged with a trivial defense." Colonel Moore advised the defense counsels to go ahead with available witnesses, and to call the officers they sought only if evidence showed their testimony was necessary.

To his credit, Major Smith intervened. "To clarify the record," the prosecutor declared, he saw no reason why the defense should not call the witnesses it had requested, and "present their testimony in any sequence they wished." The TJA was not merely being concilia- tory. Having lived through the trial of Sergeant Smith, he realized that the court's intransigence was creating a political uproar that had already elevated this second trial to front page status in the daily *Stars and Stripes*. The Lichfield trials had, in fact, displaced the Nürnberg tri- als to the back page.

Within two days, the courage of Smith, Johnson, and McGee had produced an effect. Under Secretary of War Kenneth Royall an- nounced that the first of the accused officers would go on trial within a week, adding that "there never was any intention other than to see that there was vigorous prosecution." Moreover, to expedite the tri- als, the War Department would "dispatch fifteen or sixteen lawyers to London to be available to *either* the defense or the prosecution"—thus making it possible for as many as four courts-martial to be in session simultaneously. On the same day, April 10th, the army announced that "All future trials of Lichfield defendants will be held at Bad Nauheim, Germany, a few miles north of Frankfurt," to "expedite" handling of the cases. The real reason, obviously, was to move the tri- als out of the limelight of the London press; but this would prove to be an advantage for the defense, since the trials would be moved out of the jurisdiction of the London area command. And, whatever the outcome of the Jones trial, it would be subject to review by the Con- tinental area command, not by the London staff judge advocate un- der Colonel Thiele.[6]

Meanwhile, Major General John T. Lewis quietly flew from Paris to London with his staff judge advocate, Colonel Clarence Brand, to testify in the Jones trial. His only part in the Lichfield proceedings, he testified, had been "to prepare a report on the administrative features of the case" for General Eisenhower in October, 1945. He also de- clared that then-General Claude Thiele had been "exempt from his command so far as court-martial proceedings were concerned," thus obliquely denying he had interfered in the Smith trial.

Just when the army thought it had judiciously poured oil on turbulent political waters, a new crisis made headlines when, on Thursday afternoon, April 11th, the five prosecution witnesses scheduled for the Jones trial refused to testify. Claiming persecution and mistreatment at the London Area Guardhouse, which was commanded, they alleged, by a captain who was frequently drunk, the witnesses said they feared reprisals when they served out their time in an area detention camp. One had been sentenced to twenty years.

Their refusals startled the court and brought the trial to a halt. On Friday, when the court attempted to reconvene, an unexpected recess was called "at the request of a high official," who was unnamed. The following Tuesday, having received assurances from the U.S. forces European theater judge advocate, Brigadier General Edward C. Betts, that they would not be "persecuted," the reluctant witnesses agreed to take the stand.

General Betts had spent an entire day with the soldiers in their cells in London's ancient Marlborough Jail. The building had originally been designed for the temporary detention of prisoners, and, as an army IG report later observed, it was "not suitable as a place to detain prisoners for long periods." General Betts ordered the witnesses transferred to better quarters in Southampton. It was another embarrassment for the army.

When the witnesses took the stand at last, it was almost an anticlimax. They told of being beaten by Jones (one said he was punched in the stomach for twenty minutes) and of being afraid to report the beatings. Another testified that a prisoner received no medical attention after being severely beaten in the guardhouse courtyard.[7]

On Wednesday, the prosecution had a surprise witness—Sergeant Judson H. Smith. His testimony was uneventful, repetitive of his previous accounts. He told of being instructed to "get tough" with prisoners, of attending "orientation courses" teaching how to use clubs and rifle butts, and, "If a prisoner was a repeater, we had orders from the lieutenant to 'work them over.'"

The next day, Lieutenant Granville Cubage took the stand to say he "was disgusted with the 'get rough' policy" at Lichfield, but had been instructed to make the prison "as miserable as possible."

"Solitary confinement and extra duty," he asserted, "were the only methods of punishment until the summer of 1944. But then a new policy that guards could use clubs was laid down by the commanding officer." Asked to repeat Colonel Kilian's famous policy-setting command, Cubage elaborated on his previous account:

"We can be just as tough as any Disciplinary Training Center. I know what they do at DTCs and we'll do the same here. More prisoners like that one and you know what to do. Take him down to the rifle range, or some place, and work him over. Just don't break too many bones."

On Friday, April 19th, a remarkable thing happened. Shortly after the court closed for a vote on the verdict, Colonel Moore, president of the court, was dismissed at his own request. In what was described as "the most turbulent session of the twelve-day old Lichfield trial" of Sergeant Jones, he asked that his fitness be challenged because of "a series of events that had occurred that might have influenced his vote, consciously or unconsciously."

"Neither the defendant nor the government can get full justice from the court as it is now constituted," he stated on the record. Questioned by the prosecutor, Major Smith, who agreed to make the challenge, Buhl went on to excoriate Major Benito Gaguine, asserting that he questioned the "ability, adequacy, and competency of the law member." Colonel Moore then stood up and left the courtroom.[8] Although it had not been announced in the increasingly sparse news releases about the trial, reporters learned the same day that a captain on the Jones court had earlier excused himself, declaring he "might be biased."

The court, now down to four majors and two captains, found Sergeant Jones guilty. He was sentenced to serve six months at hard labor, and to forfeit $18 a month from his pay. But then the court drafted a document recommending leniency for Jones "in consideration of the excellent combat record of the accused, his probable mental reaction upon return from combat and being confronted with the conditions at Lichfield," as well as the probable culpability of the officers at the 10th Reinforcement Depot. They recommended that the reviewing authority remit Jones' sentence and restore him to duty at his staff sergeant rank.

The court had taken the action following an emotional appeal by Lieutenant McGee:

The American people are beguiled by these Lichfield cases simply because some people won't come forward and tell the truth. Lichfield prisoners got the biggest break of their lives when they weren't shot in combat. They get their second biggest break when they were not lined up and shot as deserters. If the Lichfield policy is the army's fault let's be honest about it and say so, and let's apportion the blame. But don't take it out on two sergeants way down the ladder. Let's put the blame where it should be.[9]

McGee's logic—and rhetoric—sounded a lot like that of his former partner, Earl Carroll.

25

ACT TWO

After Art White's piece reporting the witness strike on April 11th, 1946, no *Stars and Stripes* articles on Lichfield were signed—although stories on the trials ran through September of that year. But it was apparent that the policy of permitting the paper's staff to publish anything already in the public press was still in effect. All Lichfield stories for the remainder of 1946 were attributed either to AP, UP, or to a new entity called "The Stars and Stripes Bureau."[1]

On the other side of the Atlantic Ocean, as predicted by both Kilian and Carroll, there were now demands for a congressional investigation. The prestigious *Army and Navy Journal* agreed. A congressional subcommittee publicly criticized the Army's entire court-martial system as being designed to discriminate against enlisted men.

A Colonel Irvin Schindler, heading a team of fifteen "expediters," was flown in from Washington to Frankfurt. He told his crew that "General Eisenhower and Secretary Patterson want these trials over with and out of the newspapers"—adding, unnecessarily, "the trial has been getting a lot of bad publicity."

Meanwhile, in the plush five-story Park Hotel in Bad Nauheim, centerpiece of a former Hessian spa, a scene reminiscent of an overblown set for a Chaplin/Essanay silent movie was being prepared. But it soon became clear that secluding the trials in a remote part of Germany was not going to accomplish the army's objectives. *The Stars and Stripes* carried an Associated Press dispatch verbatim:

BAD NAUHEIM, April 24 (AP)—A "four-ring big top" has been set up here for the Lichfield trials, which many veterans may regard as a crucial test of the Army's recently criticized judicial system.

With four court-martials in progress simultaneously in four adjoining rooms, six officers and eight enlisted men will be tried individually on charges of mistreating fellow-American soldiers who were prisoners in an Army guardhouse in Lichfield, England during the last year of the war.

Four court rooms have been prepared on the ground floor of a palatial hotel in this summer resort near Frankfurt, with gaudy red plush-covered seats for the spectators. There is a grand piano in one chamber.

On the second floor, several press rooms have been equipped with teletypes, typewriters, and telephones. Over the hotel entrance hangs a showy sign, "Lichfield Trials."[2]

The Stars and Stripes published an impressive list of fourteen Lichfield defendants, together with their hometowns. They included:

Colonel James A. Kilian, Chicago
Major Herbert W. Bluhm, Chicago
Major Richard E. Lo Buono, East Pittsburgh
Captain Joseph A. Robertson, Akron, Ohio; Toledo, Ohio
1st Lieutenant Leonard W. Ennis, Peekskill, New York
1st Lieutenant Granville Cubage, Oklahoma City, Oklahoma
Corporal Louis L. Robson, Kansas City, Missouri
T/5 Ellis D. Adcock, Hot Springs, Arkansas
Pfc Thomas E. Warren, Plainview, Texas
Pfc Austin D. Gheens, Newport, Tennessee
Pfc William C. Loveless, Parma, Missouri
Pfc William B. Norris, Birmingham, Alabama
Pfc Arthur B. Duncan, Elizabethtown, North Carolina[3]

The enlisted men were charged with offenses similar to those for which Sergeant Smith had been tried. The language in the specifications included such familiar words as "wrongfully and unlawfully imposing, and causing to be imposed . . . cruel and inhuman disciplinary treatment upon the prisoners," sometimes with the addition of detailed unsavory specifics. The charges against the officers dealt with their issuing the orders to enforce Lichfield's "get rough" policy—orders that resulted in the actions of the jailers.

Amid the trappings of the spa, the trials began to take on a carnival atmosphere. Helpful GIs, who were given to putting up satires of the sequential, 1930s-vintage "Burma-Shave" signs along German highways (e.g., "Parts for jeeps / are hard to get / Red Cross girls / harder yet") had customized some of them with helpful directions: "Five miles to Lichfield Trials," "Four miles. . . . ," etc.

A second resort hotel was taken over to house defendants, witnesses, and staff personnel for the trials. Nearby, the former clubhouse of a posh German civilian rifle range had been converted into a temporary guardhouse for the witnesses who were still prisoners. An officer with a contingent of twenty-four men had been detailed to guard the eight soldiers who would be housed in the facility.

The first officer to be tried was to be Lieutenant Leonard Ennis. His defense counsel, Colonel Edward Chayes (who had interrupted the Smith trial from the spectators' gallery) publicly accused "higher army authority" of hurrying the trials to the extent that the accused "are very much afraid they are not going to get a fair trial." But as *Time* pointed out:

The [army's] desire for haste was not matched by an equal yearning for efficiency. Defense counsels complained that documents and witnesses, available any time during the last six months, were still to be produced at Bad Nauheim. Last week, on this score they won a 26-day continuance in Ennis' case, and asked 30 days for Cubage.

There might be a method in the Army's apparent madness. Said a prospective witness: "They want you newspaper guys to get fed up and clear out. When there's no more interest in these things in the U.S., they'll start slinging mud."[4]

The trials began slowly because of continuances granted by the courts. Since Colonel Kilian's trial was postponed until June 17th, some of the witnesses who had been locked up at the spa's rifle range were released from custody and quartered at a small hotel on Ritterhaus Strasse in Bad Nauheim. One of them, Private Joseph Mallory, who earlier had escaped from the London guardhouse facility, got into trouble again. This time, in a dispute involving their mutual German "fräulein" girlfriend, Mallory shot Private Albert Rose in the leg. The incident put Rose in the hospital and Mallory went back into the stockade.[5]

Meanwhile, General McNarney, commander of U.S. forces in Europe, made headlines when he announced the findings of General Lewis's IG investigation, which included "mishandling of the cases, and a failure of some of the intermediate commanders." Citing their failure at the outset "to recognize the seriousness of the situation and to direct complete investigation and take prompt corrective and punitive action as required," Lewis recommended an administrative reprimand for officers whose actions he found wanting. But General Eisenhower decided to withhold action on General Lewis's recommendations, in the belief that "the trials themselves will elicit further facts and evidence which might indicate that more drastic action should be taken against certain officers."[6]

When Lieutenant Granville Cubage's trial got underway the last week in May, another witness strike began. As thirteen successive witnesses, including some Lichfield cadre who had been guards or jailers, were sworn in, each refused to answer questions. The fourteenth answered every question with "I don't remember," at which point the prosecution asked for an adjournment.

AP journalist Don Doane quoted one of the witnesses, Sergeant Saul Russ: "We witnesses are being held in the guardhouse and treated as dangerous criminals while these accused officers are running around free. We were always under suspicion. Then, 12 days ago, six of us were arrested and thrown into the guardhouse." The six had been accused of making "an unauthorized trip to London." The witness strike lasted ten days. When it seemed to be resolved on June 8th, Sergeant Russ was the only witness who offered an explanation for changing his mind: "I wanted to do what I could to see that Ennis gets what he deserved."[7]

A steady stream of dispatches issued from the encampment of newsmen at Bad Nauheim. Lieutenant Ennis found himself in the limelight when prosecutors in both the Cubage case and his own formally complained about his "going down and fraternizing with witnesses and trying to influence" them. But, to keep from derailing his trial, the court announced it would "disregard these intimations of improper conduct" until proof was offered. None was forthcoming.

When Colonel Kilian was called as a defense witness in the trial of Pfc William B. Norris, he refused to answer questions, stating that, since he himself was awaiting trial, his testimony might jeopardize his defense. When Captain Joseph Robertson was summoned the next day, he also declined to testify, saying forthrightly that "answering questions might tend to incriminate me." But Kilian wanted no part of that. He insisted his testimony "would *not* be incriminating because I have done nothing wrong." The court ordered Kilian to answer the questions put to him.

"Under duress and in order not to jeopardize my rights," he said, "I will take advantage of the 24th Article of War and refuse to answer." The 24th Article of War permits a witness to refuse to answer a question which might incriminate or degrade him, or which is not material to the case. The court upheld his refusal without inquiring which caveat the Colonel wished to have apply.[8]

Such was not the case with General Prisoner Otto Holt, who gave as his reason for refusal to cooperate, "I was identified as a defendant instead of a witness in a newspaper picture." (*The Stars and Stripes*, which repeated the error in an INS photo caption, had printed a public apology in its June 11th issue.) When the court threatened Holt with military punishment if he refused to answer, he defiantly told the court, "I've already got ten to twenty years, so I don't think six months would hurt me much."

The witnesses who did testify told familiar stories—some with new twists. After being taken into a latrine for a beating that broke his jaw, Private Fred Moore and another prisoner were then forced to mop up their own blood as they were asked a "test question": "What happened to your face?"

"We had been in Lichfield quite a while, so we said we'd fallen," Moore testified.

Mike Koblinski testified in both the Cubage and Ennis trials, repeating his description of the prison officer's practice of poking inmates in their combat wounds with his club. Koblinski made an Associated Press headline (repeated in *The Stars and Stripes*) with his assertion that "they've got concentration camps right in the U.S. Army."[9]

Aubrey Richey showed the court the scars on his head, explaining that Ennis "knew I had been beaten. He grabbed my collar, twisted it, and pulled me up. He put me in solitary confinement for eleven days without any medical attention." Richey said that Ennis once told him, "I hope you do try to escape because I want to shoot you anyway."

Jailer William Norris's trial ended with a finding of guilty for beating prisoners, one of whom suffered a broken jaw. Like Judson Smith, Norris had been a coal miner. He had enlisted in the army in 1940, and had seen action in Normandy before being sent to Lichfield. Taking the witness stand in his own defense, Norris admitted the beatings, but contended he had "acted under orders of superior officers and in accordance with the Lichfield policy." He was sentenced to forfeit $15 pay per month for four months—a total of $60—but no confinement was prescribed.

Norris's light sentence was one of the factors that precipitated yet another witness strike, this time interrupting Lieutenant Ennis's trial. Colonel Samuel Metcalf, president of the court, called each witness before him, asking the reason for his refusal to testify. The president asked each man the same questions: "Do you realize I am an officer in the army and you are a member of that army?" After getting an affirmative answer, he commanded each witness, "I order you to answer the questions." When each refused, he was cited for contempt and sentenced to additional confinement.

Interviewed by reporters in their barbed wire compound, the witnesses complained of injustices: "Guards convicted of beating us get fined $60 while I go AWOL [an unauthorized trip to London while waiting to testify] and get 20 years," one witness was quoted as saying. "We're imprisoned on trumped-up charges we're supposed to have committed here at Bad Nauheim, while the defendants against whom we're asked to testify walk free—laughing at us," said another. "The Lichfield trials are strictly a frame job," Pfc Peter Claim complained. "They are the biggest frame job I've seen in the army and I want justice."

Deprived of cigarettes, radios, newspapers, and PX rations since they were confined in the area guardhouse, some of the imprisoned witnesses told reporters they thought the trials should be moved to the United States. Most of the witnesses soon changed their minds about refusing to testify, however.

"It wasn't doing us any good to refuse to testify," said Robert Cox. "We decided there was no sense us getting more time in the guardhouse for refusing to testify when nobody gives a damn what we do anyhow." As of June 9th, twelve witnesses were willing to talk, but five were still holding out.[10]

The trial of Lieutenant Cubage moved along. In his opening statement, Cubage's defense counsel, Lieutenant Colonel William Parker, told the court his client "had authorized nothing outside the scope of Army Regulations." Colonel Parker's plea was not sufficient to prevent the court from bringing in a verdict of guilty. But, in a three-hour deliberation, the members radically modified the original charges, eliminating all references to "cruel or unusual punishment" and clearing Cubage personally of "aiding in any improper punishment." The court ended up finding him guilty of "wrongfully and unlawfully performing his duties as a prison officer in that he authorized imposition of unauthorized punishment, which punishment consisted of striking prisoners with clubs, forcing them to stand with nose and toes against the wall for protracted periods, and requiring them to endure silent mess."

On June 15th, Lieutenant Cubage was sentenced. He was fined $250 and administered a reprimand.[11]

The resumption of Colonel Kilian's trial two days later eclipsed most of the news on the trials of the other defendants. Their verdicts appeared on the back pages of *The Stars and Stripes,* next to the conclusion of articles on the commandant's trial that were continued from page one.

The most severe sentence of any guard of enlisted rank went to Pfc William Loveless, who was fined $100; T/5 Ellis Adcock would forfeit $80 of his pay. Both guards had figured prominently in beatings described earlier. Other jailers got smaller fines. The lightest sentence imposed was on Pfc Adolph Zortz, who received a reprimand.

Meanwhile, things were not going so well for the witnesses. Private Theodore Taylor was fined $140 and sentenced to six months in the guardhouse for making an unauthorized trip to London (having skipped a meeting during which army regulations were read). He was also convicted of using profane and insulting language to the officer who called him on his absence. When, on June 21st, witness Joseph De Felice was fined $240 for violating a "restriction to quarters" order and for showing disrespect to an officer, the Associated Press dispatch pointed out that the guards he had testified against had been fined $60 and $80, respectively.

Two weeks later, six other witnesses were sentenced to six months at hard labor for making an unauthorized plane trip to London.[12]

While the above trials were going on, Captain Earl Carroll had returned to his former duties as a volunteer defense counsel aiding GIs in the Army of Occupation (in Germany) who found themselves facing court-martial. It was the military avocation he had shared with partner Morris McGee some months earlier.

"Every GI who got in trouble wanted me to defend him against the military despots," Carroll told the author many years later. "I got more GIs out of trouble than anybody in service." It became a kind of game, Carroll said.

"I would go to a jail or a stockade and ask to see a prisoner.

"'General so-and-so says you are not to be admitted,' the officer in charge would tell me.

"'Are you denying these men their right to counsel of their own selection?' I would ask. 'This is their Constitutional right. You deny it and I will prefer charges against you.'

"He would immediately start to make telephone calls. I would sit down and wait.

"'We will admit you but we will send in someone with you,' he'd finally say.

"'I have a right to a confidential conversation with my client,' I'd tell him. 'You park your ass outside.' And they would!"[13]

"Carroll would do anything to win a case," his friend, AP journalist Donald Doane said in a later interview. "I remember writing up his famous 'midnight court-martial.'

"General Bresnahan (who was a first-class SOB) got mad at seeing junior officers and noncoms riding army vehicles to work instead of walking. One morning as the general was riding to work, he saw two young officers alight from a jeep. The general turned to his driver. 'I want those men arrested, court-martialled, and sentenced,' he ordered. But since his enlisted driver wasn't an MP, the general made the arrest himself.

"Carroll suggested to the accused officers that they demand a general court-martial, which they did. Because of the heavy docket of the military judiciary at the time, in order to get the trial cleaned up by the required date, Carroll, who was their defense counsel, had the case scheduled at *midnight*.

"At the trial, Carroll told the court that since the general was the arresting officer and the only witness, the court would have to call him to testify. The general wasn't about to show up at that unseemly hour. Instead, he sent his emissary.

"'Upon the direction of the commanding general, I move the charges be dismissed,' the emissary told the court. And they were.

"Carroll was sometimes a hero but always a showman," Doane said.[14]

26

KILIAN'S TURN

Colonel James A. Kilian's trial resumed on Monday, June 17th—the same day it was disclosed that the witnesses confined to the Bad Nauheim guardhouse (now nineteen of them) had been digging a tunnel in a plot to escape.[1]

There were seven full colonels on the court under its president, Brigadier General Robert M. Montagu of Louisville, Kentucky. Trial judge advocate was Major Joseph S. Robinson, a lawyer in civilian life, from New York City. Kilian's defense counsel was Lieutenant Colonel Raymond E. Ford, of Fort Pierce, Florida, also an attorney.

Kilian had unsuccessfully challenged the eligibility of Colonel William Beck, Jr., of Griffin, Georgia, the law member, because of "possible prejudice" against him. With typical arrogance, he also tried to challenge three other members of the court based on his claim that they were "either of lower [permanent] rank" than he was, or that they were beneath him on the Regular Army promotion list.

Ford began by asking for another month's delay in the trial because the army had failed to furnish his client with "documents, witnesses, stenographers, and the legal assistants he had requested," and because Kilian had not yet received a reply to his letter to President Harry S. Truman, asking the commander in chief to investigate the trials. The motion was denied.

Colonel Ford also lost his second motion, that the trial be transferred to the United States—but not before presenting a dazzling parade of high-ranking character witnesses, including General Joseph T. McNarney, commander of all U.S. forces in Europe, Major General John T. Lewis, Western Base commander, Major General Withers A. Burress, Inspector General for the European Theater, Brigadier General T. F. Bresnahan, Commanding General of the Continental Base Section, and his staff judge advocate, Colonel Lester J. Abele. On the first day of the trial, even Kilian's defense attorney, Colonel Ford, took the stand as a volunteer character witness on behalf of his client.

General McNarney, who sat silently in the witness chair for nearly an hour while the defense counsel and the prosecutor argued over legal technicalities, appeared startled when Ford asserted that "a fair trial is impossible under existing conditions."[2]

"There can be no valid reason why this trial and the trials of the other accused were not transferred from London to the United States," Ford declared, "except that the United States Army authorities desired to conduct this trial away from the people of the United States—away from the free public press, and where the highest degree of influence and control was and is possible."

All the while, Kilian sat at the defense table, teeth clenched, glaring at the court through his round, steel-rimmed, GI glasses. The fifty-four-year-old commandant had not been pleased when an Associated Press correspondent described him as "short, red-faced," but he was both.[3] Beyond facing charges in this court, Kilian had been cited for contempt of court a few days earlier in another Park Hotel courtroom, when, for the second time, he had refused to answer questions in the trial of an enlisted man, this time refusing to plead the 24th Article of War, but stating instead that his testimony would "embarrass" his own defense.

In the stormy emotional atmosphere of the courtroom on the second day of the trial, most of the contention was between defense counsel Ford and law member Beck, who frequently ruled against the defense counsel, and who even prevented him from reading aloud an exhaustingly long motion (members of the court and reporters had been given printed copies of it). He also forbade the defense counsel to question General Lewis about details in his report to General Eisenhower.

Ford also failed to make the prosecution pin down what he called "vague and uncertain" charges against Kilian, and to eliminate all references to "mistreatment of persons unknown," but he did manage to get a one-day postponement while the court looked into the whereabouts of defense witnesses who had not yet shown up.

Meanwhile, in adjacent courtrooms, the trials of other officers were proceeding. Sergeant Judson Smith testified in the trial of Lieutenant Leonard Ennis that "Lieutenant Ennis gave me two direct orders to work a man over. That means to hit the prisoner. Ennis was there when I hit the man. He saw his order executed."

The Lichfield trials had continuing problems with witnesses. Newspapers disclosed on the third day of the Kilian trial that the Bad Nauheim provost marshal had had no success in discovering which of the nineteen prisoner witnesses had actually dug the partially completed tunnel discovered earlier in the week.[4]

When the Kilian trial resumed and the colonel was finally asked for a plea, his voice rang out in his characteristic "barrel-organ" timbre with a resonant "NOT GUILTY!"

Exhibiting more prudence than might have been expected, Captain Carroll did not appear in the spectators' gallery. Instead, he busied himself with his gratuitous defense counsel services in another part of Germany.

On Saturday, Kilian's prosecutor was finally able to begin presenting his case. The session included testimony by Corporal Robert Henney of Toledo, Ohio, who had instigated the first investigation of Lichfield when he wrote a letter to the *Toledo Blade* in January, 1945, while he was on furlough. Henney's letter had recounted his seeing a naked man beaten with a rubber hose. He repeated the story on the witness stand, producing a number of objections by Colonel Ford which were overruled. Major Robinson read into the record earlier testimony by Lieutenant Ennis, who said that Kilian once reproved him for "not being tough enough."

When the trial resumed on Monday, Judson Smith testified about Kilian's interference in his own London trial, telling the court how the colonel had assembled the nine enlisted defendants in his London hotel room to coach them on their testimony. "Let's all stick together, get this thing over with, and go home," the former commandant had urged them. Smith said the guards had actually planned to plead guilty before Kilian called them together and persuaded them to lie. Under cross-examination, the former provost sergeant wearily told the court, "I wish I didn't have any more to do with these trials."

Sergeant Smith sat silently in the witness chair for two more days while Kilian's defense counsel and his assistant, Major James C. Burnette, continued to argue for their motion to quash the charges against their client. At one point, they demanded a copy of a classified War Department message they claimed would support their contention that Colonel Kilian would be unable to obtain a fair trial. The War Department refused to make the document public.

"I am trying to show how this case has been perverted," Ford pleaded. "These charges against Kilian were brought illegally and by design of certain people whom we will name and bring into this court."

The assertion brought the prosecutor, Major Robinson, out of his chair.

"I wanted to keep all that out of this case," the TJA angrily declared, "but if this continues, the government will be forced to bring in witnesses and show that the accused made every effort to stifle the charges against him using his connections with other people in the army." General Montagu ordered the prosecutor's remarks stricken from the record and instructed the members of the court to disregard them.

Sergeant Smith was followed to the witness stand by Sergeant James M. Jones, the one other guard who was already serving time in prison for mistreatment of prisoners, and by one of those prisoners, Sergeant James B. Gallardy. Jones confirmed that, as directed by Lichfield officers, he had removed nineteen prisoners from sight during an IG inspection because they bore marks of beatings by guards. When Sergeant Gallardy took the stand, his testimony became the subject of one of Don Doane's poignant AP dispatches, reprinted in *The Stars and Stripes:*

BAD NAUHEIM, GERMANY, June 26—(AP)—A wounded veteran of the Normandy invasion today told the military court trying Colonel James A. Kilian, former commandant of the U.S. Army's Lichfield detention camp, he was thrown into the camp guardhouse for seven weeks and "treated like a dog" for coming back five hours late from a 24-hour leave.

The witness, Sergeant James B. Gallardy, of Summerhill, Pa., scornfully refused to wear into the courtroom his numerous decorations, including the Bronze Star, which he won during seven months of combat in France and Germany.[5]

Doane went on to describe Gallardy's testimony, including all the now-familiar complaints: prisoners being beaten with clubs and fists, being made to stand "nose and toes" against the wall, enduring seven hours of rigorous calisthenics daily, during which he and others were required to hold their arms horizontal for twenty minutes at a time, and being allotted five minutes for meals in absolute silence.

Introduction of further testimony from the court record of the Smith trial during the next two days further raised the emotional temperature in the courtroom. As Ford argued that such testimony should be stricken on the grounds that it had been "illegally obtained," a scene unfolded that embarrassed both the defense and the court. It was described in a UP dispatch by a reporter who was in the spectators' gallery:

Kilian, his face red with anger, bounded to his feet and shouted, 'I ask the court's permission to make a statement!' He was physically restrained by Ford, who pushed him back into his chair and attempted to calm him.[6]

When order was restored, Major Robinson told the court why he believed Kilian had decided to make life miserable for prisoners at Lichfield. He would present evidence, he said, to show that his "rough and tough" policy had not been the commandant's first choice. But his earlier attempts had been reversed by his superiors—a position held from the very beginning by Earl Carroll, a close friend of Robinson who later became his law partner.

Robinson said Kilian's first proposal had been to send AWOL offenders into action with a gun at their backs. When that one was vetoed, his second course was to try men for desertion under the 58th Article of War "even if they were only a few minutes late in returning from a leave." When advised that both actions were illegal, he resorted "to making life so rough at the 10th Reinforcement Depot that no man would want to come back." It was a position remarkably sympathetic to the position of the defendant—and not unlike Carroll's attitude toward Sergeant Smith.

Building his case, Robinson began calling Kilian's key officers to the witness stand. Lieutenant Cubage confirmed that the colonel did, indeed, reward guards for shooting prisoners, and that the jailers joked among themselves about that being the easy way to get a promotion. He also told the court about Colonel Kilian's attempts to create a mistrial in the Smith case "so that no one else would have any worries," as Kilian had put it. Cubage repeated his well-publicized testimony about the commandant's suggestion that he take an incorrigible prisoner "down to the rifle range and work him over—and just don't break too many bones," adding that his commanding officer had clarified his order, saying, "I don't mean for you yourself to take him out, but you've got some good men down there. They can do it."

When Major Richard Lo Buono, the former Lichfield provost marshal, took the witness stand, he appeared more than a little frightened. When asked what Colonel Kilian had said in 1944 about guardhouse policy, he begged the court, "Must I answer that?" Told that he must, he hung his head and responded almost inaudibly, "He said I would have to be rougher on them. And I replied, 'I just can't do it.' That's the substance of it." Additional questioning revealed that the commandant had promptly relieved him of his job.

As he testified, Lo Buono studiously avoided the gaze of Kilian, who noisily sucked a pencil during the former provost marshal's testimony. Although the provocative gesture made the papers, including *The Stars and Stripes,* the defendant was not admonished by the court. Asked while this was going on whether "anything was done to cause you to be in fear of Kilian," Lo Buono refused to answer.

The next day, July 12, Major Robinson called Lieutenant Ennis to the witness stand. Sitting across the room from his former commandant, Ennis now sought to water down his testimony. Robinson called him on it, stating that the former prison officer had changed his testimony "at least twenty times" from what he had said during the Smith trial—reading examples from the earlier transcript to demonstrate the witness's conflicting answers.

Lieutenant Colonel Ford tried unsuccessfully to interfere. It was a stressful day for all concerned, as journalist Don Doane reported:

BAD NAUHEIM, July 12—(AP)—A defense lawyer was held in contempt of court and a prosecution witness was threatened with a contempt citation today in an angry session of Colonel James A. Kilian's court-martial on charges of cruelty to Lichfield, England, guardhouse prisoners.

Tempers strained during the stormy 26-day trial flared into violent outbreaks in which hot words were shouted back and forth across the tense courtroom.

Held in contempt was Lieutenant Colonel Raymond E. Ford of Fort Pierce, Florida, Kilian's attorney, who charged the military court's law member, Colonel William Beck, Jr., of Griffin, Georgia had "prearranged" a technical ruling in favor of the prosecution.

A few minutes later Lieutenant Leonard W. Ennis of Peekskill, N.Y., interrupted a bombardment of prosecution questions by shouting from the witness stand:

"I'll take another court-martial rather than go through this. I refuse to answer any more questions."[7]

The president had promptly called a recess and held a closed conference with the witness. When the trial resumed, Ennis apologized to the court and promised to answer questions "to the best of my ability. But I ask the court to protect me against these interferences by the prosecutor."

It got worse. Before the day was out, Robinson challenged one of the judges, Colonel Hardin Sweeney, with whom he had clashed earlier in the trial. The prosecutor moved for Sweeney's removal, stating that the member had shown prejudice by "words and actions" in questioning prosecution witnesses, citing Sweeney's longstanding friendship with Colonel Kilian.

Sweeney was furious, and, over the weekend (the Saturday session was canceled), he told reporters he was "contemplating preferring charges [against Robinson] under the 95th and 96th Articles of War for making false public accusations tending to bring discredit on an officer of the army to the injury of his reputation, and also of conduct unbecoming an officer and a gentleman." Sweeney had Robinson summoned to the office of Colonel William Thompson (the Lichfield trials coordinator) on Saturday, where, in the presence of Thompson's adjutant, Sweeney officially notified the prosecutor of his charges.

Robinson won. On the following Wednesday, Sweeney voluntarily withdrew from the court after General Montagu formally announced, "The court sustains [Major Robinson's] challenge, and Colonel Sweeney will withdraw."

As he departed, Hardin Sweeney, a Regular Army full colonel, made a surprising gesture. "I bear no animosity toward the trial judge advocate," the dismissed judge announced as he strode across the courtroom to shake the hand of Joe Robinson—a civilian lawyer who held the temporary rank of major in the Army of the United States.

As the trial continued with a reduced cast of one general and six colonels, Sweeney's expulsion failed to restore peace to the courtroom. That same afternoon, when Ford, with fists clenched, ran across the room apparently intent on punching Robinson, Kilian himself jumped up and rushed across the courtroom to restrain his lawyer. Although the president hastily called a recess, it didn't help. The two lawyers rushed out of the courtroom and faced each other menacingly in the hotel lobby, in what might have become a fistfight if a staff lawyer had not stepped between them.[8]

In yet another strange and unanticipated development, at noon on

July 31st a fire broke out on the fourth floor of the Park Hotel. It was quickly brought under control and extinguished by the Bad Nauheim fire department. In the rubble, American counterintelligence agents found a white phosphorous incendiary grenade, in what they called "a deliberate attempt to destroy the building." The agents questioned several hotel employees but were unable to solve the mystery. The incident produced a column headline in *The Stars and Stripes* the next morning: "PLOT TO DESTROY LICHFIELD COURT."[9]

Shortly after the fire scare subsided, Colonel Kilian's missing adjutant, Lieutenant Colonel Robert Norton, was finally located and summoned to Bad Nauheim. Described by Major Robinson as "one of the inner circle in the 10th Reinforcement Depot," the young lieutenant colonel testified that he had never seen any evidence of prisoners being cruelly treated in the depot guardhouse. But the former adjutant admitted under cross-examination that he had never been inside the guardhouse.

Denying he had ever heard of a "rough and tough policy," Norton said he knew that Colonel Kilian often inspected the guardhouse, and he was sure the commandant was readily available to any prisoners who wanted to see him. Norton's unswerving loyalty to his former commanding officer may have been influenced by the fact that Kilian had promoted the thirty-two-year-old chemist from second lieutenant to lieutenant colonel in just twenty-six months.

At last, on August 29th, the most tumultuous of the Lichfield trials ended, and Kilian's court went into deliberation. The military world and the civilian press waited in suspense. Two hours later, court was reconvened.

Colonel Kilian was found guilty of "aiding, authorizing, and abetting" the cruelties of which nine enlisted guards and three subordinate officers had been convicted. Drawing a razor-thin line, the court found him not guilty of "knowingly" condoning brutality, but guilty of "permitting" it. He was fined $500 and issued a reprimand. As *The Stars and Stripes* pointed out, "The court acquitted Kilian of 'aiding, authorizing and abetting' the cruelties for which nine enlisted guards and three subordinate officers were previously convicted."[10]

In a statement to the court (but obviously directed to the press), the former commandant said, "I have a clear conscience about what happened at Lichfield. I wouldn't have been tried at all except for the tactics used by Captain Earl J. Carroll."

His last observation was undoubtedly true.

Kilian later attacked the legality of his own verdict and invited a congressional investigation of all the Lichfield trials. His claim of "illegality" was based on a technical argument by his defense counsel, Colonel Ford, who was preparing an appeal. The appeal was based on Ford's failure to persuade the court to delete "mistreatment of persons unknown" from the charges against his client.[11]

"To hold a commanding officer criminally responsible for unauthorized offenses of subordinates of which he had no knowledge merely by virtue of his position is to establish a dangerous precedent," Ford's appeal read. "Officers will rightfully shun the original responsibility of command position; discipline will be destroyed in all grades."

When asked whether an officer isn't "responsible for everything within his command," Ford conceded that while that was true, and could rightfully lead to an officer's demotion, that didn't make him *criminally* responsible.[12]

During the concluding weeks of the Kilian trial, verdicts on other officers charged were also brought in.

- Major Herbert Bluhm, Lichfield's post inspector, was acquitted.
- Major Richard Lo Buono, provost marshal, was fined $200.
- Lieutenant Leonard Ennis, prison officer, was fined $350.
- Captain Joseph Robertson, prison company CO, was acquitted.

Meanwhile, in a move by the War Department to "equalize punishment," Sergeant Judson Smith was pardoned after serving six months at hard labor and, with Sergeant James Jones, was restored to duty. When an Associated Press correspondent brought Judson Smith the word that the army had suspended his three-year sentence, Smith smiled and responded with his characteristic brevity, "That's good news."

Later, Smith told reporters, he might reenlist. And he might have tried, but Smith's AGCT score would have been too low to qualify him for reenlistment under the standards in effect at the time. He left the army three months later with an *honorable* discharge—further reversing the earlier sentence of the court.

Richard Lo Buono left the service the following month, in December, 1946. Granville Cubage was separated in April, 1947. But Leonard Ennis remained in the army until July, 1969, making him eligible for a full pension upon his retirement.

THE FURTHER ADVENTURES OF EARL CARROLL

Public reaction to the Lichfield trials was a major factor in convincing all of the armed services to reassess the military justice system after World War II. Within the military services, the widespread view of the Lichfield trials as a miscarriage of justice gave momentum to the spirit of reform. Commenting on the Kilian verdict, retired Colonel Nathan W. MacChesney, a recognized authority on military law who served in the Judge Advocate General Department through two World Wars, told the Army Advisory Committee on Military Justice that "A $500 fine is a travesty on justice. This case is typical of the lack of standards in military tribunals." Gilbert Harrison, vice-chairman of the American Veterans Committee, advised the same group that the Lichfield trials were "a whitewash of horrors." Earl Carroll agreed with both assessments.

A major result was the issuance of the *Uniform Code of Military Justice* in 1949, replacing the Articles of War in an all-new *Manual for Courts-Martial.* In contrast to the thin, pocket-size paperback that had not been revised since 1928, the new manual, within two years, had grown to an eight-by-eleven-inch volume three inches thick. Integrating military law with the federal criminal justice system, "The Red Book" specifies far more detailed pretrial procedures and an elaborate post-trial, appellate review system that today results in about three cases per year being appealed all the way to the United States Supreme Court.[1]

During the Kilian trial, Major Joseph Robinson received a letter smuggled out of a Frankfurt, Germany, jail by a visitor, an appeal for help from a Pfc Daniel P. Walczak, of Detroit, who had been jailed for more than a month without any charges being filed against him. His previous letter, "forwarded through channels" to an officer-lawyer, he said, had apparently never been delivered. Walczak claimed he was one of a group of thirteen prisoners, both soldiers and civilians, being held indefinitely without charges by the army (which, in its military government role, constituted the only legal authority in Germany). One of the American civilians, William C. McKinley of Bessemer, Alabama, said he didn't know why he was being held, and army officials had no record on him.

Much too busy as Kilian's prosecutor, Robinson sent the letter to Earl Carroll, who accepted the assignment with relish. Undeterred by Kilian's formal preparations to court-martial him for "maliciously instigating" his trial, Carroll left for Frankfurt at once.

The army tried to prevent Carroll from seeing the prisoners. Twice, he was denied entry at the jail. With characteristic flamboyance, Carroll sent his habeas corpus writ to the United States Supreme Court, together with a registered letter to the chief justice. Naturally, Carroll made it public. It read in part:

A grave situation exists in the occupied area [Germany]. There is a growing attitude in this area that the military are above the law. There are no civilian counsel practicing in this area, nor are there any civilian courts.

Under the court-martial system a man is not entitled to counsel until the case is referred to a court for trial. In this theater there have been many instances of persons confined eight or nine months before their cases were referred for trial. During this period the accused is not only deprived of counsel, but is kept in confinement and is completely helpless to prepare his own defense. In most cases they do not know the charges upon which they are being held.

Many American civilians as well as military persons are being held in confinement for protracted periods of time. The real issue in this matter is whether or not American citizens by reason of their presence in this occupied territory are reduced to the same status as enemy aliens resident here.[2]

The army responded with several statements. Captain Harold Chase, assistant staff judge advocate of the Frankfurt prison command, said there were "reasonable and probable grounds to believe that these imprisoned individuals have committed serious crimes." But when unfavorable publicity appeared in the press, Colonel Owen Summers, commandant of the European Theater Headquarters Command, issued a much more moderate statement—after personally interviewing six of the complainants. "It is unfortunate," he said, "that these investigations take entirely too long," adding that legal counsel would be provided and the prisoners' complaints would be investigated.

Carroll was told he had been refused entry because of his timing. Lieutenant Colonel W. F. Fratcher, staff judge advocate of the command operating the prison, now said "he could see the prisoners during regular visiting hours on Sunday, like any ordinary visitor."

Carroll's publicized habeas corpus resulted in stateside press inquiries to the War Department in Washington, which produced a nonstatement declaring that "any comment from the War Department will be withheld until an official report is received from the European Theater."

A week later, Carroll was making what the army saw as new mischief. Another of his clients, Captain Morris Marmorstein, a combat veteran, had been accused of making a false company ration report by General Thomas Bresnahan—the general who earlier had court-martialed junior officers for riding in a jeep instead of walking. Bresnahan was now commanding general of the Continental Base Section. The young company commander was actually facing court-martial for a relatively common petty administrative ploy designed to make sure his troops were adequately fed.

When Carroll submitted a "demand for redress," which would have required the general to testify in the trial, it was returned marked "not favorably considered." In the same mail, Carroll received an order declaring him "unavailable" as defense counsel because his "expertise as a trial judge advocate was needed to educate civilian lawyers being brought into the theater." The order immediately assigned him to "special duties," which consisted of writing orientation lectures.

Unfazed and obviously well coached, Captain Marmorstein personally handed a formal "complaint of wrong" to an aide of General McNarney, Bresnahan's boss and commander of all U. S. forces in Europe. Claiming it was impossible for him "to secure a fair and equitable trial" in Bresnahan's command, Marmorstein's letter asked McNarney (1) to transfer his case to the next higher command for trial, (2) to reassign Carroll as his defense counsel, and (3) to forward his complaint, "together with the wrongs herein complained of," to the War Department. The letter further stated that Carroll, "in truth and in fact" (a trademark Carroll expression that shows up hundreds of times in the Smith trial record), *was* available, contrary to General Bresnahan's claim that he was not.

That action worked to the detriment of another of Carroll's clients, Ralph K. Betz, of Willoughby, Ohio, a twenty-six-year-old combat veteran facing a charge of illegally entering Germany, having returned to Europe as a civilian after leaving the army (probably to find the girl he had left behind). In protest, when deprived of his defense counsel, the former GI refused to defend himself.

Since Carroll had been declared unavailable as the man's defense counsel, he made his point by sitting through the man's entire trial as a spectator. Betz was sentenced by the military court to ninety days in prison and deportation thereafter. Don Doane quoted Carroll in an AP dispatch as saying afterward that "military justice is neither military nor justice."[3]

At last, the army had had enough. On September 6th, 1946, General McNarney announced that, in response to a (May 20th) letter in which Carroll had requested redeployment, the captain had been sent home. He was, in fact, already in midocean at the time of the announcement, having left Bremerhaven on the *General Steward* two days earlier with scarcely time to pack.

Unlike some of Colonel Kilian's replacement troops, Carroll had not been put on board ship under armed guard, but he might as well have been. He had not gone quietly, however. According to the *New York Times,* Carroll, while on board ship had "radioed numerous protests to high officials and friends in the U.S. that he was being 'Shanghaied out of Germany' because of his crusade against 'grave abuses' in the justice system of the U.S. Army and of the military government in Germany."[4]

Anticipating the possible conflict that Carroll's departure might create with Colonel Kilian's pending court-martial charges against him, Colonel W. K. Ghormley, chief of staff of the Continental Base Section, announced that "Since Colonel Kilian's charges would probably be referred to the U.S. for pretrial investigation, and since most of the probable witnesses in the proceedings are in the U.S. or will be returned to it," Carroll's redeployment to the States would pose no problem. Once Carroll was back in the United States, Kilian's court-martial charges were quietly dropped and the captain was cashiered out of the army within weeks.

Instead of going back to his law practice in San Francisco, Earl Carroll soon returned to Germany to open a civilian law office in Frankfurt under the army's new program to admit American lawyers—a program initiated at least in part as a result of Carroll's public complaints. His practice was supposed to be limited to military clients and American civilians, but this was hardly enough to sustain a thriving law practice—especially since Carroll prided himself on defending GIs without charge. Soon Carroll began branching out.

The Nürnberg Tribunal had sentenced several German industrialists to imprisonment and had confiscated their industrial holdings. One of these tycoons was Friedrich Flick, who had owned German coal mines, a wagon works that built rail cars, and other war-related industries. Carroll was soon involved in his case, cooperating with German attorneys whose appeals had been percolating through the legal echelons of the U.S. judicial system. Pleading a writ before the

United States Supreme Court, Carroll was successful in having Flick's property restored in 1949 after promising that Flick, said to be the richest man in Germany, would sell his munitions-related holdings and buy into Mercedes Benz instead. Flick, having served seven months in prison, gratefully paid Carroll $750,000.

Friedrich Flick also brought Carroll to the attention of his friend, Alfried Krupp, inheritor of the giant munitions dynasty headquartered in Essen. Dating back to 1811, the firm was famous for its role as a prime purveyor of arms. In the nineteenth century, it had developed a process for casting steel cannon—an innovation that helped Prussia defeat Austria in 1866 and France in 1870. In World War I, the firm was famous for making Germany's huge "Big Bertha" artillery pieces.

Under Hitler, Alfried and his father, Gustav, had rebuilt and modernized the Krupp Works. Alfried had been imprisoned since the beginning of the Nürnberg trials in April, 1945. Although sentenced to twelve years in 1948, he was released with credit for time served from Landsberg Prison (where several of Hitler's generals were also serving time) in August, 1950, thanks to a general amnesty authorized by U.S. High Commissioner John J. McCloy.

Stripped of his industrial holdings, Krupp still retained some $150 million in cash, and Flick arranged for Carroll to meet the former munitions manufacturer on the French Riviera, which, according to William Manchester, Krupp was thinking of buying—all of it.[5]

Krupp already had an American lawyer on his staff—the former Major (later Colonel) Joseph Robinson, prosecutor in the Kilian trial. Like Carroll, Robinson had left the army and returned to Germany to practice law. Within a year, Carroll and Robinson had Krupp's property restored, after the pair successfully pleaded that the original tribunal had been illegal, essentially because U.S. judges had been holding court in a foreign land.

Krupp paid the two lawyers handsomely for their services. Estimates of the actual fees vary with the source, but, in 1954, an American magazine said that it was to have been five percent of everything Carroll could recover—"roughly $25 million." The *Chicago Daily News* and *New York Daily News* published the much more modest estimate of $2 million each, while Don Doane, based on his own sources at the time, believed that Carroll got $1.5 million and Robinson a million dollars. One of Earl Carroll's conditions in taking the case had been that he would get his fee in cash. And he did. Not surprisingly, it led to a classic Carroll fight with the U.S. Internal Revenue Service.[6]

Carroll remained in Europe for several years, using some of his new wealth to support his hobby of helping GIs in trouble. His civilian lawsuits included a divorce case for a European tin fortune heiress. She was one of many women who were totally captivated by the flair and boundless energy of this maverick personality, and they lived together in Switzerland for a time.

By 1955, Carroll was back in his San Francisco law office in the Mockadnock Building at 681 Market Street. There he became counsel for the San Francisco Apartment House Association, handling mostly accident claims—a singularly unglamorous role for Earl Carroll. On extended vacations, however, he traveled to Africa and to both the North and South Poles. And he went to Japan, China, and Alaska to defend GIs in military courts.

In 1957, Earl Carroll returned to Paris to marry Marianne Simon, daughter of Jacques Simon, who had served in French intelligence during both World War I and World War II. Simon was, as Carroll was fond of saying to anyone who would listen, "the first French official arrested by the Germans when they invaded Paris." Marianne and Earl Carroll first settled in Miami, living there until 1961, when they moved to Connecticut.

Meanwhile, Carroll's nemesis, Colonel James A. Kilian, had retired in 1951 with a service-connected disability. President Harry S. Truman had personally blocked his promotion to brigadier general. Kilian died of cancer in Walter Reed Army Hospital March 19, 1958.

Earl Carroll's house in Connecticut. (Photograph by the author, 1979)

Lake in front of Carroll's house. (Photograph by the author, 1979)

Earl Carroll at home in Connecticut. (Photograph by the author, 1979)

EPILOGUE

When I became serious about this book, I realized that I needed to talk to some of the principals in the story if they could be located—if, indeed, they were still alive. James Alphonse Kilian was, of course, no longer available. But I found his prosecutor, Joseph Robinson, at his law office in New York. Robinson was very helpful and invited me to come to New York to review his own Lichfield files. Through him I located Carroll's former law partner, by then Municipal Judge Thomas L. Foley, in Hayward, California.

But it was Carroll I really wanted to talk to. With the help of the California State Bar Association, I finally found him. Earl Carroll had retired from his law practice and was living in Greenwich, Connecticut. I called him at once and made an appointment to see him.[1]

I arrived at Earl Carroll's beautiful Connecticut home late one afternoon in the spring of 1978, driving my rental car into his sweeping horseshoe driveway. Built of fieldstone in French Provincial style, Carroll's home had a steeply gabled slate roof with a massive circular stone tower dominating one corner. The home fronted on a picturesque little lake with overhanging trees.

I walked up to the front door with mounting excitement. But there was no response to my ring. After waiting a discreet several minutes, I rang the bell again. I knocked. Nothing. Disappointed, I walked back to the car.

As I put the key into the ignition, a heavy wooden door suddenly opened beneath a stone archway on the basement level of the house. A male figure stood in the doorway, silhouetted against the brightly lighted interior.

Smiling apologetically, Earl Carroll welcomed me into his rathskeller. He was now seventy-four years old, more slightly built than I remembered, with thinning white hair. It had been more than thirty years since I had seen him in that grubby courtroom on London's Grosvenor Square. He had apparently forgotten our appointment.

When I introduced myself and reminded him of our telephone conversation, Carroll seemed delighted to see me. He shook my hand and led me inside. Waving me to a seat in front of a massive stone fireplace at the end of the room, Carroll proceeded to pour me a liqueur glass of what I believe was Cointreau. Smiling and gracious, he poured another for himself. He exuded charm. But there was a certain vagueness about him. He didn't seem to remember my name or why I had come to see him.

When I reminded him I was researching the Lichfield story, he quickly warmed to the subject and suggested that I contact his friend Donald Doane, whose Washington address he looked up and gave me. But when I asked my first question about the Smith trial, he quickly skipped to its conclusion and was more interested in talking about his later exploits defending soldiers in trouble.

Carroll said he had first realized that many GIs needed help when he was still active in his role as an Air Force captain. He spoke about his disappointment with the military after he finally managed to wangle his way into the army as a flight instructor. He felt the army placed too much emphasis on discipline instead of motivation by genuine leadership.

"Having an occasional drink with troops under my command, I found that many of them had problems," he said. "But whenever you made an attempt to help them, the army acted like you were committing a crime.

"The army seemed to strip individuals of sympathetic understanding for others. I couldn't understand why life in the army should be any different from ordinary life as a civilian."

Focusing his attention on that period of his life, he started reminiscing about his own background, volunteering most of the biographical information detailed in earlier chapters. But I didn't learn very much more about the Lichfield trials before I had to leave for the airport. Having combined my visit with a business meeting in Norwalk, I obviously hadn't budgeted enough time.

I thanked my host and departed, promising to send him a complete set of the Lichfield articles I had gleaned from *The Stars and Stripes*.

It was almost a year before I was able to go back to see Earl Carroll.

I arrived on a Tuesday afternoon in January, 1979. But this time I had done my homework, having read the fourteen volumes of trial transcripts and having had dinner with Don Doane—who graciously sent me a set of all of his 1946 Associated Press articles on the Bad Nauheim Lichfield trials.

Carroll was raking leaves in his yard when I arrived. Again, he didn't seem to remember that I was coming. But, welcoming me, he put down his rake and invited me inside—picking up the remains of a warm twelve-pack of beer he had left on the side porch.

Opening a bottle for each of us in the adjacent kitchen, he led me into a large room he called his study. With its huge fireplace on the side wall and three-story beamed cathedral ceiling ascending into the roof gable, it reminded me of Winston Churchill's study in Chartwell, a room created in 1086. Cobwebs on the lamp shades and foot-scuffed trails in the dust on the carpeting were evidence that it had been quite a while since the place had been cleaned.

I was struck by two interesting appliances, one on an end table and the other on Earl's desk (he wanted me to call him "Earl" but couldn't seem to remember I was "Jack"). Each was a heavy wire framework stand that held a gallon bottle of liquor mounted on a horizontal pivot so that the heavy flagon could be tipped forward to pour out a drink. One of the giant-size bottles bore a Beefeater Gin label; the other was good Scotch.

Suddenly I understood the reason for Earl's vagueness. There was no advancing senility here as I had suspected. Carroll was a certifiable alcoholic of W.C. Fields dimensions. Indeed, his personality reminded me a little of the Elwood P. Dowd character in *Harvey*. But it had little effect on his long-term memory, or on his way with words, as I would find out during the next several hours while we sipped his expensive Scotch together. My problem would be deciphering my notes, whose longhand gets increasingly difficult to read as the evening progresses. We never got to the restaurant he promised to take me to. I ended up missing my plane, checking into a nearby hotel for the night, and calling my wife to say I would fly back the following morning. It was a memorable experience.

This time I immediately steered our conversation to the Lichfield trials, which I now knew something about.

"They were a colossal whitewash of the army command," Earl volunteered in a kind of opening statement. "They expected the prosecutors to put Smith and the other GIs in jail—regardless.

"The Smith trial was rigged. But I refused to be a tool. [President] Leone was pretty decent. Not a bad guy—but the army was on his neck for not being tough."

"You were sure more aggressive than Leland Smith," I suggested.

"Poor old Lee," he soliloquized. "He had a Colonel Prichard breathing down his neck. 'When are you going to be a lawyer instead of a God damn stooge?' I asked him.

"'We're in the army and we have to follow orders,' he told me. "'But they're not legitimate orders,' I argued.

"'No, but I'm a reserve officer and I've got a pension coming,' he said. So he left it up to me."

I asked Earl about the disappearance of Major Bluhm. He lit his pipe.

"That was before we got smart," he said with the cocky grin I suddenly recognized. "The army would ask us who we 'might want to have available' for trial. If you were stupid enough to give them a list of witnesses, the army would be sure they were gone.

"After that we learned to play the game differently. We'd give them a probable list of their own probable witnesses!"

He enjoyed his confrontations with the military establishment—and he obviously enjoyed telling about them. Like the time he was summoned to the judge advocate general's office: Frustrated because "the army had closed witnesses' mouths," Carroll had used one of his by-then standard tricks, slipping a story to the press via Don Doane. *The Stars and Stripes* had come to him for verification. He gave them what they came for.

"How dare you release this?" the officer had demanded.

"If you appoint me, I'm supposed to try a case. If the truth doesn't please you, that's too bad. You classify it and I'll show you how to make a first class story out of your classification!"

And he got away with it.

"'Maverick Carroll,'" he mused. "A name I enjoyed more than any other appellation they could have placed."

He was summoned before military authorities more than once, he said.

"McNarney was mad as hell at me. He considered me to be a 'great interferer with military justice.' I asked him about that." (General McNarney was commander of the army's entire European Theater at the time.)

"'I'd be interested in your concept of what justice is,' I said.

"'I'm not interested in being cross-questioned. I'm here to investigate.'

"'What are you investigating?' I asked.

"'I'm not interested in answering your questions,' he snapped.

"'If you have that kind of chip on your shoulder, you aren't going to get very much information out of anybody,' I told him.

"'That'll be enough from you, Captain!'

"And it was."

Carroll blew a cloud of smoke and smiled, replaying the experience in his mind. The smile faded as he turned to me, focusing his eyes on mine.

Indulging in what was obviously playacting, but on a subject about which he was deadly serious, he suddenly put me on the witness stand; and I had the firsthand experience of being subjected to a Carroll interrogation. It made enough of an impression that, before leaving for the airport the next morning, I pored over my notes of the night before and wrote it all down on hotel stationery:

"'Justice,'" Earl began, "is a rather elusive term."

He pointed his pipe stem at me, spacing his words:

"What is *justice?*"

Trying to scramble out of the mist produced by the Scotch, I made an attempt:

"Justice is the discipline by means of which the rule of law is administered in society."

"That's justice?" He looked disappointed. Maybe a little disgusted. "You ought to be able to do better than *that.*"

"Okay, maybe I was trying to define the court system. I'll give you a simpler one: Justice is *being fair.*"

"What does that mean. What is fair?"

"Oh, come on. That's a Great Books question. My wife and I used to lead a Great Books group: 'What is an inalienable right?' Do you think there are any?"

He sucked a draught from his pipe and looked thoughtful. It was an act. He resumed control at once—turning my question around and aiming back it at me.

"'Inalienable rights. Are there any?' That *is* a good question. Do *you* think there are any?"

The Scotch had obviously dulled my inhibitions:

"Yes," I said. "Survival! Survival is an inalienable right. And it supersedes everything else for most people. But for some—those they love—their families—sometimes even their own principles are more important than survival. If it were not so, we wouldn't have posthumous awards of the Congressional Medal of Honor." It sounds a little sophomoric and puffy, but it's what I said.

He nodded, actually agreeing! I had made it. But, then, Earl had been drinking Scotch too. He rephrased it, making his own pronouncement.

"People's *thoughts* are more important than survival." It reminded me of the quote attributed to Einstein and I told him so: "Imagination is more important than knowledge."

Getting back to his point, he told me the answer.

"Justice is *equity.*"

My *Random House Dictionary* defines "equity" as "the quality of being fair; impartial," but I didn't have the reference, and I wasn't about to argue the point with my interrogator. Besides, it got us back to the Lichfield trials—and Carroll's evaluation of military justice:

"Any system of justice is what a particular group of people who are gathered together to sit in judgment consider it to be. The so-called system of *military* justice was a great misnomer. It was distorted into a punitive instrument to enforce discipline that the officers failed to enforce themselves—because of their lack of ability. It was a crutch to substitute for their leadership skills. Instead of leading, they insisted that 'military *discipline* must be preserved above all'!

"I refused to prosecute Judson Smith because the whole theory of prosecution was wrong.

"I always thought the law was man's basic instrument of justice. But it was grossly distorted in the army. There it was an instrument to enforce authority. And the army, unfortunately, put people in positions of authority who didn't have the competence to understand what authority really means. As a result, they allowed the circumstances of the moment to obscure the real objectives of justice.

"The whole military structure is really quite an artificial thing—governed by expediency more than anything else. You can't have justice in a tribunal where participants have an ax to grind. In the army, there is a very simple answer to all of the problems that are raised. But it all depends on whose ox is being gored."

The Smith trial, he said, was a classic case in point. He began reviewing its principals.

"Cubage, that little bastard, was a stooge." He defined a "stooge" as an officer who meekly went along with a corrupt establishment instead of standing up it.

Smith was a "pitiable" character because he couldn't help himself. Earl agreed with Don Doane: "Smith wasn't bright enough to know he was doing wrong." But even if he had been, Carroll added, he couldn't have done anything about it.

"The guards picked were psychos. They were no good for combat. They were good-*size* bruisers. And they were told that 'anybody we put in jail deserves anything.'"

Ennis was "Kilian's strong man—his enforcer; a complete stooge, but crafty. 'Cute,' but not smart. A little crazy."

Carroll finally got to James Alphonse Kilian.

"Kilian was a bastard of a commander. He had been in the Regular Army a long time, and he was 'old army'-wise. He had friends in high places. And he knew how to *use* friendships.

"He had real contempt for officers who came in from civilian life during the war. And he didn't hide it. He had no use for government political heads."

"Don Doane told me," I interrupted, "that, although he didn't agree with them, he thought Kilian had his own set of principles, and that he had integrity in his own way." Earl didn't disagree:

"I never disliked Kilian as a man. I've had many a drink with him. But *I* rejected his principles, too.

"'Military discipline is everything.' That's what Kilian believed. From his standpoint, without discipline an army is just a ragged mob having no order or responsibility to authority."

"What do you think," I asked, "about the 'moral' of *The Caine Mutiny Court Martial*—that if a country is going to have wars, you really need guys like this?"

Earl said he had to go along with that.

"In some ways, I really liked the guy," Earl continued. "He had real guts, and integrity as he viewed it. He sure had the courage of his convictions. Most officers were afraid to open their mouths. He wasn't.

"But he was a man obsessed with what he considered his duty and responsibility. He took a lot of responsibility that should have been taken by his superiors who chickened out. It's difficult to condemn a man governed by such thoughts. Who are we to judge? Every man is entitled to his own opinion and judgment.

"No, what I objected to was the *system* Kilian represented. I felt bad about having to tear that guy apart. He wasn't acting only on his own. He was acting on orders he received that went all the way to the White House. *He* was the *scapegoat.* My quarrel was not with Kilian (what the hell can a Colonel do?) but with his superiors who hid behind their rank. Kilian was not a villain. He was a *tool*—just like *Smith!"*

"What about the argument, and the Article of War—and the thrust of the prosecution in the Nürnberg trials—that says an officer, *or* a soldier, is only obliged to carry out those orders that are *lawful* orders?"

"That," Earl declared, using one of his trademark words, "is an exculpatory statement! If you are in the army, you are bound to follow orders. Following orders can't become an individual decision of every private. That's ridiculous."

He went on to enunciate a position that made Eisenhower's famous warning about the "military-industrial complex" sound tame— a personal conviction that may have accounted for much of Carroll's notorious conduct after the war.

"The worst organization for a human being to be made a part of is the military establishment, because he is compelled to lose his entire identity, and any sense of right and wrong. He becomes a *roboton*—a roboton who is the subject of whatever modern Caesar has seized the power of command.

"There was much military arbitrariness during World War II that was not reported. The Lichfield trials pushed a dark cloak aside."

The identity of "The Beast of Lichfield" was clear enough in Earl's mind:

"We were governed under so-called wartime conditions by an absolute military dictatorship that was invulnerable to any form of civilian inquiry or criticism. They took the position that they were the sole and independent defenders of this country, and their processes of defense were beyond question or inquisition by any civilian authority. The military authority arrogated itself to a position of supremacy above and beyond all civilian inquiry, including that of the presidency—whose titular position as supreme commander was regarded by the military as a ceremonial role. *They* were the guardians of national security.

"A military establishment is based primarily on total authoritarianism, and as such must forever pose a threat to any democratic government to which it may be attached."

He did have a way with words.

Carroll's equating commandant Kilian and defendant Smith, characterizing *both* as "tools" and "scapegoats," provided a new insight into the Lichfield trials—a different perspective from the one I had entertained since sitting in that first courtroom in 1946, watching Carroll destroy the man that I, like many others, perceived to be the villain of the piece.

Earl Carroll died a few months later. He drowned in the lake in front of his home on May 21, 1980. His body was found five days later.

After his honorable discharge in November, 1946 (the same month Earl Carroll left the army), Judson H. Smith returned to his wife, Evelyn, in Lynch, Kentucky, (population 1,614), and to his Harlan County roots. There he went back to work in the Kentucky coal mines from which he had once hoped the army would allow him to escape.

Smith died March 19, 1954, of internal injuries after being crushed between a shuttle car and a ceiling brace in a mining accident. He was forty years old.[2]

APPENDIX A: *Findings in the Trial of Sergeant Judson H. Smith*

Of Specification 1, Charge I: a. Not Guilty

Of Specification 1, Charge I: b. Guilty

Of Specification 1, Charge I: c. Not Guilty

Of Specification 1, Charge I: d. Not Guilty

Of Specification 1, Charge I: e. Not Guilty

Of Specification 2, Charge I: Guilty

Of Specification 3, Charge I: Guilty

Of Charge I: Guilty

Of Specification 1, Charge II: Guilty, except the words "with intent to do bodily harm," and except the words " by willfully and feloniously," substituting therefor, respectively, the word "wrongfully," and except the words, "with a dangerous weapon, to wit." Of the excepted words not guilty; of the substituted word guilty.

Of Specification 2, Charge II: Guilty, except the words, "with intent to do bodily harm," and except the words, "by willfully and feloniously," substituting therefor, respectively, the word "wrongfully," and except the words, "with a dangerous weapon, to wit." Of the excepted words not guilty; of the substituted word guilty.

Of Specification 3, Charge II: Guilty

Of Specification 4, Charge II: Not Guilty

Of Specification 5, Charge II: Guilty

Of Charge II: Guilty of Specifications 3 and 5; Not Guilty of Specifications 1 and 2

Of Charge II as to Specifications 3 and 5: Guilty; as to Specifications 1 and 2: Not guilty, but guilty of a violation of the 96th Article of War.

Of the Specification of Additional Charge I: Not Guilty

Of Additional Charge I: Not Guilty

Of the Specification of Additional Charge II: Not guilty

Of Additional Charge II: Not Guilty

SENTENCE

The court was closed, and upon secret written ballot, two-thirds of the members present at the time the vote was taken concurring, sentences the accused to be dishonorably discharged the service, to forfeit all pay and allowances due or to become due, and to be confined at hard labor at such place as the reviewing authority may direct, for three (3) years.

In accordance with sub-paragraph *a.* of Paragraph 80, MCM, 1928, for the information of the reviewing authority, the following statement of the reasons for the sentence is formulated for inclusion in the record:

As to sub-paragraph *b.* of Specification 1, Charge I, as to Specification 2, Charge I, as to Specification 3, Charge I, as to Specification 1, Charge II, as to Specification 2, Charge II, and as to Specification 5, Charge II, the court found that the accused acted in accordance with orders, or in accordance with an established policy, from his superior officers, and considered this in mitigation.[1]

APPENDIX B: *Dramatis Personae*

FIRST TRIAL

The Defendant

SERGEANT JUDSON H. SMITH—The accused. Provost sergeant at the Lichfield prison. A Kentucky coal miner in civilian life; a man who reenlisted in the Army early in the war, having served two previous hitches during the Great Depression.

The Court

Panel of Judges

COLONEL LOUIS P. LEONE, Infantry—President of the Smith court, or chief justice; a Regular Army career officer.

MAJOR WALTER E. HOPPER, JR., JAGD[1]—Law member, assigned by the office of the Judge Advocate General; a kind of legal parliamentarian who rules on all questions of law and procedure; advisor to the president.

MAJOR WILLIAM L. TAYLOR, Transportation Corps—Member of the court.

MAJOR BENJAMIN E. PERS (M.D.), Medical Corps—Member of the court.

CAPTAIN MILTON BLUM, (M.D.), Medical Corps—Member of the court.

CAPTAIN JAMES L. CHAVASSE, Corps of Engineers—Member of the court.

The Prosecution

MAJOR LELAND SMITH, Quartermaster Corps—Trial judge advocate, or chief prosecutor; a lawyer in civilian life.

CAPTAIN EARL J. CARROLL, Army Air Corps—Assistant trial judge advocate, or assistant prosecutor; in civilian life a lawyer, stunt pilot, and musician. Carroll changed the direction of the Lichfield courts-martial.

The Defense

1ST LIEUTENANT FRANK M. JOHNSON, Infantry—Defense counsel, a young civilian lawyer, recently commissioned, with limited legal experience.

1ST LIEUTENANT JOSEPH E. CASSIDY, AUS[2]—Assistant defense counsel, with a background similar to that of defense counsel Johnson.

Witnesses

ADCOCK, T/5 ELLIS D.—An indicted prison guard at Lichfield.

BAIZER, STAFF SERGEANT ASHUR H.—An NCO on temporary duty as a guard in the Lichfield prison.

BAKER, GENERAL PRISONER ADD—A Lichfield prison inmate.

BAKER, GENERAL PRISONER JOHN—A Lichfield prison inmate.

BARRON, LIEUTENANT COLONEL STEPHEN F.—a Catholic chaplain.

BEACH, GENERAL PRISONER ALBERT E.—A Lichfield prison inmate.

BERNARDO, PRIVATE JOHN—A Lichfield prison inmate.

BLUHM, MAJOR HERBERT W.—Lichfield post inspector; a late-arriving witness.

BUCKMASTER, PFC JOHN P.—An MP and former inmate who returned as a volunteer witness, sentenced for attending an off-post party *with* permission.

CALOGERO, PRIVATE ANTHONY—A prisoner in the Lichfield guardhouse convicted for being AWOL ("jumping ship") three times.

CAPPELLO, PFC THOMAS P.—A Lichfield prison inmate.

CHAVES, GENERAL PRISONER LESTER J.—A Lichfield prison inmate who sometimes conducted calisthenics for the other prisoners.

CHAYES, COLONEL EDWARD—Courtroom spectator who interrupted the Smith trial claiming to be counsel for Lieutenant Ennis.

COMFORT, CAPTAIN WILLIAM I.—a Catholic chaplain.

COX, GENERAL PRISONER ROBERT E.—A Lichfield prison inmate.

CROSSCOPE, PFC JOHN F.—A Lichfield guardhouse detail clerk.

CUBAGE, 1ST LIEUTENANT GRANVILLE—Police and prison officer at Lichfield, a student in civilian life.

DAMON, PRIVATE PHILIP A., JR.—A temporary guard in the trustee barracks.

DUNCAN, STAFF SERGEANT JIM L.—Another Lichfield guardhouse detail clerk.

ENNIS, 1ST LIEUTENANT LEONARD W.—Lichfield prison officer who succeeded Cubage; a career soldier and former provost sergeant in Hawaii.

FURNARI, GENERAL PRISONER GASPAR—A former Lichfield prisoner.

FRIEDMAN, 1ST LIEUTENANT ALBERT B.—Courtroom spectator who became a witness.

GALLARDY, STAFF SERGEANT JAMES B.—A wounded combat veteran who was a prison inmate; one of the few who complained to authorities.

HAYS, 1ST LIEUTENANT WARNHAM E.—An officer (with no legal training) who was assigned as defense counsel for all prisoners awaiting court-martial.

HENNEY, T/5 ROBERT—A technician temporarily assigned to guard duty in the prison who vented his outrage to his hometown paper, the *Toledo Blade*.

HOLLOWAY, PRIVATE SAM—A prisoner who was awaiting court-martial.

HUMMELL, LIEUTENANT COLONEL WILLIAM G.—Assistant theater inspector general, USFET, who had an office next door to the court, and who was subpoenaed as a witness; a Kilian collaborator.

JONES, STAFF SERGEANT JAMES M.—An indicted Lichfield jailer.

KARDON, PRIVATE LOUIS L.—A former Lichfield prisoner who volunteered as a witness, returned from Germany on order of General Eisenhower.

KILIAN, COLONEL JAMES A.—Commandant of the 10th Reinforcement Depot at Lichfield. Regular Army (Cavalry) officer who served in both World Wars, and who had received the Legion of Merit in World War II.

KOBLINSKI, GENERAL PRISONER MIKE—Wounded combat veteran who was a prison inmate.

LO BUONO, MAJOR RICHARD E.—Provost marshal at Lichfield, ostensibly in charge of police and prisons; a graduate student in civilian life.

LONDON, LIEUTENANT ALVIN A.—An MP officer who testified for the defense.

LUTNICK, PRIVATE IRVING—An army photographer who took evidentiary photos for Captain Carroll.

MacMILLAN, GENERAL PRISONER DANIEL—A career criminal convicted seven times in two years for car theft and other crimes.

MALLORY, PRIVATE JOSEPH M.—A Negro [the army's official designation for African-American soldiers at the time] inmate involved in a mess hall incident.

McGINNIS, PFC CHARLES—A Lichfield prison inmate who witnessed a confrontation between a prison guard and Sergeant Smith.

McNIGHT, PFC RUFUS B.—A Lichfield prison inmate.

NEWLANDS, STAFF SERGEANT JOHN M.—An NCO on temporary duty as a prison guard.

PETRAS, PFC HENRY—A former Lichfield inmate who had spent a month in solitary confinement, where he suffered grave mistreatment.

RICHEY, PRIVATE AUBREY L.—A Lichfield prisoner who was beaten unconscious and placed in solitary confinement after returning from the hospital.

RIDGE, 1ST LIEUTENANT DONALD—A witness called by the defense in an attempt to disparage the character and testimony of Daniel MacMillan.

ROBERTSON, CAPTAIN JOSEPH A.—Commanding officer of the 316th Prison Company, proprietor of a Toledo dry cleaning shop in civilian life.

ROSE, PRIVATE ALBERT J.—A Lichfield prison inmate.

RUSS, PRIVATE SAUL L.—A wounded combat veteran who was a prisoner in the Lichfield guardhouse awaiting trial for being AWOL.

SHILLING, MAJOR JOHN—A courtroom spectator who became a witness.

SCHWERFTBERGER, PFC ROBERT W.—A former Lichfield prisoner.

SCOTT, SERGEANT ROBERT E.—An indicted Lichfield jailer.

SMITH, GENERAL PRISONER CLARENCE B.—A Lichfield prison inmate.

TANNAHILL, CAPTAIN NORMAN B. (Medical Corps)—A physician on the Lichfield medical staff.

TAYLOR, PRIVATE THEODORE—A former Lichfield prisoner who became a volunteer witness, a Negro soldier for whom a lineup was arranged.

WARNECKE, CAPTAIN RUDOLPH E. (Medical Corps)—Post surgeon at Lichfield.

Act Two

ABELE, COLONEL LESTER J.—Staff judge advocate for General Bresnahan; a witness in the Kilian trial.

BECK, COLONEL WILLIAM, JR.—Law member in the Kilian trial.

BRESNAHAN, BRIGADIER GENERAL T. F.—Commanding general of the Continental Base Section; a witness in the Kilian trial.

BURNETTE, MAJOR JAMES C.—Assistant defense counsel in the Kilian trial.

BURRESS, MAJOR GENERAL WITHERS A.—Inspector general for the European theater; a witness in the Kilian trial.

FORD, COLONEL RAYMOND E.—Colonel Kilian's defense counsel.

GAGUINE, MAJOR BENITO—Law member in the Jones trial, whose actions contributed to President Moore's resignation.

KILIAN, LIEUTENANT COLONEL JAMES A.—Commandant of the 10th Reinforcement Depot; defendant in his own trial. Regular Army (Cavalry) officer who served in both World Wars, and who had received the Legion of Merit.

LEWIS, MAJOR GENERAL JOHN T.—Western Base commander; a witness in the Jones and Kilian trials.

McGEE, FIRST LIEUTENANT MORRIS C.—Assistant defense counsel in Jones trial.

McNARNEY, GENERAL JOSEPH T.—Commander of U.S. forces in Europe; a witness in the Kilian trial.

METCALF, COLONEL SAMUEL—President of the court in the Ennis trial.

MONTAGU, BRIGADIER GENERAL ROBERT M.—President of the court for the trial of Colonel James A. Kilian.

MOORE, COLONEL BUHL—President of the court in trial of Staff Sergeant James M. Jones, who was dismissed at his own request.

ROBINSON, MAJOR JOSEPH S.—Trial judge advocate in the Kilian trial; a friend and later law partner of Earl Carroll.

ROYALL, KENNETH C.—Under Secretary of War, who oversaw later Lichfield trials.

SWEENEY, COLONEL HARDIN—A member of the court in the Kilian trial; a friend of Colonel Kilian who withdrew from the court when challenged.

Offstage

BOLTON, PRIVATE ERIL L.—A Negro soldier inmate who died of a massive intracerebral hemorrhage.

BROWN, MAJOR GENERAL ALBERT E.—Commanding general, Ground Forces Replacement Command, who visited the Lichfield facility.

DOANE, DONALD P.—Associated Press correspondent who later became a senior writer and editor with *U.S. News and World Report*.

GHEENS, PFC AUSTIN D.—An indicted Lichfield jailer.

KEARNEY, MAJOR RICHARD D.—Staff judge advocate for the European theater of operations, on the staff of General Thiele.

KING, CAPTAIN ROY E. (Sanitary Corps)—Lichfield sanitary engineer.

LAMPROLOS, FIRST LIEUTENANT GEORGE W.—Special defense counsel, who made preliminary preparations, including witness lists, before the Smith trial began.

LOVELESS, PFC WILLIAM C.—An indicted Lichfield jailer.

MENUNES, SERGEANT JOE M.—A Lichfield jailer implicated in Bolton's death; many inmates thought his name was "Nunes;" others called him "Unice."

NORRIS, PFC WILLIAM B.—An indicted Lichfield jailer.

NORTON, LIEUTENANT COLONEL ROBERT—Colonel Kilian's deputy at the 10th Reinforcement Depot; a witness in the Kilian trial.

ROBSON, CORPORAL LOUIS L.—An indicted Lichfield jailer.

ROSENTHAL, ED—*Stars and Stripes* journalist.

SIMS, PRIVATE WILLIAM D.—A Negro prisoner who was severely beaten.

SWOPE, COLONEL JOHN G.—Assistant inspector general, European theater of operations, who inspected Lichfield twice in 1945.

THIELE, BRIGADIER GENERAL CLAUDE M.—Commanding general, London area office; appointing authority for the Lichfield courts-martial.

VARNER, LIEUTENANT COLONEL LAWRENCE—A representative of the Inspector General's office commissioned by General Eisenhower to investigate Bolton's death.

WARREN, PFC THOMAS E.—An indicted Lichfield jailer.

WHITE, ART—*Stars and Stripes* journalist.

NOTES

Prologue

1. Facsimile of Special Order 316, creating a general court-martial at the UK Base, London, England, reproduced from *Record of Trial of Sergeant Judson H. Smith, 35455208, 19th Reinforcement Depot, APO 413* (London, England: General Court-Martial appointed by the Commanding General of the United Kingdom Base, Volume 2, 31 May 1946).

2. The Germans' final V-2 rocket of the war hit Orpington, England, southeast of London, on March 27, 1945, the last of a missile campaign that killed 2,700 British civilians. See Peter Young, ed., *World Almanac Book of World War II* (New York, NY: World Almanac Publications; Prentice-Hall, 1981), 334.

3. "Nürnberg," the German spelling for the Bavarian city, was used almost universally by American publications at the time; it was pronounced accordingly on the radio and in common parlance. "Nuremberg" became a more popular reference after release of Stanley Kramer's film, *Judgment at Nuremberg* (United Artists, 1961).

4. Arthur Noyes, "20 Top Nazis Go on Trial Today," *The Stars and Stripes,* 20 November 1945, Southern Germany edition; Lester Bernstein and Stoddard White, "Charges Read in Trial of 20 Nazis; Defendants to File Protest Today," ibid., 21 November 1945.

5. Ed Rosenthal, "Yanks Tell of Beatings at Lichfield Trial," ibid., 20 November 1945.

6. Although the name of the Army Air Corps was technically changed to "Army Air Forces" in 1942, when General George C. Marshall, chief of staff, reorganized the army's branches into Ground Forces, Air Forces, and Service Forces, the change was generally unknown in other arms, and it did not significantly affect army administration. Officers' commissions continued to be held in the Army "Air Corps," as is apparent in the reproduction of Special Order 320 of 6 December, 1945 (see Chapter 1), appointing "Captain Earl J Carroll, 0512149, AC" as assistant trial judge advocate. Passage of the National Security Act of 1947 and the National Security Act Amendments of 1949 later established the Air Force as a separate military department within the reorganized Department of Defense. For further reference, see *Columbia Encyclopedia*, 5th ed., s.v. "Air Force, United States Department of the"; see also James E. Hewes, *From Root to McNamara: Army Organization and Administration, 1900–1963* (Washington, DC: U.S. Government Printing Office, 1983).

7. In his reference to "the United States Army," the president of the court is reminding the witness that he holds a commission in the prestigious Regular Army, as distinguished from the Organized Reserve, the National Guard, or the Army of the

Army of the United States.

United States (the World War II "expansion army" in which temporary commissions were issued).

8. For the lengthy confrontation between the assistant trial judge advocate, Captain Earl J. Carroll, and Colonel James A. Kilian during the Lichfield commandant's second appearance on the witness stand (beginning on February 6, 1946), see *Record of Trial of Sergeant Judson H. Smith*, 2:3332 ff.

Chapter 1: The Trial

1. Facsimile of Special Order 320, appointing Captain Earl J. Carroll, Air Corps, to the Smith general court-martial as assistant trial judge advocate, is reproduced from *Record of Trial of Sergeant Judson H. Smith*, vol. 2.

2. William Manchester, *The Arms of Krupp* (Boston: Little, Brown and Co., 1964, 1968), 625.

3. Biographical information on Earl J. Carroll was provided by Adjutant General's Office, *Official Army Register* (Washington, DC: U.S. Government Printing Office, 1954), and in two interviews by the author with Mr. Carroll at his home, Greenwich, CT, 21 March 1978, and 2 November 1979; also interview by the author with journalist Donald P. Doane, Washington, DC, 12 April 1978; also telephone calls to the California Bar Association, Los Angeles, and to Carroll's former partner, Judge Thomas L. Foley of Hayward, CA, both in 1978.

4. Lieutenant Cassidy apparently had not yet been assigned to a service branch (see Special Order 316 at the beginning of the Prologue), such as Infantry (Inf) or Quartermaster Corps (QMC), but held his temporary commission at that time simply in the Army of the United States (AUS). The Army of the United States, as originally established by 1932 Congressional legislation, included the Regular Army (United States Army), the National Guard, and the Organized Reserve. The meaning of the entity changed, however, when the draft was created in 1940, and the AUS became the "expansion army" for World War II, to which draftees were assigned and in which temporary officer commissions were issued.

5. Biographical information on Judson H. Smith was obtained from a number of sources, including the Registrar of Statistics, Commonwealth of Kentucky (see Certificate of Death File No. 116 54-4599, 3/22/54); Harlan County vital statistics personnel in Cumberland, Kentucky, telephone calls by the author; Donald P. Doane, interview by the author, Washington, DC, 12 April 1978; and Sergeant Smith's own testimony during the course of his trial; also telephone calls to the Veterans Administration Record Center, St. Louis, MO, 1979.

6. Richard D. Kearney, Major, JAGD, Staff Judge Advocate, *Review of the Staff Judge Advocate*, from *Record of Trial of Sergeant Judson H. Smith*, vol 1.

7. Military law at the time of the Lichfield trials was governed by Office of The Judge Advocate General of the Army, *A Manual for Courts-Martial, U.S. Army* (Washington, DC: U.S. Government Printing Office, 1943).

8. Ibid., 223, 225.

9. The charges against Sergeant Smith are reproduced from General Court-Martial Orders No. 52, Headquarters, London Area Office, Western Base Section, US Forces European Theater, APO 413, U. S. Army.

The eight others referred to in Specification 1, who, initially, were codefendants with Sergeant Smith, included Staff Sergeant James M. Jones, Sergeant William B. Norris, Sergeant Robert E. Scott, Corporal Lewis L. Robson, Technician Fifth Grade Ellis D. Adcock, Private First Class Austin D. Gheens, Private First Class William C. Loveless, and Private First Class Thomas W. Warren. To avoid self-incrimination while serving as witnesses, these other Lichfield cadre were eventually tried separately under a "motion of severance" filed by the defense. Names of the six alleged victims in Specification 1 were Sergeant Saul L. Russ, Private Terold R. Seiler, Private William D. Sims, Private Aubrey L. Richey, Private Anthony R. Calogero, and Private First Class Henry Petras.

Two additional charges were added after investigation by 1st Lieutenant Anthony B. Dreier, Coast Artillery Corps:

ADDITIONAL CHARGE I: Violation of the 96th Article of War.

Specification: In that Sergeant Judson H. Smith . . . did . . . on or about 15 December 1944, wrongfully and unlawfully commit an assault upon Private John L. Bernardo, then a prisoner under his control, by striking him on the back with a whip.

ADDITIONAL CHARGE II: Violation of the 93rd Article of War.

Specification: In that Sergeant Judson H. Smith . . . did . . . on or about 1 October 1944, with intent to do bodily harm commit an assault upon Private First Class Peter Henry Claim, then a prisoner under his control, by willfully and feloniously striking the said Private Claim on the buttocks and legs with a dangerous weapon, to wit, a billy club.

10. "Personnel: Crime and Punishment," *Time,* 31 December 1945, 20 ff.

Chapter 2: The Depot

1. "Personnel: Crime and Punishment," *Time,* 31 December 1945, 20. Other historical background on Whittington Barracks was collected during the author's visit to the facility in the fall of 1978, augmented by correspondence with Major M. K. Beedle, MBE (Retd), regimental secretary of The Staffordshire Prince of Wales Regiment, Whittington Barracks, Lichfield, Staffordshire, England WS14 9PY; specifically Major Beedle's letter of November 14, 1979.

2. Information about the pup tent stockade at Fort Custer was provided by Edward L. Clark, who was an officer at the Michigan post at the time.

3. Detail about the latrines and solitary confinement cell at the Lichfield Depot is provided in evidentiary photographs accompanying the *Record of Trial of Sergeant Judson H. Smith,* and in the trial record, vol. 14.

4. Sources of biographical information on James Alphonse Kilian include Adjutant General's Office, *Official Army Register* (Washington, DC: U.S. Government Printing Office, 1954), 897; the University of Missouri, Office of the Registrar and the university's Department of Records, Columbia, MO, telephone calls, 1979; the University of Missouri's *1914 Yearbook*; Washington County Clerk's Office, Blair, Nebraska and Omaha, Nebraska, where earlier records were kept, telephone calls, October–November, 1979; telephone calls to the Veterans Administration Record Center, St. Louis, MO, 1979. Information on the military record of James Kilian's father, Julius Nicholas Kilian, comes from Francis Heitman, *The Historical Register & Dictionary of the United States Army* (Washington, DC: U.S. Government Printing Office, 1965, reprint of 1903 edition), 597.

Chapter 3: The Case for the Prosecution

1. Sources of information on pretrial correspondence include the author's interview with Earl Carroll, Greenwich, CT, 2 November 1979, and *Record of Trial of Sergeant Judson H. Smith,* vol. 1.

2. Trial testimony summarized in this chapter is extracted from the *Record of Trial of Sergeant Judson A. Smith*, 2:17 ff.

3. This and all subsequent references to *The Stars and Stripes* are from Library of Congress microfilms of the European and Southern Germany editions of the daily newspaper, 1945–46.

Chapter 4: The Defense Begins

1. Trial testimony in this chapter is extracted from the Record *of Trial of Sergeant Judson H. Smith*. Defense presentation 3:126 ff; testimony of Lieutenant Cubage, 3:132 ff; Carroll's entry into the trial, 3:147 ff; Carroll's cross-examination of Colonel Lo Buono, 3:184 ff.

2. The journalist quoted is Donald P. Doane, a European theater correspondent with Associated Press at the time; interview by the author, Washington, DC, 12 April 1978.

Chapter 5: The Chain of Command

1. Testimony in this chapter is reproduced from the *Record of Trial of Sergeant Judson H. Smith*. Testimony of Major Richard Lo Buono, 3:173 ff; for that of the two Lichfield chaplains, Father Barron and Father Comfort, see 3:232 ff.

Chapter 6: The Commandant Appears

1. *Time*, 31 December 1945, 20.

2. Colonel Kilian's testimony in the *Record of Trial of Sergeant Judson H. Smith*, 3:277 ff.

3. Testimony of the two Medical Corps officers, Captains Warnecke and Tannahill, ibid., 3:295 ff.

Chapter 7: The Beast of Lichfield?

1. Donald P. Doane, interview by author, Washington, DC, 12 April 1978.

2. Testimony of Lieutenant Ennis, *Record of Trial of Sergeant Judson H. Smith*, 3:312 ff.

3. Art White, "Officer Admits Making GIs Jog A Wall," *The Stars and Stripes*, 9 December 1945, Southern Germany edition.

4. Ed Rosenthal, "Lichfield Defense Witness Disappears," ibid., 11 December 1945.

Chapter 8: The Accused Takes the stand

1. For Technician 5th Grade Adcock's testimony and that of the other jailers, see *Record of Trial of Sergeant Judson H. Smith*, 3:312 ff; testimony of the accused, Sergeant Judson Smith, ibid., 3:365 ff.

2. Ed Rosenthal, "Lichfield Defense Witness Disappears,"*The Stars and Stripes*, 11 December 1945, Southern Germany edition.

Chapter 9: Rebuttal Witnesses

1. Rebuttal testimony begins with testimony of General Prisoner Lester J. Chaves, *Record of Trial of Sergeant Judson H. Smith*, 4:498 ff.

2. Ed Rosenthal, "Papers Banned in Depot's Jail, Witness Says,"*The Stars and Stripes*, 13 December 1945, European edition.

3. Bulleted items summarize the testimony of rebuttal witnesses, including General Prisoner Lester J. Chaves, G/P Robert E. Cox, Pfc Thomas P. Cappello, Pvt. Joseph M. Mallory, G/P Mike Koblinski, G/P David A. Higgins, Pfc John P. Buckmaster, Pfc

Joseph J. De Felice, Pfc Rufus B. McKnight, G/P Clarence B. Smith, G/P John Ayers, G/P Albert E. Beach; *Record of Trial of Sergeant Judson H. Smith,* 4:498–5:1061.

4. "Witness Tells Lichfield Trial Of Knife Battle," *The Stars and Stripes,* 15 December 1945, European edition.

Chapter 10: The Court vs the Press

1. "Colonel Said to 'Forget' Beatings, Sergeant Testifies at Lichfield Trial," *The Stars and Stripes,* 16 December 1945, Southern Germany edition.

2. "Inmate Beat to Knees, MP Says at Trial," ibid., 19 December 1945.

3. "Lichfield Murder Suspected: Probe Opens in GI Death" (1st ed.); Ed Rosenthal, "Death Laid To Beating At Lichfield" (2nd ed.), ibid., 18 December 1945.

4. Art White, "S and S Story Is Refused as Mistrial Basis," ibid., 20 December 1945.

5. Information about the "loophole" in censorship rules for the army newspaper was provided by journalist Donald Doane in an interview by the author, Washington, DC, 12 April 1978. Mr. Doane had been an Associated Press correspondent in 1945–46.

Chapter 11: Lo Buono Cracks

1. Testimony of recalled witness Major Richard Lo Buono, *Record of Trial of Sergeant Judson H. Smith,* 5: 1066 ff.

2. "CO Threatened To Hang Him, Major Asserts," *The Stars and Stripes,* 23 December 1945, Southern Germany edition.

Chapter 12: Kilian's Ubiquity

1. Testimony of T/5 Robert Henney, *Record of Trial of Sergeant Judson H. Smith,* 5:1224 ff; that of Major Herbert W. Bluhm, 6:1246 ff.

2. "Lichfield Major Denies Hiding," *The Stars and Stripes,* 12 December 1945, European edition.

3. "Personnel: Crime and Punishment," *Time,* 31 December 1945, 20 ff.

4. Recall testimony of Major Richard Lo Buono, *Record of Trial of Sergeant Judson H. Smith,* 7: 1476 ff.

5. Ed Rosenthal, "Major Tells Of Fear for Lichfield CO," *The Stars and Stripes,* 4 January 1946, European edition.

6. Testimony of Major John Shilling, *Record of Trial of Sergeant Judson H. Smith,* 7:1609 ff; that of 1st Lieutenant Albert B. Friedman, 7:1663 ff.

7. Ed Rosenthal, "Perjury Trial Demanded for Maj. Lo Buono," *The Stars and Stripes,* 5 January 1946, European edition.

Chapter 13: The Lineup

1. Testimony of General Prisoner Add Baker, *Record of Trial of Sergeant Judson H. Smith,* 7:1728 ff.

2. Art White, "Lo Buono Is Accused of Watching Beating," *The Stars and Stripes,* 9 January 1946, European edition.

3. Art White, "Ex Prisoner Identifies Lo Buono From Lineup, Names 4 in Courtroom as Brutality Witnesses," *The Stars and Stripes,* 10 January 1946, European edition.

Chapter 14: Recantation

1. For the substance of this chapter, see *Record of Trial of Sergeant Judson H. Smith,* 8:1926 ff; also Lieutenant Granville Cubage's testimony, 9:1978 ff.

2. "Court Orders Charge Against Lichfield CO," *The Stars and Stripes*, 16 January 1946, European edition.

Chapter 15: Intrigue

1. For Lieutenant Granville Cubage's testimony, see *Record of Trial of Sergeant Judson H. Smith*, 9:1978 ff.

2. Lieutenant William G. Hummell's testimony, ibid., 9:2072 ff.

3. "Pointing to the Stars," *Time*, 14 January 1945, 21 ff.

Chapter 16: Reaction

1. See *Record of Trial of Sergeant Judson H. Smith*, 9:2126 ff. Detail on the court's communications with the appointing authority, ibid., 9:2156.

2. Collateral information was contributed by Earl Carroll during the author's interviews with him in Greenwich, CT, 21 March 1978, and 2 November 1979.

3. "Lichfield Court Admonished on Blast at Kilian," *The Stars and Stripes*, 17 January 1946, European edition.

Chapter 17: The Court Stands its Ground

1. For the court record detailing the events reported early in this chapter, see *Record of Trial of Sergeant Judson H. Smith*, 9:2187 ff.

2. Lieutenant Cubage's testimony, *Record of Trial of Sergeant Judson H. Smith*, 9:2234 ff.

3. "Kilian Ordered Lichfield Beatings, Officer Testifies," *The Stars and Stripes*, 19 January 1946, European edition.

Chapter 18: Purgatory

1. Lieutenant Cubage's testimony after his voluntary return to the witness stand, *Record of Trial of Sergeant Judson H. Smith*, 9:2234 ff; that of T/5 Ellis Adcock, ibid., 10:2362 ff; testimony of Staff Sergeant James Jones, ibid., 10:2531 ff.

2. Art White, "Lichfield Guard Sang to Drown Out Cries of Prisoner, Court is Told," *The Stars and Stripes*, 22 January 1946, European edition.

3. Sergeant Smith's voluntary return to the witness stand, *Record of Trial of Sergeant Judson H. Smith*, 11:2701 ff,

4. Art White, "Bad Treatment Known to IG, Guard Charges," *The Stars and Stripes*, 30 January 1946, European edition.

5. Captain Robertson's testimony, *Record of Trial of Sergeant Judson H. Smith*, 11:2949 ff.

6. Lieutenant Leonard Ennis's recall testimony, ibid., 11:3170 ff.

7. Art White, "Lichfield Officer Admits 'You Could Kill a Man,'" *The Stars and Stripes*, 5 February 1946, European edition.

Chapter 19: The Commandant Returns

1. Colonel James A. Kilian's testimony upon being recalled, *Record of Trial of Sergeant Judson H. Smith*, 13:3332 ff; the author was present during this testimony.

2. Art White, "Kilian Is Ordered to Talk After He Balks on Stand," *The Stars and Stripes*, 8 February 1946, European edition.

3. Ibid.

4. Ed Rosenthal, "Charge Ordered Against Kilian in Refusal to Testify," ibid., 9 February 1946.

Chapter 20: Kilian Bends

1. Colonel Kilian's testimony continues from the previous chapter in the *Record of Trial of Sergeant Judson H. Smith*, 13:3617 ff. For the content on the page noted, ibid., 13:3670 ff. The author was present in the courtroom

2. Art White, "Prison Staff Duped Him, Kilian Says," *The Stars and Stripes*, 12 February 1996, European edition.

Chapter 21: Final Shots

1. Colonel Kilian's testimony again continues in the *Record of Trial of Sergeant Judson H. Smith*, 13:3769 ff. The author was present in the courtroom during the testimony reported.

2. "Kilian Sees Own Trial if Smith is Convicted," *The Stars and Stripes*, 14 February 1946, European edition.

Chapter 22: Summations

1. Summations begin in the *Record of Trial of Sergeant Judson H. Smith*, 13:3836 ff.

Chapter 23: Findings

1. Art White, "Lichfield Court Sentences Smith to Three Years," *The Stars and Stripes*, 17 February 1946, European edition.

2. The Review of the Staff Judge Advocate by Major Richard D. Kearney, JAGD, is published in the *Record of Trial of Sergeant Judson H. Smith*, 1:2. Major Kearney's page numbers in his *Time* citations do not match those cited for the same articles in notes for Chapter One in this work, apparently because Kearney was using the abridged Army edition of *Time*, from which advertising was deleted.

3. Art White, "Charges Out for Kilian, Five Officers," *The Stars and Stripes*, 23 March 1946, European edition.

Chapter 24: Aftermath

1. "Lichfield Evidence Ready in Ten Days, Royal Says," *The Stars and Stripes*, 3 April 1946, European edition.

2. "Overseas: Lichfield Fireworks," *Newsweek*, 15 April 46, 36 ff.

3. "Ike Orders Lichfield Probe as Carroll Quits," *The Stars and Stripes*, 4 April 1946, European edition.

4. Ibid.

5. Joe Mackey, "'Whitewash' Is Denied at Lichfield," *The Stars and Stripes*, 6 April 1946, European edition.

6. "War Dept. Seeks Speedy Trial of Lichfield Officers," *The Stars and Stripes*, 11 April 1946, European edition.

7. "Lichfield GIs Lose Fear And Testify," *The Stars and Stripes*, 17 April 1946, Southern Germany edition.

8. The Stars and Stripes Bureau, "Lichfield Trial Head Dismissed After Own Request for Fairness," *The Stars and Stripes*, 20 April 1946, Southern Germany edition.

9. "Court Backs Leniency for Lichfield GI," *The Stars and Stripes*, 22 April 1946, European edition.

Chapter 25: Act Two

1. Art White, "Afraid to Testify, 5 Witnesses Say At Lichfield Trial," *The Stars and Stripes*, 12 April 1946, Southern Germany edition; The Stars and Stripes Bureau,

"Lichfield Trial Head Dismissed After Own Request for Fairness, " ibid., 20 April 1946, Southern Germany edition.

2. "Lichfield's Second Act Deemed Test," ibid., 25 April 1946.

3. "Kilian, 13, To Face Trial at Nauheim," *The Stars and Stripes,* 23 May 1946, European edition.

4."Out of Mind?" *Time,* 13 May 1946, 26.

5. "Lichfield GI Witness Shot By Another Over Fräulein" *The Stars and Stripes,* 23 May 1946, European edition.

6. "'Mishandling' Found In Lichfield Trials," ibid., 15 May 1946.

7. Don Doane, "Lichfield Soldiers Refuse To Testify," AP dispatch, 29 May 1946.

8. "Kilian Won't Testify For Defendants," *The Stars and Stripes,* 4 June 1946, European edition.

9. "Witness Compares Lichfield With Concentration Camps," ibid., 11 June 1946.

10. "Lichfield GIs Explain 'Strike,'" ibid., 10 June 1946.

11. Don Doane, "Lichfield Officer Is Fined $250," AP dispatch, 16 June 1946.

12. "Lichfield Trial Witness Gets Jail Sentence," *The Stars and Stripes,* 20 June 1946, European edition.

13. Interview by the author with Earl Carroll, Greenwich, CT, 21 March 1978.

14. Interview by the author with AP journalist Donald P. Doane, Washington, DC, 12 April 1978.

Chapter 26: Kilian's Turn

1. Don Doane, "Colonel Calls Trials Partial, Lichfield Boss Asks Quashing of Indictment," AP dispatch, 18 June 1946.

2. "McNarney on Stand As Witness for Kilian," *The Stars and Stripes,* 18 June 1946, European edition.

3. Don Doane, "Legalism Delays Lichfield Trial, Kilian Postpones Evidence With Technicalities," AP dispatch, 19 June 1946.

4. "Lichfield Trial Witness Gets Jail Sentence," *The Stars and Stripes,* 20 June 1946, European edition.

5. Don Doane, "Wounded Vet Tells of Cruelties, Bronze Star Holder Testifies of Lichfield" AP dispatch, 26 June 1946.

6. "Kilian Disrupts Lichfield Trial With Outburst," *The Stars and Stripes,* 2 July 1946.

7. Don Doane, "Defense Lawyer Held In Contempt," AP dispatch, 12 July 1946.

8. Don Doane, "Judge Accused of Bias Quits; Lichfield Trials Court Room Again Scene of Turmoil," AP dispatch, 17 July 1946.

9. "Plot to Destroy Lichfield Court," *The Stars and Stripes,* 1 August 1946, European Edition.

10. "Col. Kilian Fined $500, Censured," ibid., 30 August 1946.

11. "Kilian Invites Congressional Probe of Trial," ibid., 4 September, 1946.

12. "Kilian Appeals To Washington," ibid., 14 September 1946.

Chapter 27: The Further Adventures of Earl Carroll

1. Major Ralph Kohlman, USMC, Judge Advocate General's School, U.S. Army, Charlottesville, VA, 26 July 1996, interview by the author.

2. "Captain Asks Help of High Court to See Clients," *The Stars and Stripes,* 21 August 1946, European edition; Don Doane, "13 Americans Get No Legal Aid in Custody," AP dispatch, 20 August 1946.

3. Donald P. Doane, Washington, DC, 12 April 1978, interview by the author.

4. "Carroll 'Shanghaied out of Germany,'" *New York Times,* 5 September 1946.

5. William Manchester, *The Arms of Krupp* (Boston: Little, Brown and Co., 1964, 1968), 748.

6. Ibid., 651; Donald P. Doane, Washington, DC, 12 April 1978, interview by the author.

Epilogue

1. The narrative in this chapter is based on notes made by the author during two interviews with Earl Carroll at his home in Greenwich, CT, 21 March 1978 and 12 January 1979.

2. Information on Judson Smith's death was obtained through the courtesy of personnel at Harlan County, Kentucky's Bureau of Vital Statistics in Cumberland, Kentucky. A copy of his Certificate of Death, File No. 116 54-4599 dated 3/22/54, was obtained from the Registrar of Statistics, Commonwealth of Kentucky.

Appendix A

1. The pages in this appendix are reproduced from *Record of Trial of Sergeant Judson H. Smith,* 13:3872 ff.

Appendix B

1. "JAGD" are the initials of the Judge Advocate General's Department, the army's judicial branch.

2. "AUS" is the abbreviation for Army of the United States, in which most wartime commissions were issued. Apparently Lieutenant Cassidy had not yet been assigned to an army branch of service.

ABOUT THE AUTHOR

A Registered Professional Engineer, Jack Gieck retired as Director of New Product Development for Firestone to become a full time writer/producer of nontheatrical films, founding his own company, Cinemark, Inc. Shown on the History Channel, on PBS, and at many festivals, his films and videos have won more than thirty awards. He is also the author of *A Photo Album of Ohio's Canal Era, 1825–1913*, published by Kent State University Press.

ABOUT THE BOOK

Lichfield: The U.S. Army on Trial was designed and typeset on a Macintosh in Quark XPress by Kachergis Book Design of Pittsboro, North Carolina. The typeface, Meridien, was designed by Adrian Frutiger in 1957 for the French foundry Deberny & Peignot.

This book was printed on sixty-pound Glatfelter Supple Opaque Recycled Natural and bound by Thomson-Shore of Dexter, Michigan.